TRAINING THE EVENT HORSE

TRAINING
THE EVENT HORSE

VIRGINIA LENG MBE

with Genevieve Murphy

Trafalgar Square Publishing

NORTH POMFRET, VERMONT

First published in the United States of America
in 1991 by Trafalgar Square Publishing,
North Pomfret, Vermont 05053

First published in Great Britain 1990 by Stanley Paul and Co Ltd, an imprint of the
Random Century Group

Printed and bound in Great Britain

ISBN 0-943955-38-6

LOC : 90-83638

All photographs taken by Kit Houghton

CONTENTS

PREFACE

I have always been part of a team when training horses at Ivyleaze, my mother's home near Badminton, where I have the best back-up team in the world. Our combined knowledge has been pooled for this book, which is another team effort. It could not have been written without the help of my mother, Heather Holgate, and our friend Dorothy Willis, who has been based at Ivyleaze since 1980; they have both acquired a vast reservoir of knowledge. I am also indebted to our vet, Don Attenburrow, whose painstaking research has done so much to improve the treatment and welfare of horses.

There have been many others who have given me valuable advice over the years, thereby widening my own knowledge of a wonderful sport in which you never stop learning. With apologies to all those I am leaving out, I will mention three trainers who have had a tremendous influence. Pat Manning has been my guiding light in dressage; Lady Hugh Russell was largely responsible for teaching me how to ride cross-country fences and Pat Burgess has given me an immense amount of help in show jumping.

Heartfelt thanks are also due to my wonderful sponsors at Citibank Savings. Without their continuing encouragement and support, it would have been impossible to keep a yardful of horses.

Finally, I must thank the girls – both past and present – who have looked after the horses at Ivyleaze with such dedication. They have kept our eventers well and happy, thus enabling them to give of their best in competitions.

Opposite: *It takes time for the horse to jump into water with complete confidence. Beneficial is leaping in boldly and obviously enjoying himself*

1

UNDERSTANDING THE HORSE

I was once asked to pinpoint the most important key to the successful training of a three-day event horse. Was it the lungeing, the ridden flat work, the feeding, the fitness programme or the cross-country schooling? I had no need to rack my brains to answer, 'It's a combination of them all.'

At Ivyleaze, we all have our separate tasks which contribute towards the same goal. Together we are aiming to train each and every horse in the yard to the stage where it can realise its full potential as an eventer. No specific part is more important than the others; they are all essential to the one shared aim. We endeavour to make everything that happens to the horse, from the time it is first handled right through to advanced three-day events, seem like a natural progression from what went before.

There are no short cuts to training an event horse. Each animal has to be treated as an individual and given as much time as it requires for the various stages of its education. This means that each step has to be accomplished satisfactorily before the next step is introduced. Problems, based on misunderstanding, invariably arise when you try to speed up the process. Training has to be slow and painstaking, because that is the only way we can establish the co-operation and con-

fidence which lie at the heart of all successful partnerships between horse and rider.

At Ivyleaze we firmly believe in the principle that prevention is better than cure. Those words are likely to be repeated many times in this book, because they influence our whole outlook on training. We avoid problems like the plague, because we know how difficult they are to overcome.

Horses have a sharp awareness of what is going on around them and a very long memory. If a problem arises, it may be impossible to cure completely because it is stored away in the horse's memory box, ready to re-emerge in any situation which is similar to the one which sparked it off in the first place. Refusals are just one example of something that is much easier to prevent than to cure.

Our other golden rule is never to grind on. This maxim is applied to every stage of training, at whatever level. You serve only to accentuate problems by grinding on, because the horse then becomes bored, confused or resentful. He will therefore become uncooperative.

Because each horse is an individual, it is impossible to say how long each stage of his training will take. I have attempted to give some rough guidelines simply because the reader might not know whether a particular stage is likely to take three minutes or three months – but there can be no hard and fast rule. The trainer has to listen to the horse and proceed with the utmost caution.

If the horse is not progressing, you obviously need to check that you are doing nothing wrong yourself. But, having done that, you should take stock of the fact that some horses do take longer than others. You may have expected results in two days and are therefore tempted to move on to something new when they are not achieved. If you were to persevere for two weeks – never for more than a short time per training session – the problem would probably disappear.

The rider must learn to listen to the horse. A few people are lucky enough to have an inborn instinct which enables them to do this quite easily, but most have to teach themselves to be more receptive. The partnership has to be based on mutual trust and respect, which can be achieved only through the rider's sensitivity. Abusive measures are a sign of failure, indicating that the rider's understanding and knowledge have been exhausted. The same applies to the use of gadgets, to which people tend to resort when there are shortcomings in their own training methods.

Before administering punishment, you need to be sure that the problem is not of your own making; in nine cases out of ten opposition stems from the rider's mistakes, not the horse's recalcitrance. In other words, it is not the rider who has a problem with the horse, but vice versa! For clear and careful aids to be given, the rider needs to be like a tree, with arms and legs (the branches and roots) able to move independently of each other, while the trunk remains still. Aids come from the legs, weight of the body and, finally, the hands. The use of the seat is widely misinterpreted and therefore wrongly applied; such misunderstandings are less likely to occur if you think of your weight

(rather than your seat) as an aid.

Everything is dependent on the quality of the horse's flatwork. If he is not straight over fences, there is only one reason: it is because he is not straight on the flat. Dressage is therefore the basis of all successful training. The horse will not be required to learn anything that he cannot do already. Out on his own in the field he walks, trots, canters, jumps; he performs flying changes and piaffe. Dressage simply teaches him to do these things when asked, with the weight of a rider on his back.

It is that additional weight which interferes with his natural balance. He is built in such a way that his own body is heavier in front and, with incorrect training, the rider's weight is liable to push him further on to his forehand. When that happens, the forelegs bear the burden that should be carried by the hindlegs. This in turn produces strain and stress. Horses left alone in the wild rarely sustain injuries to their tendons or ligaments; these normally occur because the horse has not learnt to carry his own weight, plus that of his rider, in a way that causes least stress.

People often refer to riders having good or bad luck according to whether their horses stay sound or go lame. Obviously there is an element of truth in this; but it is also true to say that we can help to make our own good luck by training the horse to carry himself in balance – *with* the weight of a rider on top. This will not only help to conserve the horse, it will also enable him to jump with accuracy and rhythm and to reach the level of fitness required for the endurance aspect of a three-day event.

The horse can give of his best only if worked in a calm and loving atmosphere. The actual rate of progress will depend on his temperament, size, physique, maturity, fitness and soundness. Training the horse is a slow but fascinating process and, when we succeed, it is wonderfully rewarding.

2

FINDING THE RIGHT HORSE

Since I have been lucky enough to compete on British teams, I am always looking for horses that are capable of reaching international level. It has to be admitted that I am not the easiest person in the world to please in this respect. When my mother and Dot believe they have found the ideal horse, I am still not necessarily satisfied. Possibly I have been spoilt by choice!

I like the horse to go in a certain way, so that I feel we can both hit it off together. It worries me when I seem unable to find the key to a particular horse; I begin wondering whether it would have a better chance of achieving its full potential with another rider. Master Craftsman was one such horse. I worried about him all through his novice and intermediate stages, and if he hadn't been my mother's pride and joy, he would almost certainly have been sold on. I came to realise what a dreadful mistake that would have been when I rode Crafty at the 1988 Olympic Games in Seoul. I have therefore learnt that perseverance can be rewarded!

Some of the horses we buy are unbroken youngsters whose jumping ability has to be taken on trust. We never pay vast sums of money for a horse, nor do we buy them ready-made at advanced level; we prefer to make them ourselves. The only one of our horses that

was already advanced on arrival at Ivyleaze is Griffin, whom we swapped with Ian Stark for Murphy Himself. Griffin was a little small for Ian and Murphy's boisterous temperament made him too big and strong for me; he needed a man on his back.

My goals are not necessarily shared by all other riders. Not everyone wants a horse with international potential – which is just as well, because they do not exactly grow on trees. If I were buying a horse to ride only in novice events, I would obviously be ready to overlook certain points that might be seen as shortcomings in an international eventer. But there would be some priorities that remain the same; whatever our ultimate goal in eventing, we need a horse that is honest, bold and sound.

Because there are certain factors in common, I will begin by describing the type of horse we like to have at Ivyleaze. My mother's success in finding the right material has prompted me to put her thoughts first. She has inherited an instinctive sixth sense from her father, who was regarded as one of the best judges of a horse in the West Country. Someone else's instincts are not particularly easy for the rest of us to follow, nor are they simple to explain, but my mother has done her best.

HEATHER HOLGATE'S INSTINCT

'The first impression the horse gives me is terribly important, rather like meeting a person,' says my mother. 'It's the general feeling I get when I walk into the box that creates this first impression. It's not necessarily whether the horse is pleased to see me or not; the Irish horses are usually displeased to see me, but I have now looked at so many of them that I am aware of this in advance.

'Though the head can tell you an enormous amount, the initial feeling I get comes from the whole horse. It is so instinctive, it's virtually impossible to explain. Later on, of course, I do look for specific things. I like the head to be sensible, but I've never worried about eyes. If I had been influenced by them, we would never have bought Priceless; you could hardly describe his eyes as big and generous.

'Everybody needs to realise and remember that no horse in the world is one hundred per cent perfect. I often work on the theory that the more defects you can see the better; if everything on the horse appears absolutely fantastic, there is very often a hidden problem. Bearing this in mind, I think one should be prepared to overlook things like false curbs. The same applies to splints, as long as they're not so big that they're likely to be knocked and are fully formed. Small things like this should not sway the decision as to whether you buy the horse or not, though it is obviously essential to get it very well vetted.

'Though it is always nice to have a horse that moves well, I am not personally bothered too much about whether it moves perfectly straight. Some people would be put off if they saw the horse dishing but, if most other things seemed to be going for it, I wouldn't let that bother me. I would be more concerned about its rhythm and elevation and the way it uses its hocks. Movement can be improved, assuming that the horse has good natural paces, so I am always thinking of what can be done and how long it will take.

'Unless the horse is too young, I obviously look at the way it jumps as well. I want to see whether it uses its shoulder, how high it raises its forearm, whether it tucks its forelegs up and so on. These are technical things, which I am much more aware of now than I was ten years ago when they wouldn't have worried me. I still look carefully (as I did in the early days) at the horse's face and ears as it comes into a fence. They will tell me how clever it is and whether it enjoys jumping or is slightly apprehensive.

'A good temperament is absolutely vital, whether you're looking for an international horse or a novice. In most cases those that are half bred have better temperaments than Thoroughbreds, but there are always some exceptions to the rule; I have known one or two Thoroughbreds with superb temperaments. I am always looking, first and foremost, for a really kind and generous horse; from what I've seen of eventing, I know you can't get anywhere without these qualities. In my case, it also helps if I can find a horse that my daughter likes as well!'

Inevitably, since I am the one who rides the horses in competitions, those that are sold are usually the ones that suit me least. They are certainly not discards. Among successful horses that were once at Ivyleaze was one that went to Canada, where his new owner rode him to win the national Young Riders' Championship; another was shortlisted for the 1988 Canadian Olympic team.

It is only because we need to sell some horses each year that we usually buy geldings. Mares are far more difficult to sell, so we do not go out of our way to look at them. If the right one turned up on the doorstep, however, we would not turn her down because of her sex; I happen to think that a good mare is hard to beat.

A TECHNICAL ASSESSMENT

Dot and I concentrate on the technical aspects as well as listening to our instincts; neither of us is blessed with my mother's sixth sense. I always look at the horse's legs and feet first. It seems daft to fall in love with the animal's head until you know whether it has the sound limbs and feet that are needed to carry you across country.

Feet
I would not wish to buy a horse with either boxy or flat feet. I am also put off by feet that are not part of a matching pair, because it could mean that the normal development of one foot had been retarded by previous lameness. Soft or sensitive soles are also best avoided in our sport, because the ground on cross-country courses can be rough. You can test the sole by tapping it and seeing whether the horse flinches. The horse's feet have to bear his own weight of around 500 kg (nearly 10 cwt) plus that of his rider. In trot this heavy burden rests on two feet at a time; in canter there is a moment when one foot alone bears the entire weight. It is therefore obvious that the horse needs sound and healthy feet to be an eventer.

Night Cap's head shows boldness and intelligence

Good feet for an eventer

Boxy and flat feet are to be avoided

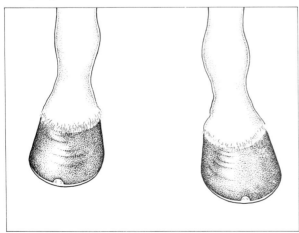

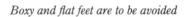

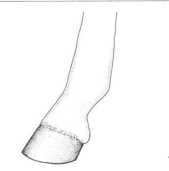

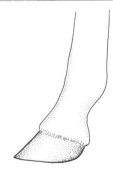

boxy feet can be prone to injury because concussion is not easily dispersed

flat feet put extra pressure on the frog and heel

Legs

I am concerned that the legs should be a good shape, with a strong second thigh. Minor blemishes would not necessarily worry me as long as there was no scar tissue in an area that might hit a fence and could not be protected by boots or bandages. Priceless had a scar on his cannon, but it was always covered by boots; it might have been a problem had it been on a knee or the front of a fetlock.

Like my mother, I would disregard a false curb, which is merely a fault in conformation. It would obviously be considered as a defect in the show-ring, but that does not concern me because I am looking for an athlete rather than a show horse. Priceless had a false curb, but we still went ahead and bought him. However, a true curb, which could be an unsoundness, would probably send me straight home without waiting to see how the horse moved or jumped.

You can recognise a true curb by standing at right angles to the horse's hindleg; from this position it can be seen as an obvious swelling at the bottom of the hock joint. The false curb is less obvious from this angle, but will be seen more clearly if you move a little nearer the horse's head. You can also try picking up the leg and bending the hock joint; in some cases, if it is a false curb, the swelling will seem to disappear.

I would prefer the horse to be physically built so that his natural way of standing brings his hindlegs underneath him. It has to be said that this is not true of Master Craftsman; his hindlegs tend to be further back than most of our other horses, but it does not seem to have been too much of a handicap!

The legs should have good bone and plenty of room for the tendons. I dislike cowhocks but would not automatically turn down the horse because of them. I would obviously turn down one with damaged tendons, because they indicate weakness and possible trouble in the future.

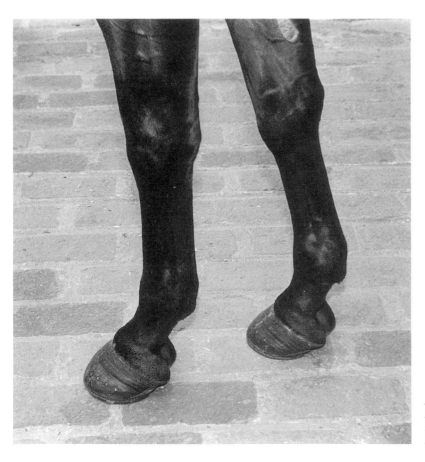

An example of good feet and limbs. Note that this horse is short between knee and fetlock, which suggests that he has strong tendons

13

Head

I like a good honest head and am definitely averse to pretty faces. Night Cap probably comes closest to my ideal. He has a lovely head, with a kind and honest look. It's the overall picture that pleases me; it would be hopeless to try to break it down into different parts.

Priceless has a real workman's head. We like to think he is similar to Arkle in this respect, even though he does have piggy eyes. However, we feel he has done quite enough to prove that a horse with small eyes can have a big heart and a sharp brain. It is the expression in the eyes, rather than their size, that can tell you a fair bit about the horse's temperament. It can indicate such things as bad temper, a suspicious nature, intelligence, or a friendly attitude towards people.

Welton Chit Chat: the ideal type of event horse, who naturally stands with a round frame

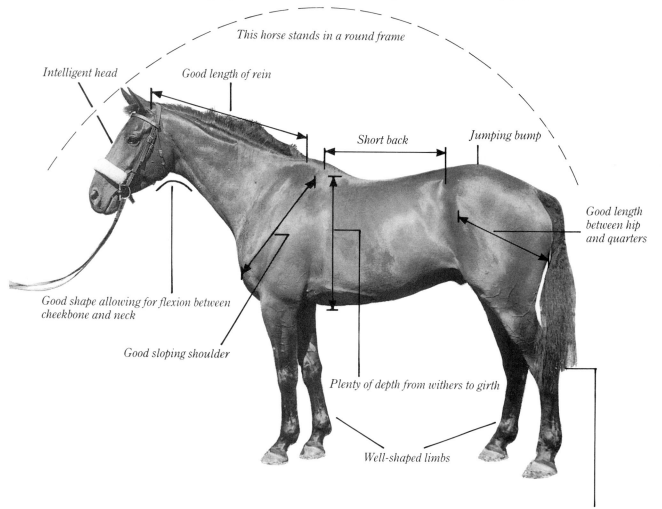

This horse stands in a round frame

Intelligent head

Good length of rein

Short back

Jumping bump

Good length between hip and quarters

Good shape allowing for flexion between cheekbone and neck

Good sloping shoulder

Plenty of depth from withers to girth

Well-shaped limbs

Hocks well let down, so fairly close to the ground

Body

My potential three-day eventer would need to have a good front, with a sloping shoulder and lean withers. Much can be done to improve the quarters, so they don't receive quite such close scrutiny. I like the horse to be in proportion, so that its overall shape looks right and all the parts appear to fit together and make a pleasing picture. I would prefer him not to be either too long or too short through his body, from nose to tail.

Griffin: another good type of event horse, with some small defects in conformation. His heavy head makes it more difficult for him to balance himself and engage his hindlegs but, because of good conformation, he is not on his forehand

Heavy head, with a tendency to carry it rather low

Slightly short in the neck

Good sloping shoulder

Short back

Good distance between hip and quarters

Jumping bump

Large cheekbone which can tend to restrict flexion

Plenty of depth from withers to girth

Good front limbs and feet

Hock rather too high off the ground

15

Movement and jumping

Next I would want to see the horse walked and trotted in hand, so that I could look at it from all angles – coming towards me, going away and moving past to give me a sideways view. I prefer the horse to move straight, but a slight dish would not be the end of the world. It must, however, have a natural spring to its trot and I would like it to give the impression that it enjoys moving.

My next request would be to see the horse ridden, by someone other than myself, so that I can assess its way of going and style of jumping. It would not worry me if the horse were not on the bit or if it failed to bend in the right direction; I would be far more interested in its natural balance and cadence. Other things, like any obvious stiffness, would be noted for future reference

Welton Houdini: another good type, also with a few faults. His natural way of standing gives him a hollow frame with shoulders down and head up, so you would expect him to find the same problem when ridden. However, thanks to his co-operative temperament, he has learnt to overcome these defects

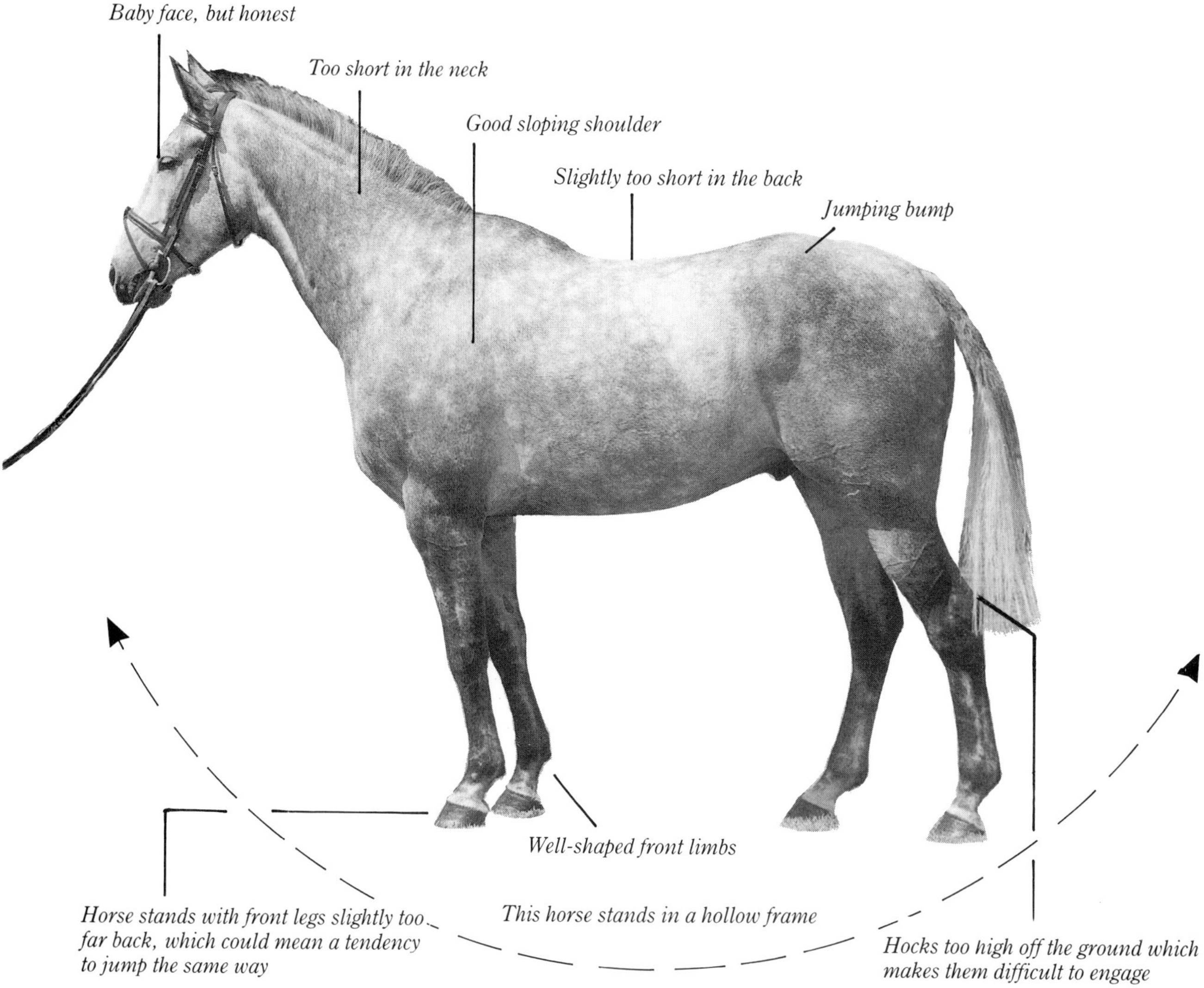

Baby face, but honest

Too short in the neck

Good sloping shoulder

Slightly too short in the back

Jumping bump

Well-shaped front limbs

Horse stands with front legs slightly too far back, which could mean a tendency to jump the same way

This horse stands in a hollow frame

Hocks too high off the ground which makes them difficult to engage

when I came to ride the horse myself.

Before that happens I would want to see the horse jump with someone else on board. If he already has some jumping experience, I would hope to see him build up from a small fence (such as cross-rails) to a decent-sized obstacle of about 3 feet 6 inches. Virtually any horse jumps with a rounded bascule when it has never been ridden over fences. The problems arise through incorrect schooling and, once bad habits have been learnt, they are hard to eradicate. At the risk of sounding ultra-fussy, I have to admit that I would not buy a horse that jumped with a hollow back or one that dangled. The latter describes a horse that fails to raise its forearm sufficiently when jumping. This would not be much of a handicap at novice level; indeed, I have known some danglers who went on to become success-ful advanced horses. I simply feel that they are less capable of extracting themselves from the sort of trouble one can easily meet in a championship three-day event, because they are virtually incapable of get-ting close to a fair-sized fence without hitting it.

If the horse refused, I would not automatically assume that it was chicken-hearted. It could, of course, be just that – but it is equally possible that the problem occurred because the rider was nervous or the horse simply lacked confidence. I would have to get on the horse myself to try to discover the root of this type of problem.

I would do flatwork first and then jumping, with my mind focused on any shortcomings I had seen while watching from the ground. Usually I can tell, more or less, if the horse is green or careless, if it lacks confi-dence or is just plain chicken. I will keep on asking myself whether I think we can make improvements, using our own methods. In our experience, very few horses are careless by nature. Mistakes that look like carelessness are usually the result of insecurity – which, apart from the odd exception, is always man-made.

Temperament

Psychoanalysing the horse on first acquaintance is never easy. Temperament is the number one priority, yet often there are only small clues to tell us whether the odd little quirk will work for us – with the help of confidence and training – or against us. Usually a bad temperament is man-made, but if you suspect that the horse has a mean or cowardly streak, it is better to find another mount.

There are all sorts of small indications that will tell you whether a horse is brave and clever. When he is led out of his stable you might ask to see him go further than his own familiar surroundings, so that you can see how he copes with different sights and sounds. Maybe you could ask for him to be led past a car – either with dogs inside barking at him or with one or two doors left open on purpose – so that you can see how he reacts. If the horse walks on confidently, you will know that he is brave.

Ears are the best indicators of intelligence. When you see a horse cock an ear at a car going up the road, you know that he is aware of what is going on. When you are aware of something, you are capable of dealing with it, so it is almost the same as being clever.

Breeding and colour

My ideas have changed over the years. Since riding Thoroughbreds, like Master Craftsman, I would be more inclined to buy one than when I rode Priceless and Night Cap, who both had some non-Thoroughbred blood. They are not, however, suitable for inex-perienced riders and many of them would not be suffi-ciently tough for three-day eventing. Having been bred to race, Thoroughbreds are notoriously lazy when it comes to schooling and you have to take care not to overdo the flatwork. Asking them to walk, trot and canter in the correct shape for dressage goes against their breeding, whereas the warm-blood horses have been specifically bred for that purpose.

I am obviously interested to know something about the horse's sire and dam, though it is far less relevant than in racing. Some sires have undesirable reputa-tions, perhaps for bad temperament or for tendon trouble in their progeny. Others are highly thought of because they have produced a number of good off-spring. Ben Fairie (the sire of Priceless and Night Cap) and Master Spiritus (who sired Master Craftsman) come into the latter category. We have horses by both these stallions, but we did not buy them just because of the sire's reputation; we happened to like them as well.

Colour is immaterial. I would personally love to ride a piebald or skewbald; they are often regarded as a bit plebeian, but I think they look really smart when well turned out. My favourite colours are grey and dark brown. I am not that keen on chestnuts, but I would certainly not be put off buying one if I liked everything else about it.

Vetting

We very rarely buy a horse without first getting our vet, Don Attenburrow, to look at it. There are few absolutely positive things we can be told about the animal but, thanks to Don's radio stethoscope, we can have the condition of its wind in black and white.

The radio stethoscope is a more effective way of testing lung function than the alternative endoscope, which involves pushing a tube down the horse's throat. The endoscope allows examination of the upper airway but since it can be used only on a horse that is standing still, its findings are inconclusive. Don's radio stethoscope, on the other hand, can test the lungs while the horse is galloping – and it is, after all, during exercise that we are concerned about his wind. It involves applying a microphone to the skin over the horse's windpipe; this transmits sounds to a tape recorder and produces a graph, similar to the one seen when a human heart is tested. Don is therefore able to see and hear the condition of the horse's lungs.

Our indispensable vet also tests the sight of our potential purchases and listens to their hearts, using a conventional stethoscope. At the same time he makes sure that there are no old injuries that might prove troublesome in the future. Unfortunately, the veterinary certificate can do no more than state that the vet has found no defect at the actual time of the inspection; it can offer no reassuring guarantee for the future. The vet is not a miracle man; he cannot promise you that the horse will be sound for the next ten years. It could slip ten minutes later and go lame.

A horse for the novice rider

The more horses you look at, the more you will learn – so try not to be in too much of a hurry to buy. You will need to enlist the help of someone experienced, whether you are answering advertisements (which do not necessarily tell the whole truth) or go to see a horse that you have heard about by word of mouth. Such help is absolutely vital if you are thinking of going to sales, where it is all too easy to be swayed by a pair of trusting eyes. Never, ever buy without getting the horse properly vetted.

If you are allowed to take the horse on trial (which obviously won't be the case if you buy from sales) you will have the chance to find out how well you suit each other. Once you have bought the horse it will become part of your life, so compatibility is important. Taking the animal on trial is, however, a big responsibility and you need to be adequately insured.

Each rider's individual circumstances, skills and ambitions are likely to be different – and all three have to be taken into account. In making the following suggestions, I am considering an inexperienced rider with limited funds, who is looking for a horse that would be fun to compete with in novice events.

The funds must not, of course, be too restricted. Buying the horse is only the first part of the outlay. It will be followed by payments for saddlery, forage, bedding, shoeing, veterinary treatment, transport and entry fees. There should then be some money left in reserve for training. Every rider, at whatever level, needs some help to iron out the faults that tend to creep in unnoticed, otherwise the horse's performance tends to get worse rather than better.

As already mentioned, there are priorities at all levels of the sport. Boldness and honesty are obviously essential – there is no fun to be had riding a horse that stops or is in any way ungenuine. I would also look for good feet and legs, because there will be a certain amount of stress and strain on them, even in novice events. You cannot guarantee that the horse will stay sound, but he is less likely to go lame if he has the right limbs and feet for the job. His conformation should be basically correct as well, because faults in this department can have a detrimental effect on the way he moves and jumps.

Breeding is not important for novice events; it does not matter in the least if the chosen animal is related to a cart-horse. Indeed, if funds are limited this could be an advantage because such a horse could live outside most (if not all) of the year and would therefore be easier and cheaper to keep than one with a large percentage of Thoroughbred blood. The cart-horse relative would also be likely to have a more equable temperament than the animal with classier breeding; very often he will move well and possess both stamina and a good jump.

There is no sustained galloping in a one-day event, but there can be plenty of twists and turns; so you need a horse that is handy rather than fast. It doesn't matter a hoot if he is a bit common and plain; it should still be possible to get round the cross-country within the optimum time once he is ready to attempt it.

Age can cover a fairly wide range. I would recommend a minimum age of six for a novice rider, because the horse should then be mature, but an older horse of up to twelve years old would be equally acceptable and would have the advantage of costing less. He may also be an excellent school-master.

Experience would be an advantage for the novice rider. Although it is not impossible for horse and rider to learn together, I would certainly advise any newcomer to the sport to start with a horse that has already done some jumping. It should also enjoy jumping; novice riders should never consider buying an animal that they have seen refusing. Horses can be pretty cute, regardless of age and breeding; they know when they have someone inexperienced upstairs and they try them out, much as a naughty child might do with a new babysitter.

Short-striding horses may have their limitations, but they also have distinct advantages for the novice rider. A horse with a long stride can be much more difficult to train over jumps than the rabbits of this world, who are far more manoeuvrable and usually meet each fence just about right. It can seem like the difference between driving an articulated lorry and a mini.

Whistling is not necessarily a drawback if the animal is to be aimed at novice and intermediate one-day events with, perhaps, a novice three-day event as the ultimate goal. This would become a handicap only if you were to attempt an intermediate three-day test, because the whistler is unlikely to be able to cope with the faster time required, although there are exceptions. Don has passed horses that were whistlers; with the help of his radio stethoscope he was confident that the condition would not have a significant effect on their performance.

Crib-biting or *weaving* would not necessarily matter either, as long as the horse was not losing weight as a result and there were no others in the yard to copy him. If you take your crib-biter or weaver to stay in another yard, you do have to warn people beforehand. Otherwise you might lose some friends through their horses picking up one of these habits.

Size is important for novice riders. Unless you have plenty of experience, you should avoid buying a horse that is too big for you. The same applies to a little horse that is a very big ride, because of his extravagant movement. He may seem perfectly amenable when you first ride him, but he could become too strong for you once he is really fit. You can often get away with a horse that is slightly small, but being over-horsed can be frightening, if not downright dangerous. Let us not forget that the sport is supposed to be fun!

SUMMARY

Basic requirements for horse with international potential

Feet:	Should be part of a matching pair. Should not be boxy or flat. Avoid horse with soft or sensitive soles.
Legs:	Good shape required and should be in proportion to the horse's body. Avoid horse with true curb; ignore false curb. Should have good bone and room for the tendons. Leave well alone if there is any sign of damaged tendons.
Head:	Look for good honest head and kind eye.
Body:	Sloping shoulder and lean withers required. Also correct conformation, with all parts in proportion.
Movement:	Look for natural spring at trot, plus balance and enjoyment of moving.
Jumping:	Look for rounded back, raising of forearm and folding of fetlocks. Should enjoy jumping.
Temperament:	Must be brave and honest. Watch how horse reacts to strange sights and sounds. His ears will tell you how aware he is of surroundings and whether he has a good brain.
Breeding:	At least 50 per cent Thoroughbred.
Colour:	Immaterial.
Vetting:	Essential.
Conclusion:	Nothing is perfect, and handsome is as handsome does.

Basic requirements for horse to be ridden by inexperienced rider in novice events

As above:	Feet, legs, head, temperament, colour, vetting.
Age:	Six to twelve years.
Breeding:	Immaterial, but undiluted Thoroughbred blood not recommended.
Movement:	Short-striding horse easier to ride, but may lack paces for good dressage marks.
Body:	Conformation should be basically correct.
Jumping:	Avoid any horse that refuses. Look for enjoyment in jumping.
Size:	Must not be too big for the rider.

3

LESSONS ON THE LUNGE

Dorothy, who does most of the lungeing at Ivyleaze with some help from my mother and myself, says that it involves being 'part of a triangle which is formed by the lunge line, the horse and the whip'. She can either widen or close up the triangle by positioning the whip closer to the horse's hocks or further away. It is much the same as in ridden work; Dot comes closer with the whip when she wants to produce more energy, just as the rider would increase pressure with the legs. If the horse were fairly busy and showing plenty of energy, the whip is kept further away on the lunge, just as the rider's legs would be passive under saddle.

We all regard these lungeing lessons as crucial, especially with young horses who are being asked to work for the first time. They are used to being handled, but they have not yet been expected to concentrate and make an effort. It is therefore the beginning of the horse's working relationship with a person and it will colour his future attitude towards both work and people.

We start to lunge the young horses at three years of age, normally in the autumn when we are approaching the end of the eventing season and will have more time to devote to the babies. They are not clipped, because they spend most of the time at grass and therefore

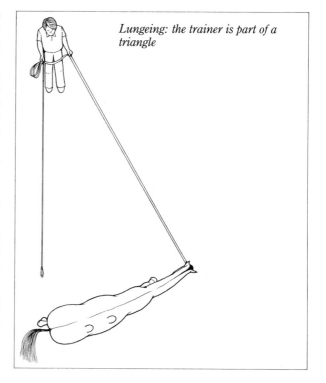

Lungeing: the trainer is part of a triangle

need their winter coats. Nor are they shod unless the ground is very hard, in which case they would wear front shoes. The hindfeet remain unshod for reasons of safety; it reduces the amount of damage they can do if they kick each other or their handler.

Those that are older when they arrive at Ivyleaze also begin their schooling with us by taking lungeing lessons. This will form an integral part of their training for the rest of their competitive lives; we therefore want to teach the horse to be obedient on the lunge. We rarely use it as a means of letting off an excess of high spirits. The youngsters can buck and play as much as they like when turned out in the field, but they are expected to listen and be obedient when they are wearing tack. If they were allowed to perform rodeo acts on the lunge, they might see no reason why they shouldn't do the same when they have a rider on top.

BEFORE THE FIRST LUNGEING LESSON

Our youngster will have been led in hand since he was a yearling (assuming he has been with us that long) so he would have become used to the human voice and to some of the basic commands such as 'walk on', 'slow down' and 'whoa'. The voice, accompanied by pats on the neck or shoulder, is also used to give encouragement to the youngster, thus helping him to form a happy association with a person.

If the horse's stable manners leave something to be desired – maybe because he is arrogant or mistrustful – he will be given part of his lesson in the stable until he learns to behave. Even with a well-mannered youngster, we make sure that someone (not necessarily the person responsible for leading him on the lunge) spends time with him in the stable to get him used to a human presence.

Before proper lungeing lessons begin, the youngster is taught to walk and halt in a straight line during short five- to ten-minute lessons given three or four times a day. We use a lightweight lungeing cavesson with a drop noseband for these lessons, with a lunge line attached to the front ring. The line is looped and held by the handler who walks close to the horse's shoulder so that he can be prodded with an elbow if he falls in (by leaning towards the handler) or barges.

Every effort is made to avoid introducing too much at once. When the youngster is led out in a lungeing cavesson for the first time, we start by walking him around the vicinity of his stable where everything is reassuringly familiar. We do not want him to be distracted by strange surroundings until he has been given a little time to become accustomed to each new item of equipment. Later he will be led around the school, in circles and large rectangles of about 20 by 40 metres – in other words approximately the same size as the small dressage arena used at one-day events.

The horse is led from both sides during these lessons in hand and he is frequently made to halt, always using the voice command as well as an indication on the lunge line – plus, if necessary, a restraining hand in front of his shoulder. The handler is aiming to make him stop without turning his head or swinging his quarters, so that he remains on the same straight line that he was following at walk.

The cavesson correctly fitted

During this pre-lungeing stage, the horse will become used to wearing lightweight brushing boots on all four legs. We use the type with Velcro fastenings rather than buckles; young horses can be fidgety and these are much easier and quicker to put on. Another new experience is encountered in the stable, which is where we let him get used to the feeling of having a lightweight canvas roller tightened around his middle. The horse will accept a saddle and girths more readily if he has been accustomed to wearing a roller in his stable, whether it is securing a rug or worn on its own.

All these experiences will make the next stage easier. By the time the horse is ready to move away from his handler on the lunge line, he will have learnt the voice commands, become familiar with the area to be used for lungeing and he will be used to going there in boots and cavesson, with the lunge line attached.

LUNGEING BEGINS

The first proper lungeing lesson begins in exactly the same way as those that preceded it. The youngster is led out as usual; he is asked to walk and halt in a straight line and he is led around the school. Having done this without any fuss, the lunge line is fed out to the horse by about 3.5 metres so that he moves on to a circle at walk without anyone alongside him.

Once this is achieved, the lesson should be ended more or less immediately, on a happy note. At all stages of training, the handler (and later the rider) must resist the temptation to keep going a little longer because everything is going sweetly. That is precisely the time to stop – before problems arise.

The horse should be rewarded after his work, perhaps by being allowed to pick at some grass on his way back to the stable or by the offer of nuts from the handler's pocket. We never give nuts before the lesson begins; they would encourage the horse to start looking for titbits instead of concentrating on his lessons.

The lesson is repeated the following day, with the horse spending a little longer circling round on the lunge at walk. At the same time a little more of the lunge line is fed out to him in order to enlarge the circle. The trainer has an assistant on hand during these early lessons on the lunge but, unless called upon to help with a particular problem, the second person remains a spectator. The assistant may have an active role to play later, if the horse is constantly falling in or fails to move at the required pace. In these instances, the second

person would walk in a small circle half-way between the trainer and the horse. If the animal is lazy and tends to hang back or keep stopping, the assistant carries the stick. This will not necessarily be used on the horse; it is usually enough for him to know that the stick is now much closer. If he always wants to go too fast, the assistant holds the lunge line so that he feels some extra restraining pressure.

Size of circle
The horse will eventually be on a circle of between 18 and 20 metres in diameter, which means that he will more or less be using the width of the small dressage arena. If the horse is big as well as inexperienced, this may seem too small for him. In such cases both control and balance can be achieved more easily by enlarging the area, which is done by the handler walking a smaller circle of perhaps 6 to 10 metres. This should be seen only as a short-term measure which might last for about two weeks; eventually the handler (after going round in ever-decreasing circles) will aim to pivot on one spot.

It is only by remaining in the same place when lungeing that you can find out whether the horse is describing a proper circle. If the lunge line goes slack, you will know that he has fallen in; when the pull becomes stronger, you will be aware that he is leaning out. You cannot be aware of such things while you are moving on a circle yourself, because you (rather than the horse) are maintaining contact on the lunge line. That process will be reversed when you stay in one spot; the horse will then take contact himself, which is a necessary part of his education. We are, after all, going to want him to take contact on the reins when he is ridden.

Length of lessons
Lessons must be kept short. Lungeing can be boring; it also puts tremendous stress on the hocks of an immature three-year-old. If the horse becomes sore, he is going to associate work with discomfort which is something we are always striving to avoid. We would therefore limit each lesson to between twenty and thirty minutes, including the initial walking in hand that would probably take up the first ten minutes. It is therefore essential for the trainer to make a note of the time before each lesson begins.

Our youngster might have two or three lessons per day, but none of them would be longer than half an hour and they could be as short as fifteen minutes. We never believe in ploughing on when a lungeing session (or any other form of schooling for that matter) is not going well. Perhaps the horse is resistant because he is tired or upset; if so, it is much better to put him away and bring him out again later the same day.

Once our youngsters have started work on the lunge, they do not have a day off for the first two or three weeks. Any break in the daily lessons could cause a setback, with the horse being a little too fresh (and therefore less obedient) after his day of rest. We believe in waiting until the horse has absorbed those early lessons on the lunge and something positive has been established.

Most horses have a natural bend to the right. Because of this, they tend to carry more weight on the left shoulder and have the left hip lower, while the quarters move out to the right. They therefore find it much easier to circle right and are noticeably stiffer when you work them on the left rein. It is important to keep changing the rein; we would never ask the horse to continue circling in one direction for more than ten minutes.

In the early stages, we are not looking for a perfect outline; we are more concerned to establish a nice rhythm and even length of stride. The horse should be both obedient and happy, as well as listening.

The voice
Horses are normally much better listeners than people and the human voice plays a major part in their training. The inflexion can be used as a rebuke or reward – and they know exactly which one is meant without the need for endorsement with stick or carrot. They also learn to recognise certain words, which makes it important for all of us who are working with the horses at Ivyleaze to use exactly the same words of command.

All our eventers are particularly receptive to the words 'Good boy'. When they hear them spoken while on the lunge, it usually signifies that the lesson will soon be ending. Some of them stop dead in their tracks as soon as they hear those two words, so we have to be careful not to say them too early.

PROGRESSING STEP BY STEP

The young horse will have worn lungeing cavesson and boots for his first lessons. If all goes well, a roller is added on the third day – fairly loosely fastened at first and then tightened if he seems quite happy. At this point he would probably be led over a single trotting pole at walk to get him used to going over something on the ground.

Trotting is added to the lesson when the trainer has decided that the time is ripe. It should not be introduced until the horse has learnt to pay attention; if he won't listen to you at walk and halt, you have not the slightest hope of getting him to concentrate at trot. It is not possible to predict how long this will take with each individual, because you can never foretell which youngster will respond quickly on the lunge and which one will be a complete featherbrain in the initial stages.

When the horse is walking and trotting satisfactorily, the roller is replaced by saddle and girths, without the stirrup irons and leathers. Depending on his reaction, this stage lasts a minimum of two days and possibly a week or more. Once he has accepted the saddle as part and parcel of everyday life, we add the stirrups. They are put up very short at jockey's length (with the leather looped an extra time around the iron if necessary) so that they are lying against the saddle flap.

Each lesson still begins with the horse being led in hand. By moving the stirrups – first when standing still and then while walking – the handler can help the youngster to get used to the mobility of the irons. Again it will depend on his reaction to this new experience whether he trots straightaway on the lunge, or goes back to walk and halt for a while.

Once he is going well at walk and trot, the stirrups can be let down gradually, over a period of perhaps a week or more, until they are hanging below the flap. They must not, however, be long enough to touch his elbow; this could cause him pain and would almost certainly create anxiety, which we are keen to avoid at all costs. It may take a week for the horse to accept the stirrups below the flap; they are bound to fly about while he is trotting on the lunge, and even if he stays relaxed, he will certainly be aware of them.

When this stage is accomplished to our satisfaction, we introduce the bridle which is fitted with a rubber bit, but with the reins removed. When the horse is ready for the reins to be added, they are tied up and attached to the throatlash so that they flap slightly on the horse's neck. Although the reins are slack rather than taut, it is at this stage that we discover whether the horse is anxious or fussy about the bit in his mouth. In many ways the whole of the training process is a voyage of discovery – for the trainer as well as the horse.

After a minimum of two days with the reins attached (or as long as is needed for the horse to be going happily), leather side-reins are introduced. They are not long enough for the horse to eat grass or, should he feel so inclined, to chew his boots. Neither are they short enough to put any pressure on the bit when the animal's head is carried normally.

The side-reins are shortened gradually over a period of several weeks, until the horse feels a slight contact and is prevented from turning his head too far to either right or left. He would also be unable to raise his head too high or to reach below his knee; though the side-reins are not being used to pull the head in towards the chest, there would be enough contact to encourage a little flexion at the poll.

The young horse requires a different length of rein in walk and trot. Whereas an advanced horse has the same frame at both paces, the novice is longer and less collected at walk and the side-reins have to be adjusted accordingly.

Having reached this stage in walk and trot only (cantering on the lunge will not be introduced until later), the young horse is ready to be backed, as described in the next chapter. We have known youngsters who could be backed within a few weeks of their first lungeing lesson, but they were exceptions to the norm. Usually you encounter some problems on the way which slow you down. The average time would be seven weeks and we have spent as long as three months on certain horses, whom we felt needed the extra time to secure the foundations of their training. The better this is established, the fewer problems you run into at a later stage.

A young horse tacked up for a lungeing lesson under saddle

Opposite: *Side reins – correct fitting for the young horse* (above), *and incorrect fitting* (below), *which leads to the horse being overbent*

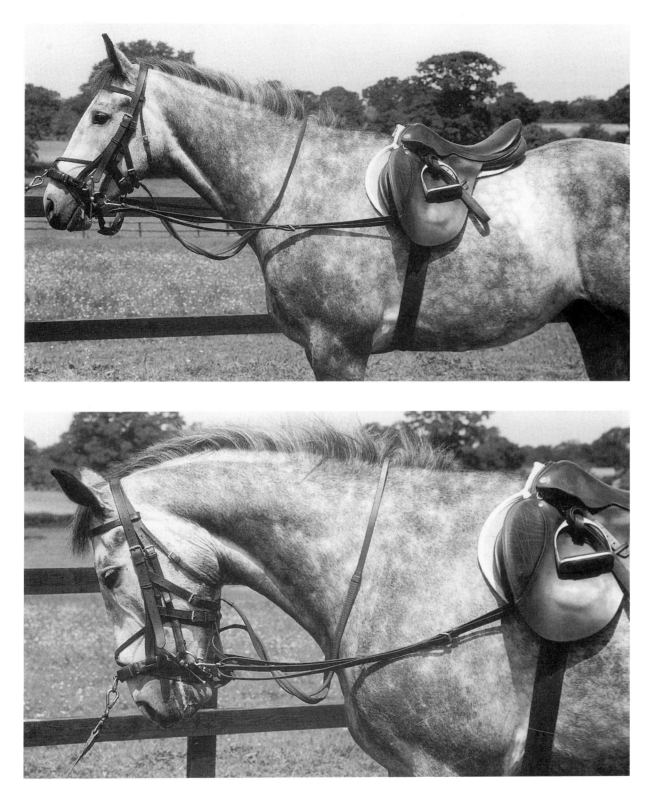

Lungeing an older horse

The mature horse that has already been backed will obviously bypass the earlier stages of lungeing. He starts with cavesson, boots, saddle and bridle, with the side-reins added a couple of days later. Very little leading is normally required before he is lunged for a maximum of ten minutes on each rein; he is used to work, so more of the lesson can be done in trot. At this stage we are trying to achieve a secure rhythm before he progresses to any serious ridden work.

As already mentioned, we will continue to use lungeing as part of the horse's training through every stage of his eventing career. These lessons supplement the ridden work and they have the same goal; whether on the lunge or under saddle we are aiming to get the horse to move in a balanced and rhythmic way, with a nice length of stride and correct bend.

Most horses favour the right rein, just as most people are more comfortable using their right hand. Because we want the horse to be ambidextrous, so to speak, it is lunged a little more on the rein it favours less. This helps to eradicate stiffness, but it should not be overdone. You can concentrate on the less-favoured rein to the extent where it becomes the one that the horse prefers; the opposite rein then becomes the problem. Sometimes the horse is so much stiffer on one side that he becomes resentful if worked for too long on the difficult rein, so that must also be taken into account. You can't expect co-operation from a horse that has been driven to resentment.

Lungeing should be regarded as an extension of ridden work, not as a separate entity. A horse on the lunge will often want to turn in and face the trainer when he halts, but it should be remembered that the rider will want him to halt without turning. So we train the horses to maintain the line of the circle they are describing on the lunge and to keep facing that way when they stop.

Sometimes we will be aiming to increase the length of the horse's stride – or, conversely, to introduce shorter strides if the horse is naturally very long and is likely to find collection difficult under saddle. The stride can be lengthened by having the horse on a slightly bigger circle (so that you are again walking some of the way with him) and by using the voice and whip to engage the hindquarters and produce increased energy. For a shorter stride, you would use a smaller circle. In this case energy still needs to be created, but the forward momentum has to be contained so that the horse becomes more springlike and less stretched out. The restraining influence comes through leverage on the lunge line and use of the voice, with words such as 'steady' and 'slow down' with which the horse is already familiar.

Dealing with problems

Some horses become stick-shy, invariably because they have been abused at some stage in their lives, and this can be a real drawback in lungeing. You have to assess whether the horse is over-reacting to the whip because he is frightened, in which case you will have to be ultra-careful. Normally the stick would be fairly close to his hindlegs and he might be given a touch on the hocks with it, if he needed a reminder to move forward. If it is pointed at the horse's shoulder, the stick has the same function as the rider's inside leg and can therefore be used to lighten a weighted shoulder (normally the left). A horse that is genuinely stick-shy will tend to run away from the whip and it has to be used with the utmost finesse.

On the other hand, he may be reacting because he is confused about what the trainer is asking him to do – or because he doesn't want to do it. It is essential to assess the situation rather than jump to a premature conclusion.

The aim is always to encourage the horse to co-operate, never to frighten him into submission. There are, however, occasions when it can be useful to give him a little assistance in frightening himself. If he stops and moves backwards on the lunge, for instance, you can use his disobedience effectively by telling him to continue going back until he bumps into something. Similarly, if he drags you across the school on the end of the lunge rein, keep him moving in that direction. As long as he is not likely to hurt himself, a slight bump can work wonders for discipline.

The training of horses requires a great deal of basic common sense, together with prudent regard for the old adage that prevention is better than cure. To take another example of a common misdemeanour on the lunge, you may have a horse that keeps swinging round at one particular spot. The answer could be to have someone strategically placed, holding a lunge whip. The assistant should let the horse see the whip, without frightening him. We don't mind him frightening himself on occasions, but we do not want him to be afraid of us. If he is to be any good at eventing, he must retain a certain independence of character; we are aiming to mould his personality, not to crush it.

Trotting poles

Once the horse has begun to establish a rhythm on the complete circle, he can be introduced to trotting over poles on the ground. They will help to loosen him and give him something new to look at and think about, as well as creating more elevation. Most horses enjoy going over things; those that don't like it will never make good eventers.

For the first lesson, we would have the pole on a straight line rather than a circle. This means that the handler has to walk or run (depending on whether the horse has been asked to walk or trot) on a parallel line about 10 to 12 feet away from the animal. If he accepts this single pole happily, more can be added, one by one, with a distance of 4-4½ feet between them.

Three poles are then placed in a fan shape on part of a circle. The average distance will be 4-4½ feet between the poles, but this will depend on the length of the individual horse's stride and it is up to the handler to acquire an eye for what is right, normally by trial and error. If you watch the horse's footfalls, you should be able to see whether the poles are too far apart or too close together and adjust them accordingly. The number of poles can be increased one by one over a period of about two weeks, until you have six on a fan-shaped curve.

Our horses do this exercise three or four times during the first fortnight, depending on their fitness and maturity. They are rarely clumsy without a rider and will normally look after themselves by lengthening their necks to look down and see where their feet are going. At this stage we are looking for the quality of stride, which includes rhythm, balance and elevation. It may be necessary to encourage the horse to lengthen its stride, which can be done by placing the poles a little further apart.

The trainer stands within the triangle and maintains contact with the horse's head

The poles can then be gradually raised (by 2 or 3 inches and later, perhaps, by 6 inches which is the highest we would have them), assuming that the horse looks as though he will be able to cope with this slightly more difficult exercise. We use our discretion and do not raise the poles for every horse, because some would find it a problem. Those that can cope with the raised poles are encouraged to loosen their backs and shoulders and improve their elevation and rhythm by this exercise.

Trotting over poles, whether lying on the ground or raised, can be arduous work for the horse. We would never do more than five minutes on each rein, always at trot, and after the first fortnight the horse would be asked to do this exercise only every three or four days. We never fail to make a careful note of the time the lesson starts, so that we can avoid the all too easy trap of creating problems by carrying on for too long. This is

an obvious temptation, because you want the horse to advance as quickly as possible; the handler therefore has to learn to be satisfied with achieving a little progress at a time.

Jumping

The Ivyleaze horses usually do some jumping on the lunge at the age of three. They start over small crossrails, with a placing pole 9 feet in front. This helps the youngster to take off at the right point, thereby giving him confidence over fences. We would then introduce him to an upright, again with a placing pole in front, which is gradually raised during successive lessons until it is about 3 feet high.

By now the horse will have been backed; he will be working with a rider as well as taking lungeing lessons. The ridden work rarely includes jumping until he has reached the age of four.

SUMMARY

Prior to first lungeing lesson

Horse led in hand, learns to walk and halt in straight line; is also led on large circles and rectangles around the school. Gets used to wearing cavesson and boots outside, and roller in his stable. Learns basic voice commands.

Sequence of lungeing lessons

(All preceded by approximately ten minutes' walking in hand.)

Horse wears cavesson (with lunge rein attached to front ring) and boots on all four legs. The lunge line is fed out so that he moves away from trainer and on to a circle at walk.

A roller is fitted (about two days later, if no problems). Trotting is introduced when horse is behaving at walk. Roller is replaced with saddle and girths (no stirrups). Add stirrups, with leathers very short so that irons lie against saddle flaps.

Lengthen stirrups gradually until they are below saddle flaps, making sure that irons cannot touch horse's elbows.

Add bridle (no reins).

Add reins, tied up and attached to throatlash.

Introduce side-reins.

Shorten side-reins.

Trotting poles

Horse is led over single pole on the ground, usually at about the stage when he is being lunged at walk in cavesson, boots and roller.

After he is wearing side-reins at the correct length for trot, the horse is taken over trotting poles placed on a straight line.

Trotting poles are introduced on the curve of a circle. If horse is able to cope, the poles on this circle are raised.

Golden rules

Keep lessons short (no more than thirty minutes, including ten minutes walking in hand).

Do not introduce anything new until each step has been accomplished satisfactorily.

Be strict with the horse – explosions of high spirits should not be allowed on the lunge.

Keep the horse happy and interested in his work (i.e. do not grind on with anything he finds difficult).

Keep to walk and trot only – cantering will be introduced at a later stage.

Lungeing over poles of varying heights and distances will improve the horse's balance and cadence

29

4

BACKING AND EARLY RIDDEN WORK

BACKING

It is normally one of the girls who gets on a young horse when we are backing it for the first time, which is good experience for working pupils. This is always done in the security and familiar surroundings of the horse's own stable, with someone holding his head.

We will have prepared the three-year-old for this moment by pulling downwards on the stirrup leathers in his stable so that the saddle feels heavier on his back. If the youngster tends to be difficult when faced with a new experience, the rider will start by lying across its saddle a few times. More often than not, however, the rider mounts from a solid, non-wobbly stool or is legged straight up to take a normal seat in the saddle. The horse is patted quietly for a minute or two, then the rider dismounts.

This would be done about three times, and if the horse behaved perfectly, we would leave it at that for the day. If he were difficult in any way, the rider might get on four or five times – always with the intention of finishing on a good note, with the horse behaving reasonably well. Should the animal find all this rather alarming, we might repeat the process later the same day.

Once the horse seems quite happy to have someone getting on and off his back, he will be led round the stable with the rider on top. Being in such an enclosed space restricts his movements, which obviously makes it much safer than being in the outdoor arena. Our horses are usually ridden in the stable for about a week before they venture outside.

We always use a mounting block for getting on the horse once it has left the confines of its stable – and for ever after when it is possible. This means there is less chance of the saddle slipping; it also reduces the risk of pulling the horse's back or digging a toe into his ribs. Obviously the animal has to be taught to accept a rider mounting from the ground, because I might need to get on him in some place where there is no mounting block available, but otherwise we try to avoid it. At an event, or when we travel by horsebox to go cantering, I either stand on the ramp of the vehicle to get mounted or have a leg-up.

The mounting block at home has an additional advantage with young horses. It is always hard to assess how much they are blowing themselves out, but if you are getting on from the ground, you have to make sure that

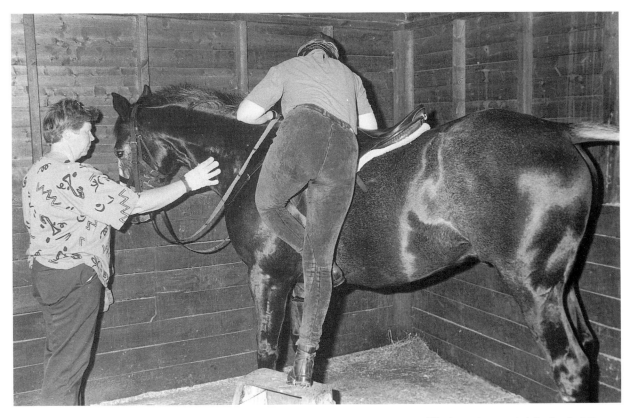

The horse is mounted for the first time in his stable

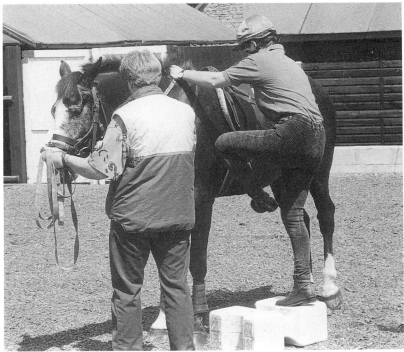

Mounting outside in the arena for the first time, with a handler to hold the young horse

the girths are tight. We do not want the horse to associate the saddle with discomfort, which would be the case if we over-estimated how much he was blowing himself out and tightened the girths like a vice. They can afford to be a little less tight when you are getting on from the mounting block, with an assistant holding the horse's head.

ACCEPTING THE RIDER

To begin with our young horse wears a cavesson over its bridle, with a lunge-rein attached. He would normally be bitted with a cheek snaffle that had a mild rubber mouthpiece. Steering can be difficult with a young horse and the shafts at either side of this bit are more suitable than rings, because they prevent it from sliding through the mouth when the rider gives the aids to turn. The equipment would also include a breastplate or neck-strap.

During his first lesson with a rider on board, the horse is led round at walk on both reins. We prefer him to be led, rather than lunged, with a rider because it enables him to walk on a larger area. At this stage, he should pay attention to the person on the ground rather than the rider on top. Until now all his instructions have come from someone on foot; he needs time to get used to the idea of transferring his attention to someone who

is out of sight and whose voice is coming from higher up and further back.

The ideal rider for our immature three-year-old would obviously need to be light. He (or she, as is usually the case at Ivyleaze) also needs to be totally laid back. These early lessons have to be learnt with someone who is relaxed and fairly passive; any hint of tension and anxiety will make it more difficult to gain the horse's calm acceptance of carrying a person on his back.

Quite often, as he walks forward with his handler at his side, the horse is unaware that there is someone sitting quietly on top. At first the handler will be giving the voice commands; then the person on the ground stays quiet and the rider does the talking. Some horses turn their heads to look up and back in order to find out what is going on. After that, they normally accept our totally laid-back rider quite calmly.

Assuming that the horse is behaving, we would expect to remove the lunge line after about a week – though the youngster would continue to wear the cavesson for two or three more lessons, just in case it was necessary to attach the line again. Although control is now being transferred to the rider, the handler still walks alongside. More often than not, the horse is unaware that he is no longer being led. When the handler moves away, transferring total responsibility to the rider, the youngster often follows. He has to be pushed back on his own separate line with a hand held out towards his shoulder.

Reassurance is all-important!

Opposite:
First lunge lesson with the rider (above)

Responsibility is transferred to the rider (below)

Lungeing over poles will help the horse to use his shoulders correctly and engage his hindlegs

A youngster takes his first jump from trot. Dangling forelegs show that he is unsure about his technique

Later the same day. Increased confidence enables the horse to jump with greatly improved style

It is important to walk the distance correctly. The horse's experience, physique, natural ability and length of stride then have to be taken into account

A difficult open intermediate coffin: rail, one stride, ditch, bounce, ditch, one stride, rail

The approach requires a short, balanced and bouncy canter to the base of the first rail

The horse needs encouragement and freedom of head and neck over the ditch, with the rider sitting up

The horse gains confidence while the rider still encourages him to go forward

Freedom of head and neck is still required, with the rider staying in the centre of balance

An open intermediate double bounce of three white verticals, with both distances at 15 feet (4.57 metres). The correct pace on approach depends on the horse's length of stride as well as the distance between elements and can only be learnt through practice at home. There is no room to make adjustments if the approach pace is wrong. The rider should stay well within the centre of balance, allowing the horse freedom of his head and neck without losing contact. Note that the horse lands equidistant between the vertical rails

LEARNING THE AIDS

Throughout these early stages the horse is learning, by constant repetition, to associate the rider's leg aids with the familiar voice commands of 'walk on' and 'whoa'. Normally he is given a moment's advance warning by using the word 'and' before the instruction. If we want to prepare him to move forward, for instance, the command would be 'and . . . walk on'.

Assuming that he has been correctly handled, the young horse is remarkably quick to learn that 'and' means some instruction is about to follow; we will continue to use it at a later stage as a preparation for transitions. It makes no difference who says the words, as long as they are always exactly the same for each command. These words form a reassuring connection throughout the early stages of training. The young horse first learns them when he is led in hand; they are repeated (not necessarily by the same person) when he is being lunged; they are used by someone else when he is ridden. The importance of using the same words during each stage of training cannot be over-emphasised. They are the great link that helps us to continue getting our message through to the horse without confusing him.

The voice is obviously an essential part of the early ridden work, when we are teaching the horse to respond to leg aids. The instruction to 'walk on', given at first by the handler, is accompanied by a light squeeze from the rider's legs. Unless the horse is whip-shy, it may be helpful for the rider to carry a short stick, which can be used to reinforce the legs by giving a light tap behind the girth as a forward aid. This message can also be underlined by the handler tapping the horse by hand behind the girth. When used on the shoulder, the stick helps to correct the horse when he has fallen in or out.

The horse again has to learn to walk and halt in a straight line, this time with a rider on top. Before the handler moves away, he must be taught to stop when the rider tells him to do so.

Though we want the horse to accept a light contact on the reins, the rider has to be ultra-careful to avoid spoiling his mouth. We would use the voice command together with a light feel on the reins – reinforced, if necessary, by a tug on the neck-strap. The handler can also help with light pressure on the lunge-rein and by placing a restraining hand in front of the horse's shoulder. If the horse were to acquire a bad mouth through the rider pulling on the reins at this stage, it would be with him for the rest of his life.

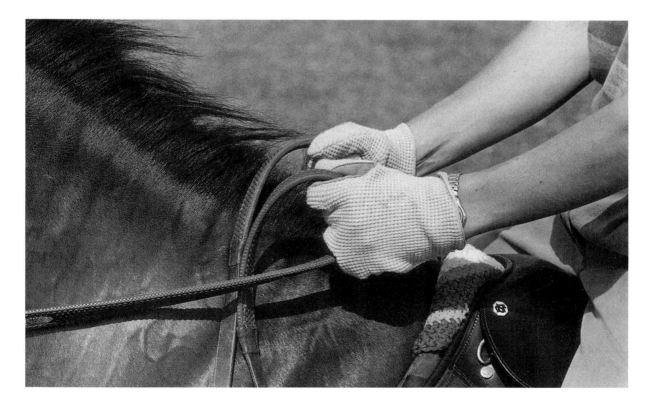

Through constant repetition, praise and discipline (plus some help from his remarkable memory), the horse will slowly learn to respond to the signals given by the rider's legs, weight of body and hands. Aids for the basic movements he will learn are described at the end of this chapter.

THE RIDER

You need to check your own position before you begin to think about what the horse is doing. This is best achieved by riding on a loose rein round the school while you are sorting yourself out.

Only a light contact, which allows a forward feel, should be attempted in the initial stages. You must be careful not to pull back on the reins but to relax your arms and let your hands move forward instead; they should maintain contact as though they were a piece of elastic extending to the horse's mouth. To do this, you need to be completely relaxed in body, arms, wrists, hands and fingers. You should hold the reins as you would a bird – gently enough to avoid squashing it, but not too lightly because it would fly away.

The amount of contact, which will vary according to the individual preference of each horse, needs to be maintained at a constant level. We sometimes help to explain this to our working pupils in the tack room, with someone holding the bit end of the reins and simulating the movements a horse might make. The pupil holds the reins at the rider's end and tries to follow these movements, with arms moving forward and back to maintain a level contact.

If you are tense on a horse, your shoulders, elbows and wrists will be tight, making it difficult for you to use your hands in a sympathetic and responsive way or to distribute your weight correctly. The effort of concentration makes it all too easy to become tense without being aware of it, so you need constantly to question yourself to make sure that every part of you is relaxed. If you are aware of some tension, take deep breaths or sing a song to help yourself relax!

Hands – correct position (left), *and incorrect position* (right), *which could lead to 'blocking' the horse*

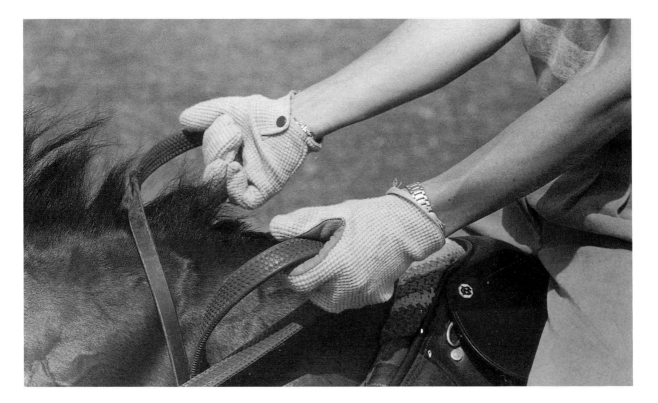

There should never be more contact through the hands than through the legs. Novice riders often try to grab the unfortunate horse between the upper leg and crutch, which gives their thighs the same action as a clothes peg and tends to move them upwards rather than down into the saddle. Instead your legs should be resting quietly against the horse's side, with thighs and knees relaxed. If you think of your ankle being on the horse, you will probably get the right part of your leg on him. The horse can be either helped or hindered by the way you use your legs or distribute your weight.

Some riders have a natural feel, which helps them to listen to the horse. Others have to teach themselves to be aware of everything the horse is doing. This awareness will be a key part of successful training because it tells you what you want to achieve and when you should start trying to achieve it. You cannot plan a horse's training on a computer; you have to listen to him, feel your way forward and be flexible.

SCHOOLWORK

You will need an enclosure of some description, whether it be a corner of a flat field or a permanent arena. The young horse requires 40 by 40 metres or (as we have at Ivyleaze) 30 by 60 metres for his schoolwork; anything smaller is too restrictive.

To begin with, lungeing will still occupy the larger part of the youngster's lessons after he has been backed. He is given two short sessions of work each day for the first week, which start with him being led or lunged for about ten minutes at walk. This is followed by five minutes trotting on the lunge. He then has a maximum of fifteen minutes' ridden work at walk, using the half of our school that is further away from the exit. If he is going well, the rider will finish the lesson early to ensure that it ends on a happy note. After about a week, he is given just one daily lesson of combined lungeing and ridden work lasting a total forty-five to fifty minutes.

During the course of the next few months the lessons will slowly change, with a decreasing amount of time given to lungeing and more of each session devoted to riding. At the start of his ridden work, he is walked on 25-metre circles and squares at the far end of the school. After that we would aim to get the youngster used to going all the way round the school, to crossing it on the diagonal and to being ridden on large loops, circles and oblongs. He is kept away from the post-and-rails at the side of the school, probably by no more than 5 feet, because young horses have a tendency to lean towards any type of fencing.

Ten to fifteen minutes' ridden work in the school is quite long enough. We do not want him to regard this as a place of tedious work, any more than we encourage him to see other areas where he is ridden as places to let off steam. Whether in the school, being ridden in the fields or later, when the horse is considered safe to take out on a hack, he is expected to listen to his rider. There will, of course, be occasions when the horse wants to do nothing of the kind. It is our job to try to combine strictness with consideration, so that he is happy in his work and wants to co-operate. We must also be on our guard to foresee situations in which arguments might arise, in order to avoid them.

If, for instance, the horse has been known to nap, you could have someone standing quietly at the exit with a lunge whip as you are riding past during the early work under saddle. If you are any good at listening to the horse, you should know when you can dispense with your assistant, always bearing in mind that you must do everything you can to avoid a battle of wills.

If our youngster is going really well at trot on the lunge and is behaving sensibly, we will include trotting at an early stage of the ridden work. This is done without making too many demands on the horse. As my mother says, 'You would obviously trot to the best of your ability, but this is not the time to have the vapours if the horse falls in coming round corners at trot, or if he loses some of his rhythm and balance.' Rome was not built in a day and we should not expect to get results from a young horse overnight.

To begin with, the rider will simply do a little trotting to add variety to the lesson in between trying to get a good walk. By the time we begin to ask for something more at trot, we will want the horse to be walking quite well, with good rhythm and balance.

Learning the basics
The horse has to learn to go forward on a light contact, which is best done by keeping him on the move and stopping as little as possible. If he is reluctant to go forward, the rider's voice and leg aids can be reinforced by using the stick behind the girth. It may also help to exploit his herding instinct by having another horse some distance in front, but within sight, for him to follow.

He must also learn to be straight, with the line of his body from ears to tail following the line he is taking. Thus on a circle, his body has to be curved to be 'straight'. Each hindfoot should follow in the same track as the corresponding forefoot, but do not be alarmed if your youngster tends to wander off that line. It is quite normal for the young horse to be crooked, as you will probably have seen for yourself when he was on the lunge.

It is only through work on the flat that he becomes straight. To do so, he has to learn how to balance himself with the weight of a rider on his back, and take an even contact on both reins.

Falling in on a turn or circle is also quite normal. It happens when the horse moves his balance to the inside shoulder and his feet usually follow by drifting inwards. His head invariably bends to the outside, which leaves his inside shoulder leading. If you watch a horse out in the field, you will see that this comes naturally to him. He automatically moves round corners with his inside shoulder leading and his head bent in the opposite direction. We therefore have to exercise great patience when we ask him to stay upright and bend his body from head to tail on the same curve as the turn or circle he is following. This is something that is not natural to him and he will need time to learn how to do it.

We are looking for a light contact as soon as the horse is backed, but we will not be asking for him to carry his head in any particular way. If you try to improve his shape before he is happy to have contact with the rider's hand, he will learn to evade the bit. To begin with, he will move his head in all directions and your hands have to follow wherever it goes. Once he is happy to accept a light feel on the reins the horse's head will remain still.

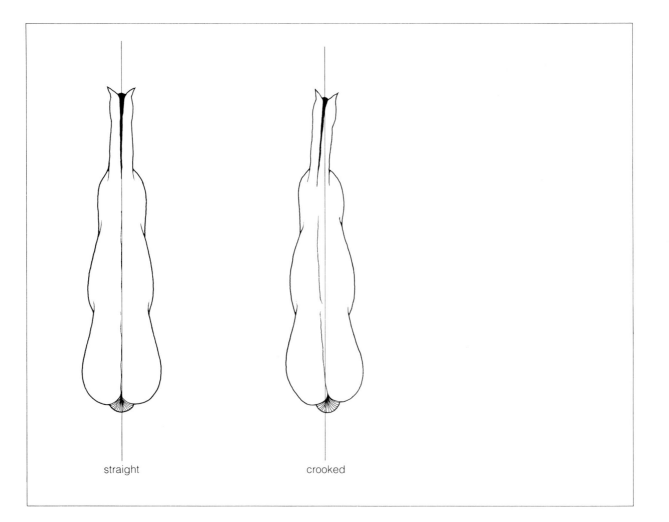

straight   crooked

Rhythm and balance

Work on the flat helps the youngster to carry himself in a way that makes it easier to support the weight of a rider. He has to learn to carry the extra load on his hindlegs and he can do this only if the rider's body is controlled, in balance and still, moving only when there is a specific reason for doing so. The horse is capable of balancing himself on his own; we must therefore avoid interfering with this natural balance through our own lack of suppleness or an inability to sit still.

Young horses are often in a hurry; they tend to go faster than the speed at which they can best achieve rhythm and balance. This is often a throwback to nature, which has given the horse an instinct to use flight as a means of escaping from anything he dislikes or distrusts. Even when happy and trusting, he may like to remind you that he was born to gallop!

It could be that the youngster's exuberance is caused by over-feeding, which is a common mistake. As will be discussed in a later chapter, we believe in giving as little hard feed as possible to get the horse fit enough for the job in hand.

When he goes too fast, the horse tends to shorten his stride. This encourages him to fall in on turns and circles, simply because that is the only way he can balance himself at the speed he is going. The trainer has to decide on the right speed for each individual horse, otherwise he will not be properly balanced with the weight of the rider. This usually means slowing down a little in trot, but not necessarily in walk.

If you do not have a metronome in your head, it may help to play some music in the school so that you can recognise whether or not the horse is in rhythm. The choice of music would obviously have to be different for walk (which is in four-time, with no moment of suspension) and trot (which has a distinctive one–two beat, with suspension between steps).

Turns and circles

Riding a correct turn is exceptionally difficult. There is only one way of doing it properly and, according to a renowned dressage expert, 3982 ways of getting it wrong – which could easily lead one to despair! The rider must be able to move each hand and leg independently, because each has a different function. When turning to the left, your inside (left) leg is used on the girth to stop the horse falling in and to keep him moving forward. The outside leg rests behind the girth, ready to be used if he swings his quarters towards that side. The inside rein asks the horse to make the turn and bend in that direction. The outside rein allows for this flexion, while maintaining contact and (if necessary) controlling the speed or correcting any excessive bending. Your shoulders need to turn with the horse and there should be slightly more weight on your inside seat-bone.

In order to get your weight in the right place, you have to overcome a natural tendency to sit on the outside seat-bone. If you try turning your shoulders to the left while you are sitting in a chair, you will probably discover this for yourself. It is natural for the right hip to collapse and for the weight to sink to that side. Your position will be crooked if you do the same thing on a horse; he will then have to compensate by going crooked himself, thus losing his balance, impulsion and rhythm.

If the horse encounters problems at a later stage, it will almost certainly be because he never learnt to do basic turns and circles correctly. They will not be achieved in one session. As already mentioned, most horses tend to be stiff on the left side. This means that they carry their quarters slightly to the right, which results in them leaning on the left shoulder. Turning to the right will seem much easier, but will nevertheless be incorrect because the horse's weight will be on his left shoulder and he will therefore have a tendency to fall out. Turning to the left will reveal more obvious faults – and plenty of them! The horse will tend to fall in with his left shoulder, tip his quarters to the left, cross his left hindleg in front of the right hindleg, lean on the inside rein and lose contact with the outer one. All these things have to be corrected.

Circles are a continuation of turns, so the same principles apply. If the horse consistently falls in when circling to the left, we use an exercise called counter-balancing. This is done by using your inside (left) leg on the girth to encourage him to lighten his left shoulder and keep moving forward, while feeling on the right rein. As a result, the horse bends to the right for one or two strides, which helps to take the weight off his left shoulder. He is then asked for the correct bend to the left, which he is in a better position to achieve because his weighted left shoulder has been released. Once he has learnt to go on a circle with the correct bend, the horse will discover that it is far more comfortable than doing it the wrong way and will therefore be happy to co-operate.

The counter-balance exercise can also be used on a straight line to encourage the horse to balance himself correctly and take an even contact on both reins. Another method to help overcome his natural stiffness is to give and take with the left hand while maintaining your leg aids; this will stop him leaning on the left rein and encourage him to take contact on the right.

Introducing canter

The horse is usually ready to canter after five to six weeks of ridden work but his physical development, as well as his state of training, has to be taken into account before it is introduced. If the horse is still physically immature, we would not attempt canter until later in the year – or we might wait until the following year. We invariably use a minuscule cross-rail, about 6 inches off the floor at the centre, when asking for the first canter strides. This is placed three-quarters of the way down the long side of the school, which will encourage the youngster to strike off with the inside leg leading.

The cross-rail saves the necessity for strong aids – and avoids the possibility of the horse going into a fast and unbalanced trot – since he will invariably land in canter over this tiny fence. Once started we would probably include canter in the lesson two or three times a week, asking for no more than one large circle to begin with.

Within the next fortnight, the horse will probably be asked to strike off in canter using normal aids (see end of chapter) instead of the cross-rails. If he is sufficiently strong and balanced, he might do two or three circuits at canter – preferably using a slightly larger area than 20 by 40 metres which is rather confined for a young horse. The trot needs to be re-established for a period of four to five minutes immediately after the horse has cantered. He may have become excited and will need this time to return to the calm, relaxed and rhythmic trot that should have been established by now.

Hacking

The length of time required before the horse can be hacked out in safety obviously depends on the individual youngster and the local environment. Usually our country lanes are reasonably quiet and we would normally reckon to take a horse out on them between eight and ten weeks after he had been backed. First he

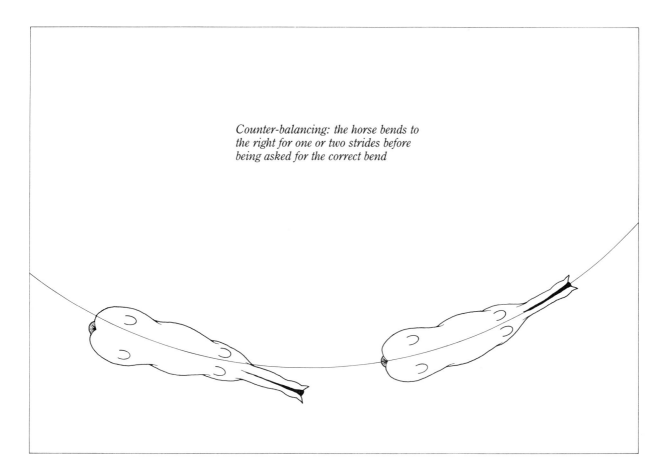

Counter-balancing: the horse bends to the right for one or two strides before being asked for the correct bend

will be taken down the drive, then a little way along the road, followed by a short trip around the village block. Assuming he is behaving sensibly, he will then venture further afield. We rarely hack a youngster out alone, so the horse will normally have one or more companions with him. These early outings last between twenty minutes and half an hour, using different routes but avoiding anything in the locality that might cause alarm.

By now the horse will be working for one hour six days a week. He will have a combination of lungeing, ridden work in the school and hacking – though not necessarily all three on the same day. The art of successful training lies in keeping the horse interested by giving him a variety of things to do; you can never hope to hold his attention if he is bored stiff with his lessons. Hacking should not, however, be seen as something entirely different. We use these outings as an extension of the school work, not as occasions for meandering along country lanes.

At this stage the youngster should be able to stay straight at walk and trot on a 20-metre circle and a large 20 by 40 metre rectangle, without falling in or leaning out on either rein. He should also be able to walk and trot on a large figure of eight. Being a baby, he will still be slightly wobbly, so little more is expected of him until the following year.

After three to four months' work, the youngster is turned away. Thanks to his long memory, we can be confident that his lessons will not have been forgotten when he comes back into work about four months later.

SUMMARY

Horse is first backed and ridden in stable.
Rider gets on outside from mounting block.
Horse is led round at walk on both reins, with handler on ground giving voice commands.
Rider gives voice commands.
Horse learns aids by rider applying them at the same time as the voice command. The stick is used only as a last resort.
Lunge line is removed from cavesson, but handler continues to walk beside the horse.
Handler moves away, transferring control to rider.
More lungeing than ridden work initially, slowly changing until horse is ridden more than lunged.
Horse ridden on large circles and squares at one end of school.
The whole school is used for oblongs, loops and riding across it on the diagonal.
If horse is sensible and trotting well on lunge, he starts trotting with rider.
Canter is introduced after five to six weeks, if horse has made sufficient progress in training and physical development.

The rider
Check position before thinking about the horse.
Aim for light contact with horse's mouth.
Relax arms and let hands follow horse's head movements.

Be completely relaxed and in balance.
Never use more contact through hands than legs.
Learn to listen to the horse.

Basic aids

Upward transitions (halt to walk, walk to trot):
Slight sink of body, with weight moved back a little.
Squeeze evenly with both legs.
Ease the reins as horse moves forward, but do not lose contact.
Trot to canter (left leg leading):
Weight on left seat-bone, slightly angling left hip forward.
Ask for a little bend with left (direction) rein.
Allow for bend by giving with right (supporting) rein.
Left leg on the girth.
Right leg behind the girth.
Allow a little with the hand as horse strikes off, but do not lose contact.
Downward transitions (canter to trot, trot to walk, walk to halt):
Prepare with one or two half-halts three strides before transition (i.e. squeeze momentarily with legs, while using hands to restrain faster movement and increase collection).
Weight up and slightly back.
Squeeze with both legs.
Retard with give and take of reins, followed by a longer retarding feel until the transition is executed.
(N.B. Your hands do not allow horse to continue at same pace, but he should not freeze up against you.)
Turn or circle to left:
Weight a little more on left seat-bone.
Ask for bend with left rein.
Right rein allows for bend and controls speed, while maintaining contact.
Left leg on girth to stop horse falling in and keep him moving forward into both reins.
Right leg behind girth to control quarters.
Turn shoulders with movement, taking care to keep weight off right seat-bone.

Aims for the trainer

At this stage we want the horse to learn to:

– go forward
– stay in rhythm
– accept contact on both reins
– balance himself with the weight of the rider
– be straight
– maintain the correct bend.

If he leans on left shoulder, use counter-balance when circling on left rein: using left leg and right rein, ask him to bend right for one or two strides. Immediately ask for correct bend to left, while weighted left shoulder is released. Counter-balance can also be used on a straight line to improve balance and encourage even contact on both reins.

Golden rule: Keep lessons short!

5

PROGRESS ON THE FLAT

The young horse is more mature, both physically and mentally, when he continues his education at the age of four. We believe in giving him plenty of time at this stage, so that he can learn without being hurried along. The better these foundations are established, the easier it will be the following year when he is preparing for his first competition.

Though he needs enough food to help him grow, his education will suffer if he is fed too much and is over-fresh as a result. He will then be too excited to listen to his trainer and the work he does will be less concerned with learning than with letting off some of his excess energy.

When he comes back into work, the four-year-old will need to get fit with a minimum of three weeks' walking. During that time, his daily work starts with ten to fifteen minutes on the lunge. This helps to make him fitter and more obedient, which also makes him safer to be taken out for a hack immediately after-wards. Work is limited to fifty minutes for the first week and then builds up to between one and one and a half hours. After the first fortnight, he still goes out for his daily hack and is either ridden or lunged in the school. Hacking is also part of his schoolwork; at Ivy-leaze we do not believe that dressage training has to be confined to an enclosed area and that you can forget all about it when you leave the arena. The horse probably finds it more enjoyable to be out on the roads or in the park, where there is so much more to see, but he is nevertheless asked to move to the best of his ability and to stay on a straight line. Once he is fit, he can do more strenuous schoolwork and hacking. He will also start the jumping lessons which are described in the next chapter.

IN THE SCHOOL

The shapes that the horse follows under saddle can now become more demanding, but the emphasis on forward movement remains. He is asked to walk smaller circles of 10 metres in diameter and to trot 20-metre circles. As well as oblongs and large 20-metre squares, he walks a smaller square of 15 metres. Diamonds, also of 15 metres, are introduced. These help to make the horse's shoulders more mobile and teach him to keep his quarters in the right place as he turns. As we have already discovered, making a cor-rect turn is by no means easy.

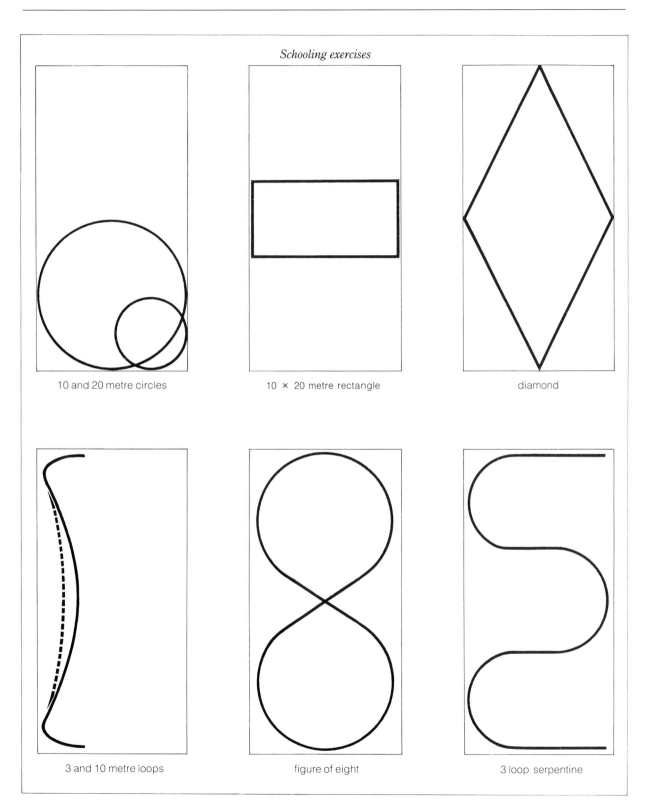

Schooling exercises

10 and 20 metre circles

10 × 20 metre rectangle

diamond

3 and 10 metre loops

figure of eight

3 loop serpentine

Next we would introduce 3- and 5-metre loops, followed by figures of eight within the small dressage arena size of 20 by 40 metres. The figure of eight incorporates two diagonals and constant changes of rein, which helps us to discover how well the horse balances himself, with the weight of his rider, in a small area.

More canter work is then introduced, both out hacking and in the school. The horse is asked to strike off, using a corner or circle to encourage him to lead on the inside leg. If he fails to do so, he will not be reprimanded. He has been asked to canter and has produced the right pace, albeit on the wrong lead; it would only confuse him to be told that was not what was wanted.

Usually he will come back to trot of his own accord if he is leading on the outside leg, and he should be

Turns and circles are difficult to perform with the correct bend, as shown here

allowed to do so. He is then trotted round the school and asked to canter at exactly the same place as before. This exercise is repeated, if necessary, until he strikes off on the required leg. He would then build up the number of canter circuits on each rein, depending on how long he can keep going without any sense of struggling.

Three loop serpentines at walk and trot are now added to the other shapes the horse was following in the school. We also like to introduce our four-year-olds to leg yielding, which is always the first lateral work they do. This exercise, in which the horse yields to the rider's leg by moving away from it, encourages more response to the aids. It also improves the horse's suppleness and elevation, at the same time helping to produce a rounder outline. At this stage, we would attempt it only at walk.

Horse and rider enjoying their work at canter

For his first lesson in leg yielding, the horse is ridden along the three-quarter line of the school and then asked to move diagonally for a few steps, crossing one fore and hindleg in front of the other. We are looking for only a little flexion from head to tail, with the horse bent slightly away from the direction in which he is going. It is always the inside of the bend (rather than the direction of the movement) which is meant when referring to the inside rein or leg – which, in this case, is on the opposite side to the direction the horse is taking.

For leg yielding to the left, he should be slightly bent around the rider's inside (right) leg, which is applied behind the girth to keep the horse moving diagonally away from it on four tracks. The outside leg, used lightly near the girth, maintains impulsion, controls the quarters and prevents falling out. The inside rein helps to keep the horse's shoulder on the correct line and asks for a slight bend, while the outside rein controls the speed.

At this stage of the horse's ridden work, we also use trotting poles – at first one on its own to be ridden on a straight line, gradually building up to about four on the curve of a 20-metre circle. These would be spaced at the same distances that were used for lungeing. Walking and trotting over these poles on the ground encourages the horse to look and see where he is putting his feet. They also help to improve his cadence and elevation, with the weight of a rider on his back. If the horse is supple and relaxed, we might add more poles or raise them off the ground by no more than 6 inches.

By now the horse's trot should have improved. We want him to be calm and relaxed, in rhythm and listening. Each horse has a distinctive one–two beat in trot and the trainer needs to know that beat in order to achieve good rhythm.

It is at this stage – assuming that the horse is performing the above movements satisfactorily and has accepted an even contact with the rider's hands – that we can also start asking for some flexion from the poll and so introduce the correct outline for dressage.

Lengthening and shortening

As soon as the horse has rhythm and co-ordination at working trot or canter, I would think about asking him to lengthen and shorten within that pace. We tend to start with canter, which is normally the easiest because it comes naturally to the horse. The walk is the most difficult, because it is harder to create energy at a slower pace; for this reason, we normally leave lengthening and shortening at walk until last.

By now the horse's jumping lessons (described in the next chapter) will have started and I will want him to be able to shorten and lengthen in canter on the flat before I think about cantering into a fence. His own length of stride dictates which of the two we work on first. If short, I would begin by asking him to lengthen for five strides and then come back to working canter. This is done by creating the necessary energy with your legs and then giving with your hands, thus allowing him to stretch his head further forward without losing contact. The horse is unable to lengthen without this extra freedom of his head and neck, because his feet cannot hit the ground any further forward than his nose. You will be looking for lengthened strides, not a faster speed; if you are failing to achieve it, you will have to come back to working canter and try again.

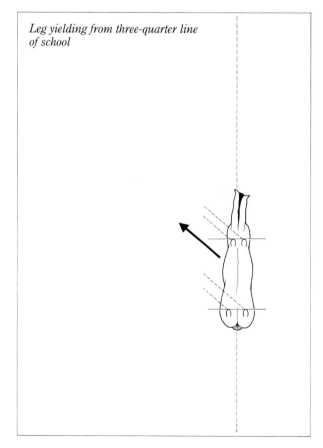

Leg yielding from three-quarter line of school

Opposite:

Good lengthening at trot, except for horse's head being slightly behind the vertical (above) *and a little overbent* (below)

Since the horse is quick to anticipate his rider, you should avoid asking for lengthened strides in the same place. Once he gets the idea that the long side of the school is the place where you want him to perform this new exercise, he is likely to start doing it without being asked. So use the short side as well and, maybe, part of a large circle.

Some horses have a naturally long stride and they need to work at shortening. In this case the rider's legs again need to create energy, but instead of encouraging the horse to stretch his head and neck forward, the hands ask for that extra impulsion to be contained in shorter and more active strides, almost like a series of half-halts. Though the immediate aim may be to help him with his jumping, shortening will also improve his working canter and be of benefit when he comes to perform serpentine loops and other more difficult movements at canter. There will be similar benefits for the short-striding horse when he learns to lengthen; these lessons will eventually produce a better medium and extended canter, as well as helping with his jumping and galloping.

Having said all this, we should not be too greedy. Flatwork can help to improve the horse's natural paces, but only up to the natural limit imposed by his conformation and action.

The rider

The rein must always be used with a give and take of the hand, never with a continuous pull. Sometimes the hand will be passive and it can be slightly restraining at the same time, while waiting for the horse to submit to the aids. The passive hand, when incorporating that element of restraint, can be an effective means of correction if the horse is leaning on the bit or unwilling to give to the rider's hand. It must always be used with sensitivity and backed up by leg aids. The restraining element is omitted if the horse is evading the bit. In this case the hand is entirely passive, waiting for the horse to come to the bit and accept an even contact. When this is achieved, the hand should yield (but without losing the contact), which is a way of conveying thanks and praise.

The level of contact you have with the horse's mouth will depend on his balance, size, cadence and individual preference. Some horses like a fairly strong contact while others prefer a much lighter one, so you have to assess your own partner's specific requirements and go along with him.

If you suddenly drop the reins and lose contact during a movement or transition, he will wonder what has happened to you and lose his balance. This is not because you are supporting him; the connection between you and the horse, established through the reins, is more like holding a child by the hand while you are crossing the road: you are holding (rather than supporting) the youngster – but if you suddenly let go of that hand, the child will be thrown off balance and will probably stop still.

You will also affect the horse's balance if you are out of synchronisation when riding a circle at rising trot. When circling left, you should sink into the saddle as the horse's right (outside) forefoot and left (inside) hindfoot touch down. Since you should frequently change the diagonal – and therefore the direction – this means sitting for one stride as you change the rein. It is always the horse's inside hindleg which produces the required energy and impulsion.

Whenever you are sitting into the saddle, you must be fluid – moving your weight with the motion of the horse's back. If you go against his natural movement, he will stiffen against you. This can lead to a tense back – and trouble.

During these lessons you should continue to concentrate on keeping the horse straight, with his hindfeet following the same track as the forefeet. Since the engine is located in the rear, it might be easier to think of the hindlegs propelling the forehand ahead, rather than following in its wake. To stay straight, you need to look forward and see your line; if you close your eyes, you are bound to go crooked.

Lungeing

We continue to use lungeing as part of the horse's schooling throughout his eventing career. It replaces one, or maybe two, dressage lessons each week and is regarded as schoolwork, not simply as a type of relaxation. While on the lunge, we can work at getting the horse comfortable in the rounded shape that we want him to adopt, which is not natural to him; when left to his own devices, he moves around with his head in the air. We can also encourage him to stay loose in his body while he goes over trotting poles, which help his cadence, elevation and footwork. It is obviously easier for him to do this on the lunge, without the extra effort and change of balance required when he is carrying a rider on his back.

Most of our lungeing is done at trot. We can work on the rhythm of this pace, with and without trotting poles. Our horses rarely canter on the lunge and they do very little walking. Without a rider on board to reinforce the aids, there is always the danger that the horse will shorten in front and not behind when he is lunged at walk which leads to uneven footfalls.

HACKING

Schoolwork is not forgotten while out hacking, which occupies most of the four-year-old's ridden work each day. The one great difference outside is that he is not constantly required to turn, but can keep on a fairly straight line for most of the ride, which is better in this stage of his training.

My mother, who enjoys riding our youngsters both in the school and out hacking, says that there are always three questions in the forefront of her mind: Is the horse in rhythm? Is he going forward? Is he straight? She is also aiming to get him on the bit and going evenly in both hands, without putting his shoulders or quarters in the wrong place. Much as she enjoys these outings, she knows that it is not the time for gazing at the countryside or planning the menu for lunch!

The rider's awareness while out on the roads has to take account of possible hazards ahead, usually in the shape of large vehicles. It might be necessary to pull into a gateway if you spot a large lorry coming towards you. We prefer to keep the horse moving because then it has less time to get itself into trouble, but you have to use your intelligence and know when it is more prudent to stop and let the vehicle go past. It is also important to choose the route out hacking in a positive way, because a horse will always know if the rider is uncertain about which way to go.

There is no time for gazing at the countryside while out hacking

Improving the paces

The walk can be the most difficult pace of all. We have had plenty of horses at Ivyleaze who proved that point, usually because their walk was short and choppy. There is no set solution to this problem; we would try several different things in the hope of finding one that worked. Equally important, we would discard any exercise that was clearly failing in its objective. It's a great mistake to grind on when you are obviously getting nowhere fast.

The horse might lengthen his stride if the rider pushes him on – or he may, on the other hand, shorten even more. Sometimes it helps to slow him to a crawl or to ride him on a long rein for three or four minutes, using the legs quietly to ask him to move on. A horse will normally walk with its head and neck down when given more rein, much as it would in its wild and natural state. The walk produced under these circumstances is usually good and sometimes excellent.

Though he will probably revert to his short stride once the reins are taken up again, the horse has shown the rider – even if only for a few strides – that he is capable of something much better. Having felt the improvement, the rider now has something at which to aim. You must make a fuss of the horse to tell him that those few strides, whichever way they were achieved, were just what you wanted. You must also resist the temptation to keep slogging on with that particular exercise in the hope of attaining a perfect walk in one lesson. Those are the very occasions when you are likely to lose the little you had achieved by asking for too much.

The horse needs plenty of variety, rather than repetition, and it is up to the rider to provide it. You could, for instance, do a circle at trot before making another attempt to establish a longer stride at walk, which is hard work for a young horse. It might help him to relax if you give him a short trot or canter afterwards. There is no easy rule of thumb; you have to listen to the horse and try to understand what is going through his mind in order to find out what is right for each individual.

Asking for an extra effort, such as a longer stride at walk, should not be restricted to work in the school. The next time, it can be attempted while you are out hacking, which is another way of breaking up the work and keeping it varied.

Sometimes, especially when dealing with a Thoroughbred horse that has been bred for racing, we encounter the opposite problem at walk. This time the stride is very long and it needs to be shortened slightly so that the feet are quicker off the ground. In this case, you need to take up the reins with a give-and-take movement and ask, with your legs, for a shorter and quicker stride.

You do not want the horse to lose his natural long walk (which you will need when extended walk is required in a dressage test), nor do you want him to start waddling, which sometimes happens when the balance changes. You also need to take care that he does not shorten too much, which you will know has happened if he either stumbles or begins to jog, because then you have to go back to square one. You therefore need to be constantly aware of what the horse is doing, always remembering that he must shorten from the back rather than the front end.

Some horses are reluctant to walk at all out hacking; instead they jog and always want to be out in front. The answer may be to trot on, until you are quite a long distance ahead of the ride. The horse will then start wondering what has happened to its companions and, perhaps, be a little less eager to go off in front next time. If this is tried a few times and it fails to have any effect, you will have to think of something else.

It could be that the horse jogs and generally behaves in a silly way because he is highly strung, which is usually the result of him having been asked to do something too soon. He easily gets in a panic, and when he does, he is prompted to have an argument. In this case it can be a good idea for the rider to make no demands, but to sit quietly and pat the horse reassuringly. Since it takes two to make an argument, the horse will usually become aware that he is wasting his time.

No horse is one hundred per cent perfect, so you are bound to encounter problems with at least one pace. If he has a wonderful swinging trot, for instance, you will probably have to work hard at improving his canter. Having done that, you should not be too surprised to find that you have lost some of the excellence at trot. Improvement in one department is often gained at the cost of a step backwards somewhere else, but you invariably regain what was lost if you are patient.

You can sometimes use the canter to achieve a better trot. If, for instance, the horse is naturally correct and balanced at canter, it can help to use that pace before trying to improve and lengthen a trot that tends to be short and choppy. The key is to use the horse's best pace, because that is the one in which he feels most comfortable.

Napping

We can never hope to conquer a horse physically, but we can usually get the upper hand mentally if we are prepared to use our imagination and common sense. Arguments are best avoided wherever possible, which is why you need to be cautious about using a stick on a horse that naps. One good smack could be the answer. Should that treatment fail I would rather use patience as a weapon and, if the horse refuses to move in the required direction, be prepared to sit on him all day.

This form of resistance has to be nipped in the bud or it will become a major – and possibly insurmountable – problem. A typical case is when a horse stops in its tracks and makes it abundantly clear that he has absolutely no intention of taking another step in that direction. Instead he tries to whip round and retrace his steps. We would not allow him to turn or to go backwards, but would make him stand facing the direction in which he was supposed to go. He is not asked to move forward, because that would almost certainly prompt him to fight back. He has to stand there until he is so bored that he eventually decides to yield to the rider's will.

There are some horses that rear when they are prevented from turning or going backwards. They don't normally rear very high, but the rider must be able to stay on without hanging on to the reins. Dismounting should be regarded only as a last resort, when you feel it would be impossible to stay in the saddle. If you do dismount you will need to run the stirrups up and take the reins over the horse's head. Should he still refuse to move forward, you have to stand and wait. Every so often you can say, 'Come on, let's go,' in a positive way, but without attempting to drag the horse forward. If he still refuses to budge, keep him standing there. We have never yet come across a horse at Ivyleaze that didn't eventually succumb to boredom and submit to moving forward.

You have not entirely lost the battle by dismounting, but it is always won more effectively from the saddle. It will be important to assess the individual horse, taking its past history into account, to ascertain whether the problem is likely to recur. If another confrontation seems probable, you will need to enlist the help of a stronger and more experienced rider who can sort out the problem without dismounting. Meanwhile, avoid having a confrontation with the horse yourself. You can always lunge him or do some other form of exercise that has not given any problems in the past.

We have enlisted outside assistance at Ivyleaze on a number of occasions. One horse that persistently napped was cured by a friend, who employed our favoured method of sitting still and doing absolutely nothing until the horse decided that it was all a big bore and submitted. We knew the rider had the temperament and discipline to deal with the problem, and that he was a strong enough horseman to sort out our wayward youngster from the saddle.

Though patience is normally far more effective than punishment, there was one occasion when the stick worked wonders for us. We had a horse that constantly swung round while out hacking and then did its level best to go whizzing back the way it had come. Having tried without success to put an end to this infuriating habit, my mother asked another friend if he could instil some discipline. She had a feeling that a few sharp whacks from someone stronger than herself might do the trick. At the first wallop, the horse unleashed a spectacular series of leaps and jumped a fence unbidden. He must have been disconcerted to find that he still had a rider on top, and at the second wallop he capitulated. Our friend rode him a few more times and when my mother got back on the horse she found he was a reformed character. We might have been able to crack the problem by other means, but the stick proved far quicker and more suitable for this particular horse's temperament.

The stick would have created a further problem instead of effecting a cure, had we used it on another of our horses, who was suspicious of people – as a result, we felt sure, of being badly treated in the past. This horse, whose brain is razor sharp, used to make the excuse of having seen something unusual while out on a hack and then whip round to the left. It would probably have been quite easy to turn him a full circle and then continue the way he was going, but we never allow our horses to do that; if they swing round to the left, they have to go back to the right in order to face the required direction. This form of resistance can otherwise lead to running out at a show jump, because the horse knows it can swing left or right and do a complete circle.

My mother dealt with this particular horse herself. She never raised her voice or got angry with him when he whipped round. Instead she sat quietly; he was not allowed to keep turning left, but there were no heavy aids from legs or stick to try to get him back the way he came. It took about five minutes before he yielded and she then rewarded him with much patting and repetition of the words 'good boy', which all our horses recognise as a sign that we are pleased with them.

SCHOOLING ON GRASS

Horses can all too easily pick up the idea that grass has only two purposes: to be eaten when they are loose in the field or to be galloped on when ridden. This is not a helpful attitude when you get to a one-day event and have to ride a dressage test on grass!

We had one horse, who was already backed when we bought him, that used to go loopy every time he felt grass under his feet. He was to test our patience and consume much of our time when we set about curing him. Three days a week, one of us would ride him at walk on grass. He soon learned to behave reasonably well when kept on the move, but if you stopped and stood still, he would immediately tense up and start plunging and rearing. There was no hint of a problem if you stopped him on the road; it was only grass that produced these antics.

We used to take this horse to the field when some of the older eventers were cantering, and he would have to walk while they went sailing past. Eventually our efforts paid dividends; you could stand him in the field while the other horses galloped past and he was as good as gold. Had we not been ready to devote as much time to him at that stage, we could have had a big problem on our hands.

Young horses, especially those that are normally schooled on an all-weather surface, need to be educated on grass. If I had no field available, I would try to persuade a local farmer to let me use a corner of his land for occasional schooling. There is no need to spend a long time there; ten minutes is enough to remind the horse that fields are sometimes used for dressage.

The next day I might take the same horse for a happy ride in the park, with a little trotting and some quiet cantering. The day after that I might do dressage in the park, which all helps to tell him that he is expected to behave whatever we happen to be doing on the day. If he always does the same thing at the same place, he will begin to anticipate instead of listening.

SUMMARY

Horse gets fit with three weeks' walking (ten to fifteen minutes on lunge, followed by roadwork).
Exercises in school include 10-metre circles at walk, 20-metre circles at trot, 20-metre squares and diamonds at walk. Also 15-metre squares and diamonds.
Three- and five-metre loops and figures of eight are introduced.
Canter work increased, with horse asked to strike off on inside leg.
Three-loop serpentines at walk and trot are added to the other shapes.
Lengthening and shortening is introduced, using horse's best pace.
Leg yielding is taught at walk.
The horse is asked for flexion from his poll.
Trotting poles are included in ridden work.
Lungeing and hacking continue.
(Jumping lessons have begun – see next chapter.)

Aims for the trainer
The priorities remain the same: forward movement, rhythm, balance, even contact on both reins, straightness.
We are looking for improved paces, and some lengthening and shortening of strides within horse's easiest pace(s).
Horse must be educated to behave on grass.
If he naps, do not let him turn a full circle.
Leave him with only one option: to go the way you want.

Aids for new movement
Leg yielding to left from three-quarter line of school, with horse bent slightly around the rider's inside (right) leg in the opposite direction to the way he is going:
Weight even on both seat-bones.
Left (outside) leg – used near girth – maintains impulsion, controls the quarters and prevents falling out.
Right leg, used just behind the girth, keeps horse moving diagonally and forward.
Left rein prevents horse falling out or going too fast.
Right rein helps to keep the shoulder on correct line and asks for slight bend.
(N.B. Inside rein and leg are on the opposite side to the direction in which the horse is going.)

6

LEARNING TO JUMP

The horse must be given confidence through every stage of his education. This is particularly vital when you are teaching him to jump; anything that undermines his self-assurance will be a serious setback, requiring a frustrating return to square one.

Our youngsters begin their jumping lessons when they are four years of age, which is when I start to play a bigger part in their lives. By the time I get on to give them their first jumping lessons, they will have learnt about co-operating with their human minders, without losing their individual personalities. The Ivyleaze method has never involved bludgeoning horses into submission.

FIRST LESSONS

The horse is already familiar with trotting poles, both on the lunge and during his early ridden work as a three-year-old. I use them again before jumping the four-year-old for the first time, though I would probably trot across them only a couple of times. They help to make the horse a little bit sharper and get him used to the weight and balance of the rider.

I normally have the trotting poles on one side of the arena and tiny cross-rails, about 1 foot high, on the opposite side. This small fence has a placing pole 9 feet in front of it, which will help the horse to take off from a point that will make the jump seem easy. Having ridden him over the trotting poles, I ask him to take the cross-rails from trot.

As with everything else connected with the horse's training, this should seem like a natural progression from the lessons that went before. If the rider gets worked up about it, the horse is likely to lose his cool and become over-excited whenever he is presented with a fence to be jumped. If he does tend to rush, I put some trotting poles in front of the placing pole; these help him to concentrate and stay within the rhythm.

I want the horse to be happy jumping the cross-rails from trot. Having popped over them a few times, I might finish jumping for that day – or I might take him over a small vertical of 1 foot high. I would not, however, start with a vertical. We always use cross-rails to begin with because their shape encourages the horse to aim for the lowest point in the centre, which helps to keep him straight.

Teaching the horse to stay straight in his early jumping lessons will be of enormous benefit later, when I

53

want to take the corner of an angled fence. Short-coupled horses usually find staying straight much easier than the longer animal with a big stride like Master Craftsman, who tended to drift to the left whenever he thought he was getting uncomfortably close to a fence. This gave him some extra space and was easier than shortening up like a concertina, which he finds particularly hard work because of his conformation. Drifting to the left or right might not be a problem over single, straightforward fences, but it could land you in all sorts of trouble when jumping corners and angles.

After two or three weeks, I would expect to be jumping three or four fences of about 2 feet high from trot, sometimes with place poles and at other times without them. These would either be single fences or built in line to form a grid. Progress obviously depends on the individual horse, who has to be given as much time as he needs to gain confidence.

I jump the youngsters twice a week until their balance and confidence are established. This must be done without interfering with the natural bascule that all horses have until they are required to carry a rider over fences. After that, I jump only once a week. I might pop the horse over the odd fence to give him some fun and loosen him up on non-jumping days, but he would have only the one proper lesson.

Jumping will occupy only part of a twenty-minute session in the school, which would also include flat work. I want the horse to enjoy jumping and look forward to it, which would not be the case if I were to make this part of the lesson any longer. Since I never do the same thing twice running, the horse has the added interest of waiting to see what fences he will be jumping next. He might have a quick jump through a grid and then do a round of little fences. He may just concentrate on grids, which can be built in many different ways to allow for plenty of variety. Constant repetition is as boring for horses as it is for people, so I am always thinking of ways in which to make the exercise more interesting.

SINGLE FENCES

I use a placing pole in front of single fences only until the horse has learnt to trot into the obstacle and pick up confidently. After that, I want to encourage him to see his own stride and learn to look after himself. Without the placing pole to put him right at take-off, the youngster invariably starts by standing much too far back

from these single fences. Then he will probably come in too close until he learns to make his own adjustments of stride.

Apart from telling the horse where to go, and keeping him in rhythm and balance, I am a passive passenger during these lessons. I need to give the youngster plenty of freedom in his head and neck, which encourages him to think for himself, maintain his balance and produce a nice rounded jump. At this stage he will be jumping little spread fences as well as verticals in trot.

On the familiar 'prevention is better than cure' theme, I refuse to allow the possibility of the young horse stopping at a fence and having to be turned back for a second attempt. For that reason, the four-year-old always starts jumping from trot, over fences that are small enough to be taken from a standstill should he grind to a halt. If you have to turn back, the horse will have learnt the last thing you wish to put into his head: he will know that stopping can be used as an alternative to jumping. I would not consider any obstacle that was too large to take from a standstill unless I was as sure as one ever can be that the horse would jump it.

The same is true whether I am jumping small fences at home or popping over little logs and ditches in Badminton Park, where we are lucky enough to be able to ride. If the horse does stop, he is not allowed to turn away but has to keep facing the obstacle until he jumps it from a standstill. In such cases the rider has to be unyielding.

BUILDING A GRID

Gridwork makes the young horse more athletic and helps him to be quicker with his feet – or to pat the ground, as we call it at Ivyleaze. With the use of a placing pole and correct distances between fences, the grid will also help to build his confidence because he will reach each of these small jumps at exactly the right point of take-off. When he becomes more self-assured, we can introduce different distances which encourage the short-striding horse to lengthen, or the long-strider to shorten.

The first grid would consist of two small cross-rails, with 18–19 feet (5.5–5.8 metres) between them, which would give room for one non-jumping stride. I would probably add a third and then a fourth cross-rail, with the same space between them, before introducing other types of fences and varying distances.

We might then change to a cross-rail followed by two

A place pole brings the young horse to the correct point of take-off and he jumps with confidence. He is allowed to use himself by being given freedom of his head and neck

verticals. The second vertical can later be converted to an oxer, after which I might add another vertical to give four fences on a line. Once the horse is happy to land and take off again one stride later, the fences can be gradually raised. The actual height and distance will be at the rider's or trainer's discretion, because you have to take account of the horse's temperament, capacity and natural balance. I have known horses that had so much confidence they were ready to jump 3 feet in the first week or so, but these were exceptions. Others might take as long as two months to reach that height.

By this time bounces will have been introduced. I always use small cross-rails when first asking the horse to bounce – in other words to jump two fences without taking a non-jumping stride between them. As already mentioned, the cross-rails help to keep the horse straight, which is particularly useful with youngsters who invariably have a tendency to wander off the line. My first bounce is always in a grid over cross-rails, set at no less than 10 feet (3.05 metres) apart. Depending on the height of the cross-rails (and remembering the bigger the fences the greater the distance required between them), I might extend this to 12 feet (4.57 metres).

The grid for this first bounce consists of three cross-rails, with one non-jumping stride to the second element and a bounce to the third. If you are feeling ambitious, you can then add a fourth cross-rail to give a second bounce. This type of exercise helps to get the horse on his hocks and makes him sharp and quick on his feet.

Once he is happy with this exercise, the bounce can be introduced into a grid that includes different types of fences, such as parallel bars and uprights. We continually alter our grids to avoid making the lessons repetitive; we also set them in a different place each time. I might, for instance, start the horse with a grid on the left-hand side of the school going away from home. If it stayed in that place, the youngster would soon begin leaning towards the post-and-rail fencing on his left and he would anticipate the right-hand turn at the end of the grid. The next time we would therefore make sure that he had to turn left at the end.

Placing poles

The grid can be made more adventurous by using placing poles before or after the fences. A pole strategically placed before a jump can encourage the horse to get close, so that he rounds his back and bascules over the fence instead of taking off in a flatter shape, more like an aeroplane. Often the youngster tends to panic slightly and take off from too far back, so this exercise helps to build confidence by teaching him that he can get closer and round his back. It also encourages him to use his shoulders in order to tuck up his forearms.

A pole placed 9 or 10 feet away from the fence on the landing side will also improve the bascule by encouraging the horse to land a little steeper. This is not recommended for an inexperienced youngster, who might well find the sight of this pole lying close to the spot where he was expecting to land such a shock to his system that he freezes in mid-air.

With a green horse, I prefer to put the pole equidistant from two fences in the grid. It can then be gradually moved in until it is 9–10 feet (2.74–3.05 metres) away from the landing side of one fence and further away from the obstacle which follows. The bigger the fence, the more room he needs to land, so you must exercise caution. The pole will be as close as 9 feet only after a small fence of up to 3 feet (0.9 metre); a distance of at least 10 feet will be used for anything bigger. Placing poles can also be used to encourage the youngster – or any horse that has a tendency to wander off line – to remain straight over his fences. This is done by laying the poles on the ground at right angles to one or more fences. Normally I use poles on the take-off side only for a green horse, if he has a tendency to drift on his approach to the jump. He has to be more experienced before I put them on the landing side as well.

The poles will probably be at the same width as the fence itself when first introduced; then, slowly but surely, they are moved in so that any deviation from a straight line is restricted. I have had the poles as close as 3 feet on an advanced horse, but I would not pull them in by more than 1 foot (0.3 metre) on either side of the stands for a baby. You can be sure that the horse will not land on one of these poles more than once; instead, he will learn to look down and see where he is putting his feet! He will therefore be encouraged to jump straight at all times.

JUMPING AT CANTER

Approaching a fence at canter is a big step forward for a young horse. I never attempt it until I am satisfied that the youngster can canter in balance on the flat and has learnt to shorten and lengthen his stride. You will know when your own horse is ready simply by asking yourself, while cantering around the school, whether you would feel comfortable jumping at that pace. The type of canter the horse is producing on the flat will give you the answer, as long as you are honest with yourself. If

The horse is dangling with his forearm, leading to the inevitable fence down (above). Fortunately most horses are apt pupils. This youngster has learnt by his mistakes and now produces a good jump (below)

it doesn't feel too great, you will know that the time has not yet come. Some of our horses do not canter into a fence until they are five; others have such a natural canter that they are ready quite early in the year they reach the age of four.

We have to use our natural instincts to feel our way forward with each individual horse. There is no programme that can be planned in advance, with set lessons on given days. I may appear to be ultra-cautious, but that is because I care for my neck too much to risk taking short-cuts with the horse's education over fences!

In jumping, as with everything else connected with horses, we have to take the animal's physical assets and defects into account. This means, for instance, accepting that the horse with a huge, long-striding canter is going to find this stage more difficult than the one with a short, choppy stride. Some, like Murphy Himself, can overcome the problems of a long stride through natural balance and athleticism. Others, like Master Craftsman, take much longer because the athleticism does not come naturally. He was bred to race and lengthen, but not to shorten.

Like most horses, Crafty was slightly on his forehand when he was younger and that made it difficult for him to shorten his stride. Beneficial, on the other hand, had a short, choppy stride which was by no means ideal for dressage but did make jumping easier, because he was never far away from the best point of take-off. Ben was one of those rare horses who was ready to pop over a 2-foot fence at canter after his first grid work. We built a 3-foot fence within the grid for Crafty, but his canter work on the flat had not progressed sufficiently to jump him over single fences at canter in those early stages.

When a young horse has had a lesson which includes jumping at canter, I invariably bring him back to trot the following week. Otherwise he might begin to find it all so exhilarating that he lights up as soon as he sees a fence. Sometimes the rider gets over-excited; the horse then gets the impression that he is supposed to screech round and go flat out into his fences. Instead, he should be learning to land in a relaxed way and maintain a rhythmic canter between the jumps.

If the horse is jumping with plenty of confidence at canter, I would consider clear-round show jumping at this stage. One of our horses, To Be Sure, did this as a four-year-old and loved it. I could feel him growing in conceit after trotting into the first two fences and clearing them. He landed over the second in canter and,

because he felt happy and balanced, we stayed at that pace for the rest of the course. Had he lost his balance and rhythm, or tried to rush his fences, I would have brought him back to trot.

I might also consider taking the horse cub-hunting in the autumn, with a view to taking him fox-hunting when he is a five-year-old. This is a marvellous form of education for young horses. It teaches them how to look after themselves across country and to find a 'fifth leg' when required to keep upright. They therefore gain enormous confidence and, because they love jumping in company with other horses, they find it great fun. Priceless had a full season's hunting as a youngster and it did him the world of good.

If the horse does hunt, he needs to do so at least ten times – if not for the whole season. Taking him out three or four times is worse than useless; he simply learns to associate grass with galloping. Given a longer period, he would discover that the sport is not just about charging across country and he would learn to settle down.

CROSS-COUNTRY FENCES

I always jump a few coloured poles at home before going out to jump natural obstacles. It is much easier for the horse to learn how to leave the ground and land back on to it without such additional problems as un-level ground or an awkward approach. He is also less likely to hurt himself over movable poles than over solid natural fences, and as I want him to associate jumping with pleasure, any pain he experienced would be an obvious setback.

The first natural fences our horses jump are usually little logs and ditches in and around Badminton Park. These are taken at trot and are small enough to be jumped from a standstill if the horse happens to stop. I would try to find some water for him to walk through as a four-year-old, and I might jump on and off a small bank. I might also take him to a schooling area that had a selection of trotting fences, but I would not attempt anything more ambitious.

The horse would need to be confident over show jumps at home, including small doubles and combinations, and he would have to be happy to take them in canter, before I would consider attempting a decent-sized novice cross-country fence.

THE RIDER

If you and the horse can establish a good style over small fences, you will have fewer problems when the time comes to jump larger obstacles. During the approach, you should be slightly in front of the vertical with your shoulders on about the same line as your knees. It is important to remain still; if your weight moves, the horse will be thrown off balance. As a result, he loses impulsion and may not have enough power left to clear the fence. At this stage your seat should be lightened within the rhythm of the canter; if you sit deep in the saddle, the horse's back will stiffen. It is your job to control the pace and direction and to keep him in rhythm and balance, so you must not lean to either side.

When he reaches the fence, the horse uses his head and neck to balance himself before he thrusts off with his forelegs. There is a natural instinct for the rider to lean further forward at this point, with the mistaken idea that it will help the horse. In fact it hinders him, putting more weight on to his shoulders at the precise moment when he is trying to use them to thrust forwards and upwards. Instead of flopping forward on that last stride, you should slightly open the angle between your body and the horse by becoming a little more upright, thus reducing the weight on his shoulders.

Almost as soon as the horse's forefeet leave the ground, his hindfeet touch down at roughly the same spot. His weight is then shifted back to his hindlegs, which contain the energy of a coiled spring for the final push at take-off. The rider's body should therefore move forward when the forelegs are in the air and before the hindlegs have left the ground. This does not mean flinging yourself forward; you simply need to go with the movement and stay in balance.

Meanwhile, your hands should also have followed the movement. They will need to go forward on the final stride, when the horse's head and neck are lowered and stretched out towards the fence. His head will then be raised and his neck arched as his forelegs leave the ground, so your hands have to come back to maintain contact. They move forward again as his hindlegs touch down in preparation for take-off, which is when his head and neck stretch out for the start of his bascule.

Your application of the aids should depend on the horse. He needs to bring his hindlegs well under his body to gain enough impulsion for take-off, but this does not necessarily mean using strong aids. Some horses prefer to have no leg aids until the last stride before take-off; others jump better if you use your legs for the last three strides. The same individual preferences pertain to the amount of contact on the reins. I have one horse who dislikes anything more than the lightest of contact on the final stride when he is lowering and stretching his head and neck. Others prefer a fairly firm contact throughout the approach. It is up to the rider to assess each horse's preference and learn to adapt accordingly.

There is nothing you can do to help the horse once he is airborne, but you can be a positive hindrance if you fail to stay in balance – or if you lean to either side and, in the process, encourage him to be crooked. You will need to remain a passive passenger until he has taken one stride away from the fence after landing. He will touch down on one foreleg and put all his weight on to the fetlock, which is pushed down until the pastern is roughly horizontal. He needs to be given time to regain his balance after landing, so you should wait until he takes his second stride away from the fence before bringing him back under control.

It will help the horse if you are able to see a stride at canter. Some people can do this naturally; others have to work at improving their eye. One useful exercise is to have a small cavalletto four to five non-jumping strides from a fence of about 2 feet 6 inches (0.8 metre). The average horse has a canter stride of 12 feet (3.7 metres) at canter, so you can measure the approximate distance by taking the relevant number of 1-yard strides yourself and allowing a total of 7–8 feet (2.1–2.4 metres) for landing over the cavalletto and taking off at the fence. The distance should obviously be adjusted if your horse has a longer or shorter than average stride.

The horse should approach the cavalletto in a rhythmic and balanced canter; you should not make the mistake (as some riders do) of hooking up and then riding like crazy. When he jumps this tiny rail – which he will do by elevating and shortening his canter stride – the rider counts down the number of strides to take-off. You can also learn to see a stride by cantering towards a thistle or past a tree and counting down the strides as though you would be jumping at that particular spot.

SUMMARY

Horse trots over poles on ground and then jumps small cross-rails (with place pole 9 feet in front) from trot.
Horse jumps small single fences from trot.
Grids are introduced.
Horse learns to see his own stride over small single fences (without place pole) from trot.
Bounces are introduced between small cross-rails in grid.
Cross-rails, uprights and spreads are included in grids, with different distances (bounce, one and two non-jumping strides).
Placing poles are used as necessary – to encourage horse to stay straight, take off later, land steeper, etc.
Small natural obstacles (logs, ditches, etc.) are jumped at trot.
Fences are approached at canter when the horse can maintain his balance while lengthening and shortening in canter on the flat.

Aims for the trainer
Horse must stay straight (no veering to left or right on approach).

He should enjoy jumping, so keep lessons short and varied.
He must not learn to refuse (start with fences that are small enough to jump from standstill).
Retain horse's natural bascule.
Improve athleticism through gridwork.

The rider
Should try to develop an eye for a stride.

On approach:	Body slightly in front of the vertical. Seat lightened within rhythm of canter. Remain still and in balance.
Last stride:	Body slightly more upright until forelegs thrust off. Lean forward with the movement when weight is on horse's hindlegs. Hands follow movement of horse's head and neck.
Over the fence:	Stay in balance – do not lean to either side.
Landing:	Do not interfere until horse has taken one stride away from fence.

7

FEEDING AND STABLE ROUTINE

The horse needs to be fit, contented and sound if he is to produce his best performance, hence the true saying that competitions are won in the yard as much as in the saddle. Constant attention, much loving care and consideration for each horse's individual needs are among the keys to success.

We have long followed the advice of our vet, Don Attenburrow, who believes that each horse should be given the minimum amount of hard feed to get him fit for the job in hand. He must have plenty of bulk as well (unless he is overweight and needs to be rationed), but the oats and event nuts have to be measured out with great care for each individual. Too little will mean that the horse has insufficient energy; too much will make him too fresh and run the risk of problems that are associated with a build-up of protein, like azoturia and lymphangitis.

You need to take the look of the horse into account – and the feel he gives you while ridden – when trying to ascertain the right quantity of hard feed. We always keep a record of the amount each horse is fed, so that we can refer back to it the next year and follow the same pattern, if it had been successful. If not, we would note that adjustments were needed. Horses that are new to the yard are always more difficult to assess because we have no such guideline.

Because we buy only the best, my mother visited the Spillers mill before deciding to use their event nuts; she had to be satisfied with the way they were made. The hay, which comes from a local farmer, has to be top quality, otherwise it will have a detrimental effect on the horses' wind and digestion. When buying the best you are paying the highest price, so we make sure that nothing is wasted.

Before the horse competes, you will need to check with your feed merchant to make sure that any prepared nuts or mix do not contain forbidden substances. Ointments and fly repellents also have to be checked for the same reason.

HARD FEED

For Ivyleaze horses, the hard feed consists of Spillers event nuts and crushed oats. We also use an event mix from which the molassine has been omitted; we prefer to have this left out because the horse can become so accustomed to having something sweet that he is reluctant to eat a feed without it.

61

As already mentioned, the quantity varies for each horse and the work he is doing; we have to rely on sight and sense and feel, especially with any animal that is new to the yard. The old-fashioned guide, which recommends one pound of hard feed per day for every mile the horse is covering, would probably not be a bad starting point – but it has to be adjusted to individual needs.

Weather conditions must also be taken into account. Our horses may have more hard feed while they are wintering at grass than when they first come back into work. They need energy-giving food as well as bulk to keep warm and retain some of their condition. We like them to have plenty of weight on them when they start the long process of getting fit again.

Amounts will also vary according to the season. There is hardly any nutritional value in the grass when we are preparing for the early spring events. Most horses therefore need more hard feed at that time of year than they will in the run-up to summer and autumn events, when the grass is at its best. Hard feed is reduced on their day off and also before and during any long journeys, which will be discussed in a later chapter.

We have a blackboard in the feed room which lists the amount each horse is fed. Even if you look after the animal on your own, it is far better to have the quantities written down rather than filed away in your head. If you are suddenly taken ill, it will then be possible for someone else to take over the feeding. At Ivyleaze, the amounts vary considerably from one horse to the next.

We have one Thoroughbred, for example, who had more hard feed than the advanced horses when he was a six-year-old; he was big, gangly and still growing at that age and he needed the extra nourishment to develop. At the same age, Ben Hovis tended to be far too fat and full of himself, so he was given very little.

If the horse is uppity by nature, it is better to cut the hard feed right back or omit it altogether. It is possible to get him one-day-event fit on grass, nuts and other bulk food without giving anything that might make him too fresh.

BULK FOOD

Needless to say, the staple food is grass – eaten in its natural state out in the fields or fed as hay or grass meal. We also use HorseHage, which has the great advantage of being 'dust-free'. The word 'dust' is used in a general sense to cover all the micro-organisms to be found in the atmosphere and, to a greater extent, in hay and straw – both of which contain fungal spores. For this reason all our hay is soaked for twenty-four hours, during which time the spores swell up. Some drop away into the water, while those that remain become harmless because they are too large to reach the lungs.

Though hay-soaking is a tiresome chore, we believe it is well worth the bother because of the enormous benefit to the horse's wind. Without those twenty-four

Left: *Amounts for each horse are shown on an old-fashioned blackboard*

Right: *HorseHage provides a useful alternative to hay*

The hay is weighed for each individual horse (left) *and then soaked to eliminate dangerous spores*

hours immersed in water, the hay spores can cause a hypersensitivity or allergy which closes the small airways and so reduces the amount of oxygen he can inhale. This, in turn, affects his performance.

Our hay is weighed for each individual horse and then soaked in a porous sack, which has his name written on it. These sacks are heavy to drag out of the water to be drained. It can be particularly difficult in the winter, when you may have the added problem of snow or ice. During the summer, the sacks of soaked hay have to be kept in the shade, otherwise the contents would either ferment or dry out and produce more spores. Since these spores can be windborne, hay has to be soaked for every horse in the yard in order to create a dust-free environment.

HorseHage is the trade name for grass that has been cut and wilted, but not dried, before being sealed in a bag. It therefore keeps its moisture content, which eliminates the problem of spores. We find it extremely useful but, because it is richer than hay, we feed it sparingly.

Assuming that the horse has no weight problem, he has as much hay as he will eat, within reason. It is fed in handfuls throughout the day, before the night ration is given at nine o'clock in the evening. During the daytime our horses are never left for more than three-quarters of an hour without something to eat; food helps to keep them occupied and stops them getting bored. By feeding little and often we are also following the normal eating habits of the horse in its natural environment. Handfuls of hay or HorseHage are given about fifteen minutes before each of the four main meals of the day; this helps to stimulate the gastric juices and take the edge off the horse's appetite, so he is encouraged to chew his hard feed rather than bolt it.

We provide bulk in the manger (as distinct from the hay-rack) with a mixture that we always refer to as 'slops'. It contains chaff, sugar-beet and grass meal. The proportions vary according to the horse's likes and dislikes; we want each one to enjoy his food and will therefore cut down on anything that he finds unpalatable enough to leave behind in the manger. The sugar-beet and grass meal, which are both used in nut form, are good for putting on weight but need to be reduced if the horse is getting too fat. Both need to be soaked before feeding, otherwise they are likely to cause colic. The beet needs to be soaked for at least twelve hours, which would be the maximum in a hot climate because it would be likely to ferment if left any longer. You should make sure it is ready by inserting your hand and checking that there are no hard lumps – otherwise the sugar-beet can cause a serious blockage of the gullet.

All the horses have chaff, which is made from oat straw and hay. It is freshly cut in an electric chaff cutter once a week and it, too, is soaked before feeding. We never feed bran, because it has little nutritional value and it upsets the balance of minerals – principally by absorbing the calcium content in the food instead of letting it be absorbed by the horse. Calcium is an important aid to bone growth, which is the main reason why Irish horses (brought up on limestone that is rich in calcium) develop such good density of bone at an early age.

During the winter we feed boiled or flaked barley, which helps to put on weight. If the horse looks too thin, he will be given smaller amounts of flaked barley during the summer as well.

ADDITIVES

We have vitamins made up for use mainly in the winter months. Fewer additives are required during the summer; at that stage the grass contains most of the vitamins the horse needs. More salt, however, is required during hot weather to replace the amount lost in sweating. We give two ounces of salt per day during the summer and only one ounce in the winter months. We also give half an eggspoon of cod liver oil and four ounces of limestone flour each day throughout the year.

THE STABLE YARD

If we were designing a stable yard from scratch at Ivy-leaze, we would put it in a sheltered spot and try to find a nice view for the horses, so they were not constantly looking at each other and getting bored. A window in the back of the stable is enormously helpful in this respect, because the horse has another scene to view. We have back windows on a couple of our stables and the horses that occupy them seem to be less bored than those who can only look out over the front door.

The yard would be close to the house – or connected by the type of intercom system that is widely used in the United States – so that the people living there could hear if anything went wrong during the night. The dung heap, the place for storing hay and the chaff cutter would have to be at least 80 metres away from the stables in order to keep the horses in a dust-free environment.

Ventilation, which is tremendously important, would preferably come from air ducts in a central line along the middle of the roof. Drainage would have to be carefully planned, with the individual drains in each stable leading to a central one. Drainage lines, shaped in a herring-bone pattern, have the added advantage of stopping the horse from slipping. We like the mangers to be approximately chest high and detachable, so that they can be taken out for cleaning. Hay-racks would also be chest high.

Right: *We use chaff in preference to bran. The feed is well mixed before being given to the horse*

Left: *All horses enjoy a really good roll*

BEDDING

There are four popular types of bedding – peat, straw, shavings and paper. Straw is bad, because it contains many spores. When the other three were tested, they reproduced only a very small quantity of spores and paper was the best of them. Equibed, a product made from sterilised waste material, was the only bedding which did not reproduce any spores. This is unobtainable at present, but it may be back on the market again in the future. When we used it, the horses were reluctant to get out of bed in the morning and the dogs wanted to rush into the stables for a lie-down.

We tried paper for a while; it is better than shavings from the point of view of spores, but a real pain when it comes to disposal. The only way to get rid of the mucked-out paper bedding is by burning. It would be a terrible eyesore if farmers were to spread it on their land, whereas they don't mind using manure in shavings as a fertiliser.

Straw has far too many damaging spores, so shavings it has to be for the time being. We do not use them as deep litter. All the wet patches are removed, together with the droppings, from the stables each morning. During the remainder of the day, the stables are skipped out several times. By regularly picking up the droppings, you avoid any unnecessary waste of shavings as well as making the beds look much better.

THE DAILY ROUTINE

Horses are creatures of habit, especially where meal-times are concerned. Priceless always knew, as accurately as if he'd been wearing a watch, exactly when he was due to be fed. If his meal was not served promptly, he liked to remind everyone by banging loudly on his stable door. We therefore keep to a fairly strict time-table in the yard at Ivyleaze.

The day's routine is always written out the night before, giving the work each horse will be doing – plus any other relevant details, such as a visit from the farrier which will obviously affect the programme for any horses being shod. The normal routine changes on the days that some of the horses canter, gallop, go for a cross-country school or to the hills for fitness work. Most of these require a journey by horsebox, so they take up more time than hacking or working in the school at home.

All the horses have a day off on Mondays, when they go out in the fields while the hard-working girls who look after them go shopping. The horses always wear protective Velcro boots when turned out; if the weather is cold, they also wear hoods and New Zealand rugs. For the rest of the week, a rota is organised which gives each horse two or three more sessions outside. Being turned out gives them the chance to enjoy a sense of freedom in their natural environment, where they can let off any pent-up high spirits and have a really good roll. If it is not their turn to be let loose, they are led out for ten minutes to pick at some grass, which helps their appetite and stops them from getting bored.

Although we like them to go out, we sometimes have to restrict sessions in the field during the summer for any horse that is inclined to put on weight. It may, however, be enough to put those with a weight problem in the smallest paddock, where they have access to less grass, while their leaner stable-mates graze on a larger area. Some of the novices go out at night and, because of our small acreage, all droppings are removed from the fields the following morning to stop the ground from becoming horse-sick.

The horses that are being aimed at three-day events wear leg bandages day and night – for warmth as well as protection, but not for support. In cold weather, this encourages circulation while the horse is standing in his box, before being taken out for exercise. Those for which no three-day event has been planned are normally bandaged only at night.

In addition to picking up droppings, all the following are done on a daily basis.

The horse's legs are checked to make sure there is no heat or swelling.
Shoes are checked for wear, plus any sign of looseness or risen clenches.
The yard is swept and tidied several times a day.
Stables are skipped out, also several times a day.
In cold weather, the horse is regularly checked for warmth, by putting a hand under the rugs to feel his shoulder and loins. More rugs will be put on if required.
Hay, chaff, grass meal and sugar-beet nuts are soaked.
Water is checked regularly and topped up as necessary – in addition to buckets being emptied and refilled twice a day.
Feed buckets are always scrubbed clean after use.
Mangers are washed once a day.
Tack is cleaned.
Numnahs, boots and bandages are washed.

We can have as many as eight horses competing at different levels, so we have an exceptionally busy yard at the height of the season and we have to start working the horses early. At such times, the rest of the day's routine goes something like this.

6.45 a.m.	Each horse is given a handful of hay or HorseHage. Day-time beds are prepared for horses that slept out. Horses that were out overnight are brought in for breakfast.
7.00 a.m.	Breakfast feeds are given. Water buckets are removed from stables during mucking out. After mucking out, water buckets are emptied, re-filled and returned to stables.
7.15 a.m.	Girls have breakfast.
8.30-9 a.m.	Horses go out for hack or work in school. Hay, HorseHage or grass is given to any horse left behind.
10.30-11 a.m.	Horses that were working in the school and/or any left behind on earlier ride go for hack. One or more horses returning from hack may be schooled. Horses that have finished work are strapped off.
12 noon	Handfuls of hay are given.
12.15-12.30 p.m.	Lunch-time feeds are given.
from 2.00 p.m.	Horses to be turned out (according to rota) go into field for half an hour to one hour. Other horses led out for ten minutes to pick at grass. Strapping for horses that were not groomed in morning.
4.45 p.m.	Handfuls of hay are given. Put on night-time rugs and bandages.
5.00 p.m.	Tea-time feeds are given. Water buckets are emptied and re-filled.
6.30 p.m.	More handfuls of hay.
9.00 p.m.	Night-time hay is taken into stables. Night-time feed is given.

OTHER ESSENTIALS

All our horses are shod approximately every six weeks. If the ground seems likely to become hard, our farrier fits pads under the shoes. Made of chrome leather and soaked in neat's foot oil, they have a cushioning effect which reduces the risk of injury on firm going. The leather is cut so that the frog remains exposed, which means that we have to be careful to prevent any grit or small stones getting through to the area between the pad and sole. This is normally achieved by stuffing a line of cotton wool around the frog.

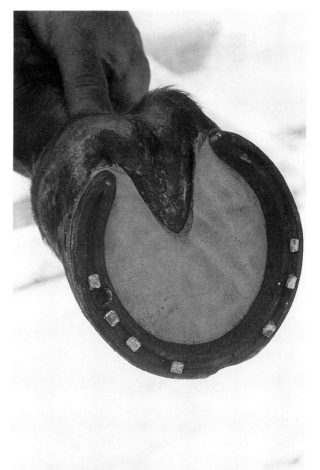

Leather pads act as shock absorbers on hard ground

The horses are also wormed regularly, according to the instructions given with the product used. Each horse is given a worm count when he first arrives at Ivyleaze and another one six months later. After that, he is worm-counted once a year, or more often if we feel it is necessary. Teeth are regularly checked so that any sharp edges can be removed by rasping.

Vaccinations are given early in the New Year, a few days before the horse begins his three weeks of walking on the roads. He therefore has plenty of time to recover before he is asked to do any strenuous exercise. Unless the weather is exceptionally cold, the advanced horses are clipped out at about the same time, while the novices are trace or blanket-clipped. If we happened to be in the grip of a big freeze, the clipping would wait until after they had finished their three weeks of walking.

A trace clip

SUMMARY

Give minimum amount of hard feed (i.e. oats and event nuts or mix) to get horse fit.

Judge quantities of hard feed by horse's appearance and feel he gives when ridden.

If guideline needed, start with 1 lb of hard feed for each mile being covered – and adjust as necessary.

Before competition, check with feed merchant to make sure event nuts or mix do not contain any forbidden substance.

Reduce hard feed on rest day.

Hard feed is given four times a day, except on rest day.

Hay is soaked for 24 hours to eliminate problems caused by fungal spores.

HorseHage can replace part of the hay ration. It contains no spores, but is richer than hay so should be fed sparingly.

A handful of hay or HorseHage is given 15 minutes before each hard feed.

Chaff is soaked to eliminate risk from fungal spores.

Sugar beet nuts and grass nuts are soaked.

Rations of sugar beet nuts and grass nuts are reduced if horse is getting too fat. Grazing is also limited if he is overweight.

Boiled or flaked barley is given to put on weight, especially in winter.

Additives: vitamins (more required in winter), salt (more in summer), cod liver oil and limestone flour.

Horses are creatures of habit, so keep to timetable.

Horses should be shod approximately every six weeks.

Pads are fitted under the shoes when ground is hard.

Horses are wormed regularly and worm-counted once a year.

Vaccinations are given in early January.

Unless weather is particularly cold, horses are clipped in early January.

8

CLOTHING AND EQUIPMENT

You do not need to spend a fortune on your own or your horse's wardrobe in order to compete in your first one-day event. Obviously, you should check an up-to-date rulebook to make sure of the exact requirements – and, equally important, to ascertain the items which are not allowed. Having once been eliminated for inadvertently using the wrong tack, I make a point of studying each year's new rulebook with the utmost care.

THE RIDER

The informal rat-catcher dress (hunting cap or bowler, tweed riding coat, shirt with collar and tie, buff breeches and black or brown boots) is currently acceptable for novice one-day events. If you want to start with clothes that you can continue wearing in intermediate classes, you will require black boots (not brown), a black jacket (not tweed), alternatively a red jacket for a man or blue for a woman, and a white hunting tie (not collar and tie). If you do not possess them already, all the items mentioned are usually available second-hand.

Except for a crash helmet (with an approved BSI

number and black or navy cover) the same clothes are worn for show jumping. For cross-country you also need the crash helmet, plus a sweater or shirt and a back protector. A hunting tie, which can be home-made quite easily, is recommended for extra protection and a bib for displaying your number is normally required. This is the one phase in which you can use exactly the same clothes from novice to championship events.

Spurs are optional in novice events, but I always wear them for competitions. They will be compulsory at advanced level, so I feel the horse might as well get used to them at an early stage. Gloves are also optional, but I wear them too – normally leather and string for dressage and string only for show jumping and cross-country.

BITTING

The bit is the most crucial piece of equipment and, unlike most other items, it cannot be adjusted if it happens to be the wrong size. So much is affected by this small piece of metal or rubber that goes inside the horse's mouth (the confidence of both rider and horse for a

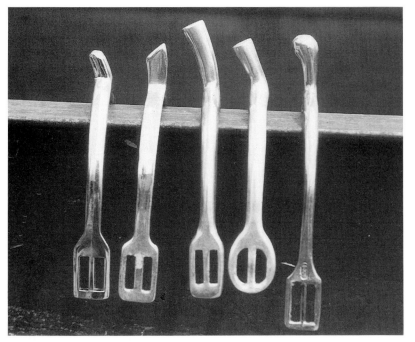

Various types of spurs

A collection of snaffle bits which are suitable for young horses. Left (top to bottom): French bridoon, rubber snaffle with cheek bars, plain snaffle with cheek bars. Right (top to bottom): small bridoon bit, rubber snaffle with D-rings, loose ring snaffle

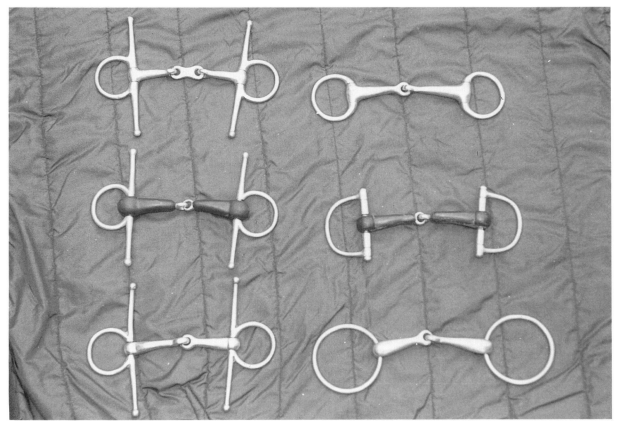

start) that it can prove more difficult to get right than all the other contents of the tack room put together.

Horses' mouths come in all shapes and sizes. One animal may have teeth that are more prominent than usual, another may be particularly sensitive on the corners or the bars of his mouth. The art of bitting has to take such things into account, so that the main action of the mouthpiece avoids any sensitive or delicate area.

If the horse has a problem with his mouth, it is up to the rider to try to pinpoint the cause before automatically changing the ironmongery. Perhaps the horse's teeth are causing the problem and need to be rasped; maybe there is a sore in his mouth. It could be that the bit is the wrong size and that he needs a wider or narrower version of the same mouthpiece rather than a different type. Or it may be the rider's hands that are creating the problem.

The snaffle should be a mild bit, but it can be severe if it fits badly. When pupils come to Dot for the first time, she frequently finds that the bit they are using is the wrong size for the horse. She is loath to put anyone to the expense of buying a new one, but correct bitting is so fundamental that she would be doing her pupil a disservice if she failed to point it out.

Sometimes the problem is in the horse's mind rather than his mouth. He may have had badly fitting tack, too strong a bit or a rider with heavy hands in the past. As a result he has formed a mental association which connects the bit with pain; he therefore becomes agitated as soon as anyone takes up the reins. His new rider may have the most perfect hands in the world, but it will still take a long time before the bad memory fades and he feels confident to take contact on the reins.

The snaffle can do as much, if not more, damage in novice hands than bits that are more severe. If, for instance, the horse is a little too strong across country and the rider is constantly pulling against him, a sore can easily be caused. It could be that a stronger bit, used with a lighter aid, would be more effective. Then, instead of pulling on the reins non-stop, the rider can give an effective aid as and when necessary. Constant pulling is like endless nagging: it is disliked but not respected. As one wise person put it, you would do better with a bucketful of hands than a bucketful of bits!

Finding the right bit

We like to keep the tack simple and the bit as mild as possible, especially in the early stages of the youngster's education when he should be learning to respond through correct training. I will be using an ordinary snaffle for the dressage, but I might feel the need for something a little stronger on the cross-country.

All our horses start with an ordinary unjointed rubber snaffle, which is the mildest bit of all. If I were looking for something stronger, I would then try a jointed rubber snaffle. After that, if I still wasn't happy, I would try the same bit in metal, if necessary followed by a loose-ring snaffle and a French bridoon. Though I have used stronger bits than these fairly mild versions of the snaffle on intermediate and advanced horses, I have never put anything more severe in a novice mouth.

We have naturally acquired a large collection of bits over the years, including different sizes as well as various types, so I can usually try out different mouthpieces without having to buy them. If you do not have your own collection, it would be better to borrow a bit or try to have one on approval. Otherwise you can incur the unnecessary expense of buying one that proves unsuitable.

It should be stressed that we prefer to stay with the mildest bit we can find, but that is not always possible. If we have to resort to a slightly stronger one for the cross-country, we will be hoping that we can switch back to a kinder bit at some later stage. This does sometimes happen, so you should not make the mistake of thinking that the mouthpiece has to become progressively stronger.

BRIDLE, BREASTPLATE AND MARTINGALE

All our horses have one exercise bridle and another for competitions. This helps to reduce the risk of a strap breaking through stress, or of any part disintegrating because the stitching has rotted. Because these things can happen, we take the precaution of checking all straps and stitching on a regular basis. Obviously two bridles are not essential, but you do need to be ultra-careful if you are using the same one for schooling, hacking and events.

Only a snaffle bridle is allowed for the dressage phase of novice one-day events. The dressage judges will probably be more impressed to see the horse in an ordinary cavesson noseband, so I would prefer to use this for the test and then switch to a grakle (cross-over) noseband for the show jumping and cross-country. I would make an exception when I am riding a horse that has a tendency to open his mouth or cross his jaw. He can do neither if he is wearing a grakle, so I might use it for all three phases. Because leather reins can become so slippery in wet weather, I prefer to have black rubber ones for dressage. They are narrower and more elegant than the wider rubber reins (normally brown) that I use for the cross-country.

All the horses wear a breastplate for canter work-outs, as well as for show jumping and cross-country. It must be correctly fitted; I have seen horses competing with their shoulders severely restricted because their breastplates were far too tight.

Some of our horses may wear a martingale or a martingale attachment, which is fitted to the breastplate for the show jumping and cross-country. We always use stops on the reins; these prevent the rings from sliding too far forward and getting caught up on the bit. I have the martingale loose enough to avoid interfering with the horse's natural head carriage, but tight enough to prevent me from getting my teeth smashed in! Turning is often difficult when the horse gets his head too high, so the martingale also helps to overcome steering problems – but I have to admit that it is there only because he is not sufficiently well schooled to go without it.

SADDLE, NUMNAH, SURCINGLE AND GIRTHS

A general-purpose saddle is perfectly adequate for all three phases of a novice one-day event; indeed, you can use one all the way through to the Olympic Games. If you do have a dressage saddle, it has the advantage of getting your leg into a better position to use for the various test movements. For that reason, I prefer to use one specifically built for dressage in the first phase, whether I am riding a novice or advanced horse. I then use the Barnsby Leng competition saddle, which I helped to design, for show jumping and cross-country. It has a flatter seat than the traditional jumping saddle, allowing me to move my weight further back at drop fences.

I always use foot grips on the stirrup irons and a fairly substantial numnah, about one inch thick, under the saddle. It is made of foam with a cotton cover, so that it can be washed easily. If the saddle has to fit two horses, you can use pads (which are available in a variety of materials) between the numnah and the saddle. Obviously, the same saddle cannot be used on two horses of a completely different size, but pads are a great help when small adjustments need to be made to stop the saddle rubbing. Pads also help to compensate for the changing shape of the horse's back as he becomes increasingly fit.

Though elasticated web girths are widely used in the racing world, I am not keen on them myself. I prefer to use two girths made of webbing, plus an elasticated web surcingle, when I am riding across country or schooling over fences at home. Normally I use leather girths for dressage and show jumping at one-day events. There is no reason, however, why you should not use your webbing pair (assuming that they are not bright pink or purple) for these two phases as well.

BOOTS AND BANDAGES

We always use exercise boots on all four of the horse's legs when schooling at home, out hacking or working in for the dressage test. They are removed at the last possible moment before the test, thus reducing the risk of a horse going suddenly lame through knocking himself.

I have seen this happen to others and experienced it myself on one occasion, when I was riding Night Cap around the outside of the arena at Locko Park prior to his test. As I asked him to strike into canter, he hit himself on an old splint and was as lame as a crow for about one minute. Since boots have to be removed before you begin your laps around the outside of the arena, there was nothing we could have done to prevent this happening. But it does underline the importance of keeping the horse's legs protected for as long as possible.

For show jumping, our horses' forelegs are protected by half-boots, which cover the tendons but leave the cannon-bone exposed. We also use over-reach boots on each horse that has shown a tendency to get a hind toe dangerously close to a foreleg. The back legs remain uncovered for show jumping.

We use tendon protectors and over-reach boots on the forelegs for the cross-country phase and also for canter work-outs, gallops and cross-country schooling. The protectors cover the cannon-bone and incorporate a special strip of plastic at the back which gives extra protection to the tendon. There is no boot in the world that could withstand the enormous impact of a horse striking directly into himself with a hindleg while at full gallop, which has been estimated at ten tons per square inch, so we have to be content with doing the best we can to protect his forelegs. We put elasticated bandages over the front protectors and they are always sewn in place to make them secure. I could never set out with confidence if the bandages were held in place by sticky tape, which some people use.

The hindlegs are protected by woof boots or back tendon protectors for cross-country jumping, whether schooling or in a competition. For canter work-outs and galloping, we would use back brushing boots.

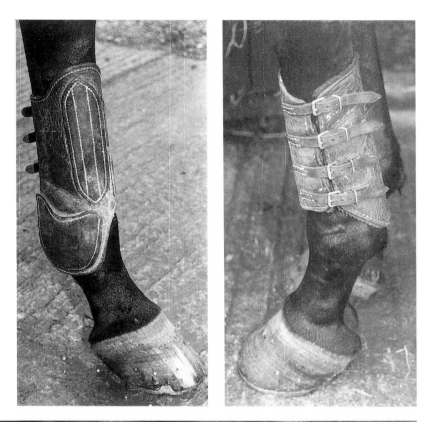

Right: *Front and hindleg Speedicut leather boots with buckles, which are suitable for cross-country at competitions*

Below: *Simple brushing boots for everyday use*

STUDS

Our horses wear studs for all three phases of eventing and any other occasion when jumping on grass. The difference they make in giving a horse a secure foothold is particularly noticeable in show jumping, whatever the ground conditions. Studs are not particularly expensive, and since they give you so much added security I would always try to have a wide variety – ranging from the pointed ones used for hard ground to the large squares or rounds used in soft going. You are then equipped for all conditions.

Our policy is to use smallish square road studs in front for all three phases. If the ground is boggy or bone hard, I might change these front studs for dressage and show jumping, but I am reluctant to do so for cross-country, although it has occasionally been known. The main cause for my reluctance is knowing that the bigger the stud, the more painful it will be if I fall off and the horse treads on me! I also want to allow his front feet to slide very slightly as he lands; if there is no such give when he is jumping at speed across country, it will put excess strain on his forelegs.

The back studs we use depend on the going. Having made our selection, we screw one stud into a hole on the outside of each shoe. In the United States they use two per shoe, presumably because the ground tends to be much harder there, which would make the foot permanently unlevel if the British system were adopted.

RUGS

The novice would need only to be trace or blanket clipped, so he requires less clothing than the fully clipped advanced horse. He would still, however, need a minimum of four rugs at a novice one-day event, a top woollen rug (which can be the one that he wears in his stable), a New Zealand rug (which he can also use when turned out in the field), a thermal rug and a sweat sheet. In the United States and other countries with a less temperate climate, a wider range of clothing is necessary.

A smart travelling rug is nice to have, but not essential. The same applies to a waterproof sheet, which is useful for keeping the saddle dry for short periods when you don't want to bother with a New Zealand rug. A quarter sheet is also useful when riding in before the dressage on a freezing cold day.

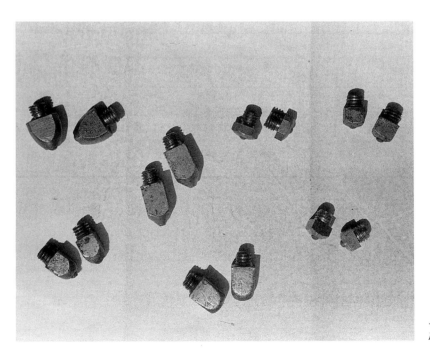

A collection of studs used for all three phases

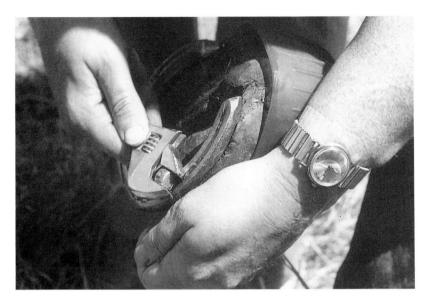

Fitting studs with an adjustable spanner

American horses have two studs fitted to keep the foot level

SUMMARY

Check up-to-date rule-book for correct clothing and tack.

Bitting:

Make sure mouthpiece does not put pressure on any sensitive area of the mouth.

Make sure the bit is the correct size for the horse.

If the horse has a problem with his mount, try to pin-point the cause.

Use as mild a bit as possible.

If a stronger bit is required for control, aim to go back to something milder at a later stage.

Suitable bits for the young horse: unjointed rubber snaffle, jointed rubber snaffle with cheek bars or D-rings, jointed snaffle in metal, loose-ring snaffle, French bridoon.

Other equipment:

Check all straps and stitching regularly.

Make sure the breastplate is correctly fitted.

If any small adjustment is needed to make the saddle a better fit, use pads between the numnah and saddle.

The martingale (if used) should be loose enough to avoid interfering with the horse's natural head carriage.

Protective boots:

For hacking and schooling – exercise boots.

For show jumping – over-reach and show jumping boots on forelegs.

For cross-country (schooling and competitions) – tendon protectors and over-reach boots on forelegs; woof boots or back tendon protectors on hindlegs.

For canter work-outs and galloping – tendon protectors and over-reach boots on forelegs; back brushing boots on hindlegs.

Studs:

Try to have a wide variety, suitable for all types of going.

9

PREPARING FOR THE FIRST NOVICE EVENT

Most horses seem to mature while they are wintering in the fields. When they come back into work as five-year-olds, they are usually ready to be asked for more quality in their paces. Sometimes, particularly with the older horses, they go brilliantly on the flat when they start working again after their three weeks of walking on the roads. Problems from the previous autumn seem to have disappeared, only to resurface a few weeks later.

At this stage we would be considering whether the five-year-old is likely to be ready for a spring one-day event in late April or early May – which will depend on his physical and mental maturity. He would normally restart his schooling in January, so there is plenty of time to get him fit should we decide to run him.

SCHOOLING FOR THE NOVICE DRESSAGE TEST

We are now looking for improved quality, with better engagement of the hocks, a round outline and smoother transitions. If we can get these things right through constant repetition, it will save a great deal of hassle later on. Though the lessons need to be varied, the trainer should never lose sight of the basic requirements.

The horse does not need to learn any new movements for the first test he will perform at novice level. We can therefore concentrate on keeping him straight, in rhythm and balanced with the weight of the rider while following random parts of the test.

If the test were to include working canter on a 20-metre circle, I would probably begin by doing that shape at walk and trot. When this is accomplished satisfactorily, I move on to canter. I also use half-circle variations at slower, then faster, paces – plus the various shapes the horse was doing as a four-year-old, which are all done at walk.

A nice outline in working canter

78

I never go through the whole test that will be used in the competition. The horse would be quick to learn it and so start to anticipate each movement. Instead I make up my own tests and practise them in a small arena of 20 by 40 metres, which is the size used for novice tests. Though lettered markers are unnecessary for schooling purposes, it makes sense to practise with some objects of a similar size – such as traffic cones or old paint tins – so that the horse is used to seeing something on the ground beside the arena.

Although some lengthened strides at trot may be required in the novice test, I do not ask for them until the horse has established rhythm and co-ordination within that pace. I would not discourage lengthened strides if he showed a natural ability to produce them, but I would not press him. Unless it comes naturally, the horse will find it difficult to avoid going on to his forehand as he lengthens, whereas we want him back on his hocks. I do, however, include periods of walk, trot and canter on a long rein, which allows him to stretch his head and neck forward and down. It is at this stage that we discover how well he can balance himself.

TRANSITIONS

I attempt only simple transitions at this stage, for example walk to trot or trot to canter. Walk to canter (or vice versa) is obviously more difficult and it will probably not be attempted until later, depending on the horse's aptitude. Before that happens I need to teach him to stay straight and maintain the same outline while making the easier transitions, whether upwards or downwards. These should not be abrupt; we want the horse to flow smoothly and rhythmically from one pace to another, which will probably take a few months to achieve. If you ask the horse to make more difficult downward transitions (for instance from canter to walk) before the simple ones are established, he is likely to lose his balance, lean on the bit and fall into a heap.

ESSENTIALS

The horse must go forward without any hesitancy; he must be obedient, in balance and stay straight. These things will have an effect on everything he does in the future. If he is not straight in his basic flatwork – if he cannot do correct turns and circles – there is little hope

of him doing shoulder-in and half-pass correctly when the time comes.

He will be similarly handicapped if he is too much on his forehand, without his hocks being sufficiently engaged. You can increase the impulsion that comes from the hocks, and so lighten the forehand, by moving your weight slightly back and down a little while your hands control the energy created by your legs, which are applied on the girth. In giving and taking with a soft hand, together with correct use of upper body weight and balance, you are containing that energy and preventing it from escaping into a faster speed. There is therefore increased power in the horse's hindlegs, which are the engine that propels him forward. Some horses have natural impulsion; others have to acquire it through training.

Work over trotting poles will also help to engage the hocks and lighten the forehand, this time without any interference from the rider. Hillwork, introduced after five weeks when he is fit enough to cope with it, provides additional help in bringing the hocks further under the horse's body. He will also discover how to balance himself, with the weight of the rider, while going up and down hills.

JUMPING

Once the five-year-olds are fit, I jump them once a week in the school – for no more than twenty minutes and often for much less. Horses that are good jumpers would not be required to go over grids and a course of single fences on the same day. They do one or the other for about ten minutes, which is quite enough.

At this age the horse's jumping muscles can become fully developed with exercise, but they must be built up gradually through his jumping lessons. He will then be capable of tackling more difficult fences. I continue to use grids – which incorporate uprights, spread fences and bounces – to improve the horse's athleticism, always approaching them in trot. The lesson is never the same two weeks running; as already mentioned, I have a better chance of maintaining his interest if he is not aware of what is coming next. I have to play it by ear, taking account of the temperament and ability of the individual horse.

If he tends to have a rather long, flattish jump, I might choose to play around with grids for one lesson. You can help to overcome most problems by building fences up within a grid. If the distances between them are correct, the horse will meet each one at the right spot and gain tremendous confidence as a result.

The actual distances will depend on the height of the fences as well as the horse's conformation, age, experience and length of stride, so you should not rely too much on the tape measure. For fences not exceeding 3 feet 3 inches (1 metre) the average distances for one non-jumping stride are as follows:

Between cross-rails (or from cross-rails to first fence): 18 feet (5.5 metres).
After first fence: 21 feet (6.4 metres).
After second and subsequent fences: 23 feet (7 metres).
For a bounce (as distinct from one non-jumping stride): 10-12 feet (3.05-3.7 metres).

All the above can be lengthened by one foot (0.3 metre), depending on the horse, but it would be rare to shorten them. The shorter the distance, the more effort will be required for him to collect himself in time for the next jump. The diagrams show sample

grids of progressive difficulty that could be used for a novice horse.

The week after concentrating on gridwork, I might do one quick grid to a round of fences. You need no more than four jumps – an oxer, a vertical and two together to form a double – to have a short course. The two single fences can be jumped from both directions and possibly the double as well, depending on how it is built.

Small indoor show-jumping contests will be used as part of the horse's training. Before that happens, I will have done some homework by introducing him to the different types of obstacles he might meet when he gets there. You have to use your ingenuity with the materials available to build something resembling a wall. Brightly painted poles and planks will help to prepare him for the vivid colours that you often see in indoor jumping. Doubles and combinations, which green horses tend to find particularly spooky, will also be included in the fences we jump during our preparations at home.

Grids suitable for novice eventers. All distances can be shortened or lengthened by one foot, depending on the horse and height of the jumps. Lower fences required for a green novice

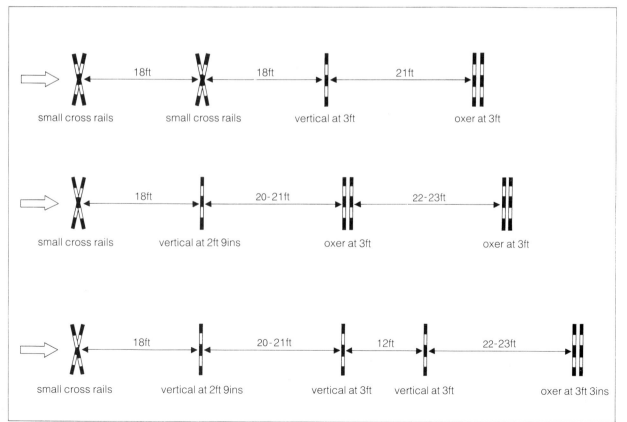

Horse competing in his first small jumping derby, which combined show jumps and cross-country fences. Such contests are an excellent way of building up confidence

Needless to say, I would pick contests with small courses for the horse's introduction to the amazing new experience of going to a show. Travelling in the lorry can be an eye-opener in itself. When he arrives, there might be as many as a hundred horses milling around, which he also finds incredible. I am sure that the baby novices feel totally exhausted when they return from one of these outings. My aim is to build up gradually to the point where the horse can jump safely round a Newcomers' course, with fences up to 3 feet 7 inches (1.1 metres). I take part in these contests with the aim of jumping clear rounds and without getting too carried away when it comes to going fast against the clock.

Flatwork should have taught the horse to stay on a straight line whenever he is moving forward. That is instilled into him at walk, trot and canter, and repeated yet again when jumping. If the horse is cantering round a corner and heading for a jump, he must come off the corner, stay straight and keep going forward. He must not be allowed to give himself extra room by veering to one side in front of the fence, because this can quickly become a habit. He has to learn to shorten or lengthen whenever necessary, so that he can stay on the same line to jump the fence.

The horse should not be reprimanded if he hits a fence. You only need to try knocking down a pole by hitting it with your own legs to know that it hurts. The horse also finds it painful – so he has, as it were, reprimanded himself. He will be anxious to avoid making the same mistake again; if he does repeat the error, it is likely to mean that your training is at fault.

Angles are not introduced until I am happy with the horse's canter and feel completely confident that he will stay on a straight line. I use two small fences for this exercise, placed as shown in the diagram. The horse takes only one fence at an angle for his first two attempts. At this stage you should avoid going too near the fence that is not being jumped, because you might then have to turn the horse away from it. This could lead to him running out at a fence when you do intend to jump it.

If he stays straight both times, the horse is asked to jump the two fences on an angle, maintaining a straight line from his approach to the first until after landing over the second. This exercise prepares him for jumping his first corner, which I would attempt only when I was happy with the way he coped with angles. I would need to have jumped at least half a dozen angles successfully before tackling a corner for the first time,

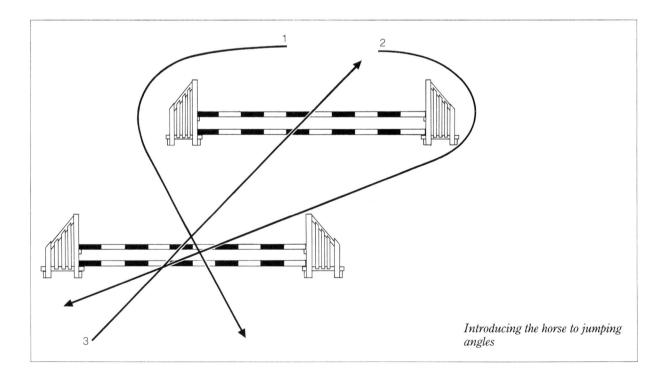

Introducing the horse to jumping angles

which is always done in the school at home using show jumps rather than fixed cross-country obstacles.

I also like the horse to learn flying changes at this stage, so that he can organise himself without any difficulty if he lands over a fence with his left leg leading and has to make a right turn almost immediately – or vice versa. This movement is taught at an early age in the United States, which I believe is a good idea. In Britain we are inclined to think that we would then run into trouble when we had to do counter-canter in the FEI dressage test, but the fact that the horse has learnt flying change as a youngster should not be an excuse; he ought to be trained well enough to stay on the outside leg when the rider tells him to do so.

I therefore encourage him to use flying change whenever he finds himself on the wrong lead for turning after a fence. The horse will normally make the change when I give the aids; if he fails to do so it should not become a big issue. He will learn this movement in his own good time and it will then become easy for him, so that he automatically uses flying change to put himself right for turns.

CROSS-COUNTRY SCHOOLING

I would probably take the horse for his first *proper* cross-country school early in his fifth year, but he would have to be confident while cantering into coloured jumps at home and popping over natural fences. I would also want to be reasonably sure that he was willing to listen to me and that he would stay straight. I very rarely use a stick on these occasions. It is far better to encourage the youngster with legs and voice, so that he can build up his own self-confidence. He is likely to be in a state of nervous tension when he goes for his first proper cross-country school, and use of the stick would serve only to make him more tense.

Unlike the rider, the young horse has not seen it all before; these strange new obstacles can therefore be a perfectly understandable cause of alarm. This obviously has to be taken into account when you select the fences to be jumped. You cannot expect him to perform the way he does in the familiar surroundings of the school at home, so you will probably need to start with obstacles that can be taken from a standstill.

I remember taking one five-year-old to Wokingham, where I attempted to ride him down some fairly steep steps. The horse stopped on top of the first step and looked down in horror. He had no idea how to cope and worked himself into a state of agitation because he didn't know what he was supposed to do. I simply patted the youngster's neck and talked to him. Eventually I could almost feel the tension drain away as he began to realise that the route ahead was not impossible after all; then he jumped down the steps. Had I used a stick, he would have started to think about what I was doing. By sitting quietly, I gave him the chance to concentrate on the steps and work out his own way of getting down. He was far less tense when faced with the same obstacle a second time.

I would never present a horse to a fence unless I believed we had a 99 per cent chance of getting over it. This is not too much of a problem at the kindergarten stage, when the youngster is asked to jump only fences that can be taken from a standstill. It becomes far more difficult when you move on to the next stage and are attempting larger obstacles, which cannot be jumped without turning back should the horse grind to a halt.

'If in doubt, don't' is one of the Ivyleaze mottos, which refers to everything we do with the horse and is particularly relevant to schooling over cross-country fences. If I am concerned that the horse might stop at a particular fence, I don't attempt it. It is far better to spend more time jumping smaller obstacles of different types than risk a setback through the horse refusing. This does not mean holding him back to the point of mollycoddling him. There has to be a balance whereby the horse keeps progressing, albeit cautiously.

This involves a form of continual assessment on the part of the rider. You also have to keep in mind the horse's experience over different types of fences, so that you can gauge the right time to present him with the next challenge. I always aim to make the horse familiar with one new experience at a time. I would therefore want to be sure that he was happy jumping a ditch on its own before attempting to jump one that had some poles above it.

The components of other cross-country fences can be separated in the same way. Before jumping off a bank into water, I would want the horse to have jumped down an ordinary step and to have paddled through water. I would probably ride him through the water at the bottom of the bank before jumping into it. If all went well, I might attempt a log into water when this particular horse went for his next cross-country school. He would be familiar with each of the three components on its own – that is the log, the drop and the water – and he has jumped down a bank into water. Assuming that he still seemed full of confidence, I would expect him to pop over the log and into water without the slightest hesitation.

I apply the same policy to every type of cross-country fence, tackling the individual components first and then putting them together. This does not mean that our horses never encounter problems, but it does help to avoid them. Before entering for a novice one-day event, I would need to be sure that the horse had successfully tackled every type of obstacle he is likely to meet on the cross-country course. But I would not try to rush him through his schooling. If the careful step-by-step process does not prepare him quickly enough for a spring event, he can wait until later in the year – or maybe as long as the following spring.

The rider should already have tried to acquire the ability to see a stride in order to assist the horse, though there will always be times when it is better to sit still and let him get you out of trouble. On one occasion, while cross-country schooling at Wylye many years ago, I plucked up courage to ask the dual world champion Bruce Davidson how he managed to see a stride from so far back. He told me that he always looked at the top part of the fence and did not take his eye off it. I then followed his example and discovered that it worked. Since then, I know that whenever I miss my stride it is because my eye has wandered for a split second.

Whether in show jumping or cross-country, I reckon that you need to have your eye on the fence from at least six strides out – and keep it there. On very rare occasions I have come down a long gallop to a cross-country fence and seen my stride fourteen paces out; because my eye was already on the obstacle, I knew that we were going to meet it right as long as I kept looking at the spot where I aimed to jump.

You should not need to look down to check the length of your reins or see which leg the horse is leading on; you should know these things by feel. Nor should it be necessary to look down in order to switch your stick to the other hand or shorten your reins. Your eye needs to be concentrating entirely on the fence, particularly if you are jumping at an angle or across a corner, otherwise you could be heading for disaster.

When you have seen your stride, you should make any necessary adjustment within the rhythm of the horse's movement. This shortening or lengthening should be so smooth and subtle that it is virtually imperceptible; you are not supposed to look up and keep kicking!

FITNESS WORK

A horse can get fit only through regular work; he needs to be ridden six days a week for two to three months to get ready for a one-day event. This may sound like a long slog, but I know of no other way to produce a horse that is capable of sustained cantering. The slow build-up also reduces the risk of strains, which are far more prevalent in horses that work only spasmodically.

If you cannot find the time to ride six days a week, you will need to enlist the help of someone who may not be able to help with the schooling but can at least walk the horse on the days when you are not available. It is easy to be deceived by a horse that is obviously fresh and seems to have a great deal of energy. This does not prove the animal is fit; usually it means exactly the opposite. He may be eager to charge off across the fields, but he would probably be on his knees ten minutes later. Unless he has been given too much hard feed, the fit horse has a calmer approach and does not expend his energy in one short burst.

All our horses are given three weeks of walking exercise when they come back into work after a holiday, but this does not mean ambling along the roads. The process of learning to go forward, keep straight and stay in rhythm continues while soft muscles become firm again. The daily sessions build up from forty-five minutes to between one and one and a half hours, with one day off each week so that the horse can relax in the field. If you have no field, he will need to be taken out for hand walks instead, preferably where he can pick at some grass.

I would probably introduce about three sessions of flatwork in the school during the fourth week – mainly at walk and trot, with a little cantering. These lessons should last no more than twenty minutes, otherwise the horse will begin to suffer from muscle fatigue. If he misbehaves, he would still be put away after twenty minutes and then brought out later the same day. He is still hacked out every day. For the Ivyleaze horses, this continues to mean walking on the roads in the early part of the year when we need to avoid Badminton Park because preparations for the three-day event are in full swing. We have no tracks for riding except in the park, where all the horses can do some trotting and cantering later in the year. We never trot on the roads except when going uphill otherwise it causes undue jarring. In an ideal world, we would use tracks and fields after the first three weeks of roadwork had helped to harden the horse's legs.

During the fifth week, the horse has one session of hillwork. His other daily sessions will include hacking, plus flatwork or jumping a small grid in the school. A canter work-out is introduced during the sixth week, by which time the horse should be reasonably fit. The last five to six weeks of his training and fitness programme involve a mixture of hacking, canter work-outs, hillwork, schooling on the flat, jumping in the school and park, small competitions and cross-country schooling. He still has a rest once a week and one hard feed is omitted that day.

A typical programme is given at the end of this chapter, but it should be used only as a rough guideline. The actual amount of work – and the way the programme is devised – will depend on the individual horse. We have been known to omit canter work-outs altogether for one particular horse who was naturally very fit and hyper-active. This horse did hillwork, which helps to expand the lungs and improve the heart-rate, as well as building up muscles. He did dressage schooling and went for hacks, which included some cantering – but there was no need for the more strenuous canter work-outs which most of the Ivyleaze horses do when they are preparing for a one-day event. As a general rule, we would expect a five-year-old to need more canter sessions than a mature nine-year-old, who might just need to be kept ticking over.

Our five-year-olds might be given a short uphill spurt, but they are never taken for five-furlong gallops. They will not be going flat out at a one-day event and galloping would make them too fit for the job we want them to do, which is a big mistake. It would probably get them thoroughly wound up as well, undoing all the work that has been aimed at making them calm and co-operative.

CANTER WORK-OUTS

It is essential to find good ground for cantering, otherwise you are likely to do more harm than good. Hard ground is the most dangerous, especially when it is uneven with the grooves you find in ridge and furrow or pits left by horses' hooves.

Whether it is smooth or ridged, hard ground can cause such problems as a sprained fetlock joint, a pulled muscle, damaged tendon or an injured foot. Very deep ground is also likely to cause sprains, and it could leave the horse equally open to risk of a muscle or tendon injury. Though we may have to take our chance in a competition, I am loath to take any risks in training. I would rather replace one of the twice-weekly canter work-outs with hillwork and search for somewhere suitable

to canter once a week. It could mean driving some distance in the lorry, but it would be worth the extra effort.

The horse needs to be thoroughly warmed up before cantering, with a minimum of twenty-five minutes' walking and five to ten minutes' trotting. He will also have to walk afterwards until he has completely recovered from his exertions.

I use a simplified form of the method known as Interval Training for canter work-outs. This involves working the horse in short bursts, resting briefly, then restarting before the heart and lungs have returned to normal pulse and respiration. This builds up the capacity of the heart and lungs without having to put undue stress on the horse's limbs.

When he makes a sustained physical effort, the heart and lungs have to work to capacity in order to pump oxygen through the bloodstream to the muscles, which release the energy required. If there is insufficient oxygen, the horse will have tired and aching muscles. By giving him a period of rest between canters, the spent energy can be restored to the muscles by the heart and lungs, which are still working overtime while the horse is walking quietly round.

Interval Training has been used for many years by human athletes and is now the accepted method for training event horses. By building up the capacity of heart and lungs through this method, the horse reaches a level of fitness that enables him to make the sustained effort required in competition. It is, I promise, less complicated than it sounds.

Our usual routine for a novice is to start with a three-minute canter, followed by a two-minute break and another three-minute canter. This builds up over five or six weeks to three five-minute canters, with a break of two minutes in between – or up to three minutes in hot weather if the horse is still blowing hard. This should be sufficient to get him fit for a one-day event – unless the terrain is flat, in which case you may need to work up to three six-minute canters. If the horse looks like being too fit, we would substitute a canter day with hillwork, trotting up the gentle slopes and walking up the steeper stretches.

The first two canters on the novice are at a speed of 400 metres per minute (15 m.p.h.) and subsequent ones at 500 metres per minute (19 m.p.h.). Nowadays I can normally judge how fast I am going, but it is still possible to be caught out. When I rode Murphy Himself, who has an enormous stride, I discovered that I was actually going much faster than I realised. It is easy enough to check, by finding a stretch of grass where you can canter while someone drives a car beside you at the relevant speed. You can do this in a field with a road alongside; there may be a hedge between the horse and the vehicle, but the rider has no need to see anything more than the aerial.

ASSESSING THE HORSE'S FITNESS

I always time the recovery rate of the horse after his canter work-out, so that I know how fit he is. The simplest way to do this is by watching his rib cage to check his respiration, which means counting the number of puffs he takes per minute with the help of a stopwatch.

You need to know his normal rate before he canters. This will probably be somewhere between ten and fifteen breaths per minute, but it could be more with a younger horse. The rate then needs to be counted after cantering, when the horse's breathing will obviously be much faster than normal. Because we do not want him standing still for too long after he has cantered, I count the breaths he takes in fifteen or thirty seconds and multiply by four or two, rather than wait for a full minute. The rate of recovery is the time he takes to return to his normal breathing.

During this recovery time, the horse will be walking quietly home. Having made a note of the time when he finished cantering, I will pull up five minutes later and count for another period of fifteen or thirty seconds. That second count gives me a clue as to when I should stop again. If he is not blowing too much I might take another count two minutes later; if the breaths are still coming quickly I would probably wait for a further five minutes. It is basically a matter of stopping every so often until the horse has returned to normal breathing and noting the time this has taken since he finished cantering. I regard this information as essential because I rely on recovery rate more than anything else to gauge the horse's level of fitness.

Given fairly cool weather, the average recovery rate for a fit horse is between seven and fourteen minutes. In order to assess his progress, you need to keep a record each time he canters. This would have to include weather conditions as well as the recovery rate, because it can make such an enormous difference. I have known a horse recover in seven minutes and one week later, in a sudden spell of humid weather, take as long as seventeen minutes.

FITNESS OF RIDER

Though the horse may appear to be doing most of the work at an event, the rider will need to be fit in order to give clear directions and other assistance from the saddle. If you have only one horse to ride at home, you will need to supplement this with some other activity. This could take the form of jogging twice a week, or you could choose to get fit through other activities like squash, aerobics, swimming, cycling and skipping. If you happen to be riding two or more horses each day, you should be fit enough to compete in a novice one-day event without any additional exercise.

Learning to fall, possibly by taking judo lessons, is another useful preparation. You are far less likely to get hurt in a fall if you have learnt how to roll out of harm's way and are not too tense.

DECIDING ON THE FIRST EVENT

It is up to the horse to tell you whether he is nearly ready to compete in his first BHS one-day event. I would want him to be confident over a variety of cross-country fences, otherwise he will need to be given more time. It is crazy to risk a fall or a stop across country through competing before the horse is ready for the challenge.

I would like his preparation to include other competitions in addition to the indoor jumping. If you can find them, hunter trials and dressage competitions (preferably with jumping) will help in his education. Mini one-day events, such as those run by riding clubs, are even more important. I always try to fit in two of these, but I don't always achieve it; when you have advanced horses to ride as well, it is not easy to arrange contests for the youngsters. I would, however, regard at least two mini events as essential for a novice rider.

I would certainly have taken my novice horse for three or four cross-country schools and would always advise an inexperienced rider to do about twice that amount. Since I do not believe in schooling round a BHS course, the youngster has to be properly prepared before he gets there. I will not expect him to win a prize at his first event, because I will be taking him fairly slowly, but I do expect him to do a reasonable dressage test and to go clear in the show jumping and cross-country.

In the United States, where you can compete in novice and training classes before the preliminary (which is the equivalent of our novice), the preparatory cross-country schooling is not so crucial. With two classes below the level at which most of our horses start, the plan of campaign is therefore very much easier to organise.

Fortunately we do have a growing number of pre-novice events in this country, which give young horses an excellent introduction to the sport. If unable to find one within easy reach, I would look for suitable courses at the ordinary BHS one-day events that are nearer home. I would want the youngster's first three competitions to be over the sort of cross-country fences that will help to build up his confidence, without asking too many difficult questions. You can find out which are the best courses for the first-time novice by telephoning fellow competitors or event organisers.

I would not run a five-year-old more than four times during the spring season, assuming that he was ready to start at all. He is still maturing at that age and it will be quite enough for his brain to cope with. If the ground was good, I might give him six outings during the autumn.

SUMMARY

Flatwork
Continue to work on basic priorities: forward movement, rhythm, balance, contact, straightness.
Now look for better engagement of hocks, round outline and smoother transitions.
Practise movements in test at slower paces (e.g. if 20-metre circle required at canter, start with same shape at walk and trot).
Make up tests to practise in 20 by 40 metre arenas.
Introduce lengthening and shortening when ready in each pace.
Work on simple transitions, aiming to make them more fluent and rhythmic.
Work to improve impulsion and lighten forehand.

Jumping
Work on grids (which incorporate uprights, spreads and bounces) to improve horse's athleticism.
Keep lessons varied – jump different grids and/or small courses.
Take part in small indoor jumping contests.
If horse stays straight, angles are introduced.
If he has jumped at least six angles satisfactorily, corners are introduced.
Horse has first proper cross-country school when confident over show jumps and small natural fences.
Before first novice event, aim to ride in at least two mini one-day events and take horse for four to eight cross-country schools (depending on experience of rider).

Other points
The rider must be fit.
The first few events must be over courses that are suitable for first-time novice, or incorporate plenty of alternatives.

Sample fitness programme
(Horse has one rest day per week.)

Weeks 1-3: Walking on roads (forty-five minutes building up to between one and one and a half hours).

Week 4: Hacking – plus three twenty-minute sessions of flatwork in the school, mainly at walk and trot.

Week 5: Introduce one day of hillwork and jumping a small grid during lessons in the school at home.

Weeks 6-10: Introduce canter work-outs twice a week. Use a varied programme which also includes hacking, flatwork, lungeing, jumping in the school, cross-country schooling, hillwork and competitions (such as indoor jumping, hunter trials, dressage with jumping and mini one-day events).

Typical programme for the last five weeks
Monday Rest day.
Tuesday Light hack and flatwork.
Wednesday Canter or workout.
Thursday Longer hack, possibly short schooling session.
Friday Hack and jumping, otherwise occasional cross-country school or show jumping.
Saturday Flatwork.
Sunday Canter or competition.

10

COUNTDOWN

As the event approaches, you would be well advised to go through a check-list in order to make sure that the horse is fully prepared. Here are some of the questions you might ask yourself.

Is the horse the right weight – neither too thin nor too fat?

Has he practised all the skills? In other words, has he done all the movements in the dressage test, gained experience at home and in competitions for the show jumping, and (most important of all) have you done your best to jump a wide variety of cross-country fences?

Have you practised in a small dressage arena of 20 by 40 metres, which is the size used for the novice test?

Does his recovery rate after canter work-outs suggest he is fit enough?

What is the state of the horse's shoes? They should not be brand new, but they should not be worn down either. If one of our horses needs to be shod, we always arrange for it to be done at least a week before the event.

Are you using the right tack? It is unwise to try using anything new at the event, so everything needs to be ridden in well in advance. New girths, boots and numnahs can rub; a last-minute change of bit can confuse and distract the horse.

Have your own clothes been ridden in beforehand? If it rains, new boots that have not yet acquired a slight stickiness can slide on the saddle.

Does the saddle fit correctly? The shape of the horse changes as he gets fitter, so you need to check this on a regular basis. A thick numnah and pads can compensate for the changing contours of the back.

Has the horse been plaited up a few times at home? If he is plaited only before a competition, you are as good as telling him that he is off to a party, so you can't blame him if he gets excited.

Do you know the rulebook inside out? If not, it is frighteningly easy to get eliminated. You only need to ride into the dressage arena with your stick or be seen jumping the practice fence the wrong way round to face instant dismissal. Regulations can change, so we all need to go through the new rulebook with a fine-tooth comb each year.

Has the vehicle been checked? Apart from checking oil, water and tyres and filling up with petrol or diesel, you need to make sure that everything is functioning. Partitions, locks and the ramp mechanism may need oiling, especially at the start of the season, otherwise accidents can occur. The vehicle also needs to be checked after the event, so that there is time for any necessary work to be done before the next competition.

Have you arranged for someone to help you at the event? Even if I were riding only one horse, I would never consider trying to manage single-handed. You do not necessarily need someone with a knowledge of horses; any willing helper who is reasonably level-headed can assist with the practice jump and lend a hand in many other ways. Those who turn up on their own are regarded as an organiser's nightmare.

If you are using spurs, have you practised at home with them? If the horse is unaccustomed to spurs, he might add some unscheduled bucks and kicks to the dressage test.

Have you learnt the dressage test? I always memorise it the day before and I get somebody to hear me go through it while we are travelling to the event.

EQUIPMENT CHECK-LIST

With so many things to take, it is all too easy to forget some vital piece of equipment – though I doubt whether many people would do as my mother once did and forget the horse! If we hadn't been forced to turn back because I had forgotten my hat, we might have reached the showground before discovering that she had failed to hitch the trailer containing the horse on to the back of our ancient Land Rover.

Nowadays the equipment – and the horses – are transported in our smart Citibank Savings horsebox, which is filled with plenty of cupboards to take everything we need. As the following list shows, you have to do some extensive packing even for a one-day event. Spares are important; you might otherwise have to pull out of the competition because of a broken strap.

For the rider
Correct clothes for all three phases
Waterproof jacket and boots
Whip (and spare)
String gloves, with spare pair if riding more than one horse
Sewing equipment (in case a button pops off)
Spare breeches (in case you take a dip in the water jump)
Bib for displaying your number
Spurs (optional at novice level)
Spare pin for hunting tie, if worn
Women also require hair nets, with spares

For the horse
Saddle(s) – if using general-purpose saddle for all phases, take spare girths and stirrup leathers
Bridle(s) – if using the same bridle throughout, take a spare (borrowed if necessary)
Spare bits
Numnah and pads
Breastplate
Surcingle
Martingale attachment, if used
Headcollar and rope
Cavesson and lunge line
Lunge whip
Side-reins
Nylon halter for washing down horse
Rugs for all weather conditions: top woollen, New Zealand, thermal, sweat sheet

Roller
Bandages
Four exercise boots for working in before dressage
Two half-boots for show jumping
Two over-reach boots for show jumping and cross-country
Two front tendon protectors for cross-country
Two back tendon protectors for cross-country
Studs and spanner
Vet box
Spare shoes
Sponges
Scraper
Towels
Grooming kit with extra hoofpick
Hoof oil
Stencil for putting diamond shapes on quarters (optional)

We always sew the strip of Velcro securely on bandages over front tendon protectors and on hind brushing boots. This prevents them from coming undone, which may otherwise happen – particularly in wet weather

Hay and hay-nets
Prepared hard feeds for lunch and tea
Buckets
Water – for drinking and washing down
Fly spray, if weather is hot
Plaiting box
Leather punch
Good-luck mascot!

Other essentials
Vaccination certificates
Omnibus schedule for copy of dressage test
Rulebook
Gas on lorry, if it has a cooker

It might seem as though you need an articulated lorry to contain all this – but believe it or not, it does fit into a fairly compact unit.

Right: *It is important to school over different types of obstacles before tackling your first event*

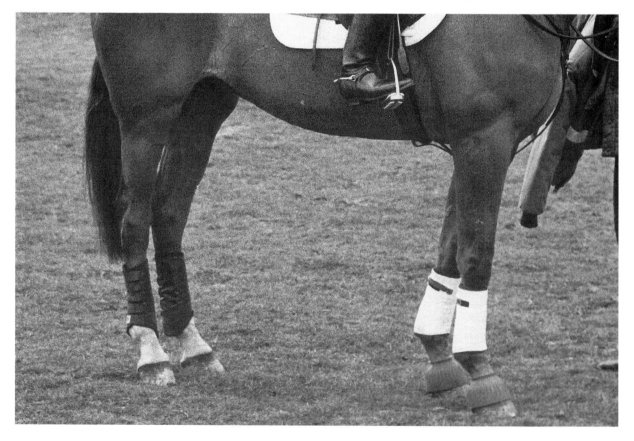

WALKING THE CROSS-COUNTRY COURSE

If the event is local, it makes good sense to walk the cross-country course the day before. You will then have more time to ponder over any fences that might worry you. Most horses and riders have their Achilles heel and by now you will be well aware of any shortcomings in this direction. Your horse may be suspicious of drop fences or ditches or water; he may have a tendency to hang on one rein more than the other. You may also have a psychological hang-up about a particular type of fence, which has to be recognised and accepted along with the horse's vulnerable spot. There will almost certainly be something when you walk the cross-country course that worries you as soon as you set eyes on it. The subconscious is quick to alert us to problems on these occasions.

If there is an alternative slow route at the fence that makes your heart miss a beat, you would be well advised to take it – especially if this is your first event. Bearing in mind that prevention is better than cure, it is much wiser to avoid the problem than to risk a refusal that could completely disrupt the horse's training. When there is no alternative, you may manage to solve the problem by standing in front of the fence and thinking about it in a positive and sensible way.

For instance, if the horse has a tendency to jump to the left and this particular fence seems difficult for that reason, you might decide to switch your stick to the left hand after the previous obstacle. Then you will be ready to slap him on the left shoulder if he feels like swerving – or perhaps, just having the stick on the left side will prevent him from drifting.

If the horse is anxious about jumping into water, you could ask yourself whether you should approach it in trot, so that he has the opportunity to see what lies ahead before you use your legs strongly to get the forward impulsion needed for the jump. Generally speaking, the faster you go at this type of fence the more likely it is that the horse will stop. He puts on the brakes because he wants to look at the fence, and once those brakes are applied it becomes extremely difficult to get one's foot back on the accelerator.

Perhaps the horse may dislike jumping from light into shadow. In this case you must again make sure that he is given every chance to see where he is going; if you are coming off a turn before jumping into a wood, for instance, you can make the turn wider to give him time for a better view. If you cannot figure out the best way to jump a particular fence, you can always ask another rider for advice. Those of us who have been in the sport for a number of years are often asked this type of question and we are happy to try to find the right answer.

You should not feel you are being feeble by trotting into certain cross-country fences; experienced riders do so quite frequently with their novices. It can be the best way to approach a jump into water or such obstacles as a coffin, downhill steps or a sunken road. The reason for using trot can be explained by taking the coffin as an example.

This type of obstacle invariably has a drop on the landing side of the first element, with a ditch to follow. The drop and the ditch are the two ingredients that are most likely to worry the horse, so the object is to get as close as possible to the first fence in order to give him the chance to see where he is going. This is best done from trot with a novice horse; he should come in steadily, with impulsion, and take off close to the first fence from a point where he can see over it. Having landed safely over this first element, you simply need to encourage him to keep going forward over the ditch and the fence that follows.

If you were to approach in canter, you might see a long stride and be tempted to go for it. If the horse is brave, he will probably take off where you ask him, which means that he will be airborne when he suddenly sees the drop and ditch. His automatic reaction is to put his undercarriage down in order to protect himself, which means dropping his hindlegs and hitting them on the fence. He will probably hurt himself in the process and will not be quite so keen to jump the next coffin he meets.

On the other hand, he may not think it such a good idea to take off some way back, at the point you suggest. Instead he might try to put in a short stride, which brings him too close to the first part of the obstacle; he therefore has a refusal. The same principle applies to any drop fence, including those into water. There is a tendency to feel that the faster you go and the further the horse stands back at such fences, the less likely he will be to have a refusal. In fact, the opposite is true. By going fast and asking for a huge leap over drop fences, you will also increase the strain on his forelegs as he lands.

Opposite above: *Unaffiliated shows help the horse to become accustomed to a party atmosphere*

Below: *The horse would have to be completely straight and obedient before attempting a corner, as shown here*

A young horse negotiating his first angle at a novice event. The rider's legs encourage the horse forward on the approach, while hands maintain contact. At take-off, the rider is climbing a little up the horse's neck but achieves a good landing. At this point four eyes are looking towards the next fence. As they move away from the obstacle, the rider's upper body is a little too far forward. The hips could be a little further back at the next take-off, but horse and rider show good style in the air

A typical grid for schooling an advanced event horse: place pole, 9 feet (2.75 metres) to cross-rails, 18 to 19 feet (5.5 to 5.8 metres) to vertical, 10 to 12 feet (3.05 to 3.66 metres) to oxer

A double bounce: cross-rails, 10 to 12 feet (3.05 to 3.66 metres) to cross-rails, the same distance to oxer. Place poles are used to keep the horse straight on approach

A good example of extended trot, marred by the horse's head being behind the vertical

An example of the correct outline

Always keep contact with the horse's mouth, while allowing freedom of head and neck

The horse should be kept in balance between hand and leg

Many falls occur by tripping up steps out of water. The horse needs to be supported by the rider's hand and leg

Jumping a corner with Master Craftsman. This one was low and very wide, demanding extreme accuracy and straightness

Should you decide that the horse might need a reminder at one particular fence, because it represents his Achilles heel, you should make up your mind not to use the stick too early. If you give him a whack six strides out, he will wonder what he has done wrong and will be reacting to you rather than the fence. By the time he switches his attention back to the obstacle, he will be almost on top of it. He is therefore far more disconcerted than if you were to give him one slap in the final stride, when it coincides with his preparation for take-off.

You have to work out a plan that suits both you and your horse. You also have to put your own doubts behind you; the horse can hardly be expected to jump with confidence if the person on top is anticipating trouble. If the doubts persist, and if there is one fence on the course that still fills you with foreboding, you don't have to run the horse. It would be better to withdraw, so that you can have more time to practise over that type of obstacle. You can always do the dressage and show jumping, and leave the cross-country for another day and a different event.

The course builder should be kind to novice horses by using distances that ride well in combinations, but it still makes sense to check them. If nothing else, it will give you some useful practice before reaching the higher levels where distances will become more crucial. The simple yardstick is to take 12 feet (3.66 metres) as the canter stride for an average horse. If you can walk a fairly accurate pace of 3 feet (i.e. 1 yard or 0.9 metre), four of your strides will be about equal to one for the horse.

Whether walking a cross-country or show-jumping combination, I put my back against the landing side of the first fence and take two paces to the spot where the horse is likely to land – which is 6 feet (1.83 metres) away from the base of the obstacle. Another four paces will be equal to one stride for the horse; if that brings me 6 feet (two paces) away from the next fence, it will probably be a fairly simple double with one non-jumping stride between the two elements.

I then have to consider all the other factors, including whether my horse has a shorter or longer than average stride. The distance is also affected by the type of obstacle, the terrain and the going. If you have two spread fences, the correct distance in the double will be shorter than between two verticals. This is because the highest point of the horse's parabola in a double of spreads will be before the rail on the landing side of the first fence and after the one on the take-off side of the next. If it is jumped downhill the horse's strides will be longer; if uphill or on heavy going, the strides will be shorter.

If all the fences seem jumpable, you will need to complete your course walk by going through the finish and beyond it so that you can decide where to pull up. You need to consider where the other horses are likely to be milling around and you have to take the location of the horseboxes into account, because your partner will probably be keen to get back to his mobile home. You will risk damaging the horse by braking too quickly; failure to pull up within the space available can be even more perilous, as I know to my cost.

I once came flying through the finish in a novice event on Beneficial, only to find that the path on the left, where I had planned to pull up, was full of people – and the right-hand alternative was obstructed by vehicles. I was forced to go straight on towards a rope, which Ben failed to see until the last moment. It tripped him on to a gravel road, where he scraped the top off both knees. My mother had to call the vet while I was taken to hospital, where they discovered a hairline fracture of my left wrist.

We knew that the danger to Ben (and yours truly) could have been much worse, but it was still upsetting to see a brave young horse hurt – perhaps psychologically as well as physically. The wounds took a long time to heal and Ben, then a five-year-old, was sidelined for the rest of the year.

TIMETABLE

Having phoned for your starting times, you will need to work out your timetable for the day. We always aim to arrive at least one and a half hours before our first horse does his dressage test, and earlier if he needs to be worked in for more than an hour or if I need to walk the cross-country and/or the show jumping before I start. We allow an extra half-hour for the journey, in case we run into fog or a traffic jam or have a flat tyre.

Unless the horse is gassy and needs more work, I plan to be on him one hour before his dressage test. Assuming that he is doing the other two phases on the same day, I get on half an hour before the show jumping and am at the start of the cross-country, ready to warm up, twenty minutes before we are due to go. The time I get mounted for this final phase will depend on how far I have to ride to get to the start.

If (as occasionally happens) the dressage is the day before, I allow one hour to warm up for the show jumping. If both dressage and jumping are on a different day, the horse needs at least one hour to warm up for the cross-country.

We are lucky enough to have the girls to help us, and we always write out a timetable for them so that they know when each horse has to be tacked up and ready for each phase. I no longer need one myself, because events have become so much a part of my routine. If you are competing in your first one-day event, it would certainly help to write a timetable incorporating details from the next chapter.

THE EVENING BEFORE

If you are due to make an early start, the horse can be plaited up the night before. You can also polish your boots and begin loading the lorry. The more you can do at this stage, the less you will have to worry about in the morning. I always have to think ahead in order to avoid any sense of panicking against time, otherwise I find it impossible to be calm and relaxed.

SUMMARY

Read check list at start of chapter.
Make sure you have all the necessary equipment, in good condition.

Walking cross-country course:
Be aware of your own and your horse's Achilles' heel.
Be prepared to take slow alternative routes (if available) at fences that worry you.
Think about each fence positively.
Consider whether some fences should be approached in trot, so that the horse has a chance to see what he is jumping.
If in doubt, ask a more experienced rider for advice.
If the horse is likely to need a reminder from the stick, plan to give it on the final stride.
Check distances in combinations, remembering that the average horse's stride is 12 feet. Allow 6 feet from fence for landing and another 6 feet for take-off.
Take account of your own horse's length of stride and the terrain. He will take longer strides downhill and shorter ones uphill or on heavy going.
Remember that the distance needs to be slightly longer between verticals than between spreads.

Walk through the finish and decide where to pull up, remembering that you will risk injury by braking too quickly.

Timetable:
Aim to arrive at least one and a half hours before the horse does his dressage (or earlier if he needs extra work before his test).
Allow an extra half-hour for hold-ups on the journey.
Aim to be on the horse at least one hour before the dressage.
Assuming you are riding all phases on the same day, allow half an hour to warm up for the show jumping and 20 minutes for the cross-country, plus the time it will take to walk to the start.
If dressage is the previous day, allow one hour to warm up for the show jumping.
If both dressage and jumping are the previous day, allow at least one hour to warm up for the cross-country.

11

THE DAY OF THE EVENT

Our horses often breakfast early on the day of the competition. The actual time obviously depends on the length of the journey and their starting times; but if we are leaving home at seven o'clock, the morning feed would be given at six o'clock. Most horses finish eating within thirty minutes, which leaves the other half-hour to get them ready for the journey and load them into the horsebox. We prefer them to eat in their own stable, but if we have to leave much earlier they are fed in the lorry, where we are lucky enough to have the facilities to feed en route.

The remaining hard feeds have to fit in with the horse's starting times. He is not fed less than one and a half hours before being ridden or less than three and a half to four hours since his last feed. When he has finished the cross-country, he has to wait for an hour before he gets another meal. The hay ration is reduced until after he has completed the cross-country, but if the travelling time is two hours or more, he may be given a small hay-net of 3-4 lb to eat on the way there assuming that he was going fairly late across country.

CLOTHES FOR TRAVELLING

The horse has to be dressed for the journey. Our eventers wear a headcollar (with rope for tying) and long travelling boots, which are shaped to cover part of the knees and the hocks as well as completely encasing the coronets. We also use tail bandages (which should not be wound tightly) or tail guards. Clothing, if required, depends on the individual horse and the prevailing temperature. Horses are like people; some shiver at the first hint of a chill breeze, while others seem to stay warm in Arctic conditions. We use only light rugs in the lorry, but weather conditions will determine whether the horse is to wear a sweat sheet, a porous thermal rug or, perhaps, one made of light towelling.

The horse is ready to travel. He is wearing leg protectors, roller and tail guard

ON ARRIVAL

One member of the Ivyleaze team has to go in search of the secretary's office to collect our numbers. If the office is a fair distance from the lorry park, this could take a quarter of an hour – but I am usually lucky enough to have somebody else to do it for me. I may have to walk the show jumping (and the cross-country if I have not already done so) before I get myself togged out for dressage and the horse is tacked up.

We always put on the bridle before unloading. Once out of the lorry, the travelling boots are removed and replaced by exercise boots. The horse is then saddled and studs suitable for the ground conditions are screwed into his shoes. If he needs extra work to calm him down before the dressage, we will have allowed time for him to be lunged for half an hour before I get on. He is likely to be far more excited than when being lunged at home, but he is still not supposed to kick and buck at the end of the line.

Most horses that behave well at home will continue to do so when lunged at an event. Occasionally, however, one of them lights up and has to be worked with slightly less restraint for maybe five or ten minutes, simply to avoid a battle which would create tension. As an alternative to lungeing a gassy horse, you could put on a cavesson and lead him around – for as long as an hour if you feel like it. He can look at all the sights until he loses interest in them. Boredom is often the best way of getting an over-excited horse to calm down.

DRESSAGE

Though I am on the horse for an hour before his test, only half that time is spent in serious work. The rest is for mooching around on a loose rein, so that the horse can absorb all the sights and sounds. Meanwhile I would need to know who is riding the test before mine (because we do not always go in numerical order), and I would make sure I knew how to get into the arena, which is often roped off. I also keep an eye on the arena to see if there is any dip in the ground and to check how close the judge's car is parked. I might trot past a parked car as part of my schooling if the horse tends to be a bit spooky.

During the half-hour of serious work I will be trying to achieve smooth transitions, correct shape, calmness, suppleness and obedience. I practise some of the movements I will be doing in the test, but not in the same order. Before I go into the arena, the horse's boots are removed and he is quickly smartened up. I get rid of my whip, so that I will not be eliminated for riding into the arena with it still in my hand. There may be a steward responsible for checking the horse's bit at this stage, which I will have found out in advance. I will also have made myself known to the dressage steward.

While I am riding the test, I am always thinking of the next movement – as well as my aids and whether the horse is straight and in rhythm. I have to keep thinking ahead so that I can prepare him for transitions, normally by giving some signal three strides before. The actual signal would depend on the animal. For downward transitions, it might mean sitting a little deeper in the saddle and putting my leg on the horse for the last three strides, but only if I were on one that did not mind me doing this. You have to know your horse and be flexible. If I am going to canter, I might prepare him by leaning a little on the inside seat-bone three strides earlier.

The smallness of the arena often comes as a shock to both horse and rider. Everything seems to happen far more quickly than at home, where you might start with two complete circles of trot before your next movement. Transitions and changes of direction come far more rapidly in the test. You may also have the added problem of an inattentive horse, who is keener on looking at the strange surroundings than listening to you. You nevertheless have to ride him as he is on the day; it is easy (but unhelpful) to flap if he misbehaves or refuses to listen. You are not in the arena for a schooling session, so you have to carry on and do the best you can.

BETWEEN PHASES

We never leave a horse tied to the lorry unless someone will be there to keep an eye on him, otherwise he goes back into the vehicle, which is where he is normally fed. Wherever he is left to relax between phases, he must be tied short enough to prevent accidents. We once saw a horse attempting to get out of a lorry through the groom's door, which might have had catastrophic consequences. If you tie the horse on a long rope outside the vehicle so that he can eat grass, you run the risk of his legs becoming entangled in it. There have even been cases of horses sustaining rope burns on their pasterns as a result. We always tie to a loop of string, rather than directly on to the ring at the side of the horsebox; if the horse runs back, he will then break the string rather than injuring himself or ruining his headcollar.

Injuries can happen in the bat of an eyelid. I remember holding Priceless at an event while someone was getting a bucket out of one of the cupboards on the side of the lorry. Because he was feeling itchy, he suddenly began rubbing himself up and down on the edge of the open cupboard, and before I could stop him, he had cut his lip. Had it been a quarter of an inch higher, the cut would have been in the corner of his mouth and he would have missed the Olympic Games.

Keeping things tidy throughout the day – and getting everything ready in advance – will avoid much unnecessary hassle. Unless the ground is too muddy, anything left out can be put under the ramp or beneath the vehicle to keep dry if it rains. You should always be aware of the weather; if it is cold and blustery, you will need to keep checking that the horse is warm enough and put on an extra rug if necessary. Water buckets – one for drinking and the other for washing off bits and sponging down the horse – should be filled in advance so that they are ready when required. The same applies to hay-nets.

SHOW JUMPING

Most novice horses have a tendency to sidle towards home (which means the exit from the ring and the horsebox while away at an event) so I would bear this in mind when walking the show-jumping course. Otherwise, if I am turning away from home I might find that I am 6 feet off my planned route; the horse therefore has to jump the fence at an angle and is more likely to have it down. If I decided to turn a little earlier, I could probably avoid that problem.

You need to know your horse inside out so that you can consider all his foibles while you are inspecting the fences. Perhaps he is more difficult to turn one way than the other, which is quite usual with novices; if so, that has to be taken into account when deciding where you will make your turns. There will be at least one double on the course, where you can measure the distance by taking 1-yard strides between the two elements – as with cross-country combinations.

Clearing a show jumping fence in good style

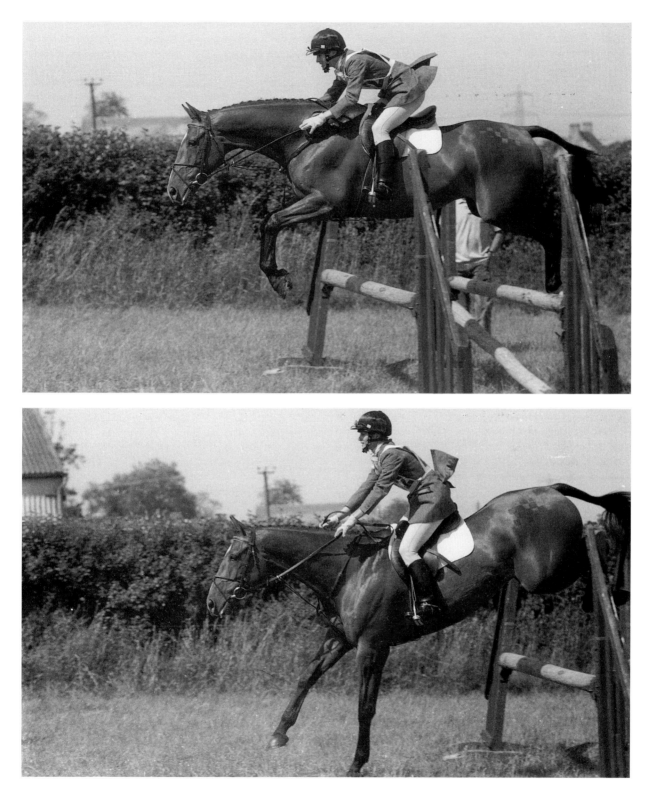

Maybe the double consists of a parallel into an upright. If you are on a big forward-thinking horse – or one that tends to balloon over parallels – you should be aware that you may need to make adjustments on the approach to avoid getting too close to the upright. On a green and slightly stuffy horse, you might have to approach it with a little more pace. You also need to consider the length of your horse's stride – and his eagerness to get on with the job – to know the pace at which you will need to approach each jump.

My course walk would also take account of the going, whether the ground was flat or sloping, the location of the practice fences and of the start and finish. Studs are selected to suit the going in the arena rather than the practice area – unless it is like concrete outside and a quagmire inside, which is hardly likely to happen. The large studs we use for soft going would cause severe jarring on hard ground.

If possible, I like to watch a couple of horses jumping before I get mounted. It may reveal some aspect I had missed when walking the course; it also gives me a chance to hear the starting signal – and to know whether it happens to be a bell, hooter, whistle or whatever. I have good reason to be diligent over such things, having once been eliminated for starting before the signal was given.

Assuming I had done the dressage (and working in beforehand) that morning, I would get on the horse when twelve to fourteen riders are left to go before it is my turn. By now the horse will be tacked up in his jumping and cross-country saddle and bridle, numnah, breastplate, surcingle, martingale attachment (if worn), half-boots and over-reach boots. I will be dressed in accordance with the rulebook, carrying a stick no longer than the allowed length, wearing the right hat and (I hope) the right number. If you are riding more than one horse, it is all too easy to forget to change the number because it is out of sight.

I always have someone to help me in the collecting ring. Though you can ask a bystander for help with the practice fence, it puts you under far more pressure if you don't have your own assistant to move the poles to the height you want them. It is also useful to have a rug brought to the collecting ring when it is cold or wet, and a fly spray when the weather is hot – together with a hoofpick in your assistant's pocket.

It is courteous to make yourself known to the collecting ring steward, who will in turn help by letting you know how many horses are in front of you. I have my first jump over the practice fence when there are six horses left to go. It may be tempting to start earlier, but it would be a mistake. You end up either jumping

too much or losing the benefit of this brief sharpening exercise. I would normally have four practice jumps at this stage (all taken at canter) – over a vertical at about 3 feet and then at 3 feet 3 inches, followed by an ascending oxer (with the back rail higher than the front) and a square oxer. If all went well, I would then walk round on a loose rein until the second-last rider in front of me had nearly finished the course. Then I would jump the vertical – once only if the horse cleared it and a second time if he made a mistake. A vertical is better than a spread fence for getting the horse sharp and quick on his feet.

Once through the start, you have to keep thinking ahead. As you land from one fence, you will need to be thinking about where to turn in order to get a good approach to the next obstacle. Having landed over the last, you must be sure to go through the finish. That may sound obvious, but I have seen people miss going between the electronic timers – usually because the horse has swerved to one side.

CROSS-COUNTRY

Before the cross-country, I need to put on my back protector and jersey, maybe change my number and spurs, and make sure I have a pair of clean, dry string gloves ready. At this point I always remove my hunting-tie pin for safety reasons; I have heard of people piercing their windpipes with a pin when falling on the cross-country.

The horse then has to be booted and bandaged. I always do my own bandaging; I regard this (and the checking of tack and equipment) as the rider's responsibility. When all this is done, I sit down on my own with the programme for a last mental run through the course. Whether I am riding a novice or advanced horse, I always go through it fence by fence, remembering any markers I have noticed and the lines I plan to take.

Someone will have checked that the cross-country is running to time. It may be cold and wet; if so, the last thing I want is to arrive at the start a quarter of an hour early and end up with a frozen horse. I always ride to the start at walk, which could take two or ten minutes, so I need to know how far away it is in advance. My twenty-minute warm-up consists mainly of cantering, with some trotting and one sharp burst at a faster speed. Then I usually have a jump or two, though this might be omitted if the show jumping has gone well (and was on the same day) or if the practice fence was

Jumping a lane crossing at a novice one-day event. A good position over the first obstacle, showing a closed leg and contact with the horse's mouth as the rider sits up and waits for the landing. The lower leg has slipped back a little on landing but both leg and hand positions are good as the horse takes one non-jumping stride. The lower leg is a little too far back at the second take-off but the hips could be further back

unsuitable – perhaps because it was flimsy or the ground was bad. If I had done both the dressage and show jumping the previous day, it would obviously be necessary to extend the warming-up time. In this case I would have to give the horse four or five jumps to get him stoked up for the cross-country.

After warming up, the girths have to be checked before I walk quietly round, with a rug on the horse's quarters and a jacket on myself if the weather is cold or wet.

I never wear a stopwatch at one-day events, whether riding in novice or advanced classes. I prefer to go by the feel the horse is giving me; I want him to stay within a rhythm and maintain a pace at which he feels comfortable. You quite often see young horses being hurried out of this rhythm – and thereby ruined – at novice one-day events. They do not necessarily achieve the fastest times by going at breakneck speed between fences, because they are more or less obliged to slow down and show jump each obstacle – thus defeating the object of the exercise.

If the horse has been taught to go in a rhythmic way across country, the miles per hour can be increased as he gains experience. We have had horses whose times proved slower than they felt at the first few events. Then, slowly but surely, they began to get faster without my being aware of it. With one particular horse, I knew that I had made slightly shorter turns and had taken less time to set him up for certain fences, because he was becoming more educated. I was nevertheless surprised to learn how much faster we had gone. The rhythm felt exactly the same; it was only the miles per hour that had changed because he had gained enough confidence to maintain a faster pace.

I always aim to set off across country as though I mean business. The first two fences are usually straightforward, and if you can ride them in a positive way and get two good jumps, the horse will be given an automatic boost to his confidence. I aim to keep thinking ahead to the next fence, but there is a tendency for me to harp back to the previous obstacle if I had a bad jump. That usually results in the next one being just as bad. Having acknowledged the first mistake, you have to try to put it behind you and be positive about the next fence.

Forward thinking on the cross-country course will include remembering the lines you planned to take. You will also be concentrating on keeping the horse in rhythm, watching out for stray spectators and for any steward waving an emergency flag to indicate that you must pull up. Spectators are always a worry at one-day events; if I am riding towards a bend in a wooded track,

I might shout something (such as 'coming round') because often people fail to realise that a horse is galloping towards them. Events would not be the same without spectators, so we should do our best to avoid mowing them down!

Having completed the course, it is essential to pull up correctly. Your horse will be in serious danger of breaking down if you kick on through the finish, then drop the reins and pat him while he comes back into trot. That is when he starts propping, applying the brakes with his forelegs and causing them undue stress. The same risks occur when you are pulling up downhill or when making a sharp turn. After urging the horse through the finish, you should sit quietly and ease him back on the bridle – on a straight line or a gentle turn.

I dismount as soon as the horse has stopped, loosen the girths, surcingle and noseband, run up the stirrups and lead him back to the horsebox. He should be fit and therefore not blowing too badly, but I will need to time his recovery rate (as we do after canter work-outs) to get a more accurate idea as to how his fitness is going. We do this with every horse at every event.

HORSE CARE

There is still plenty to do when the horse gets back to the lorry after completing the cross-country. The Ivyleaze routine goes something like this:

Remove saddle.
Put on sweat sheet or rug, depending on weather.
Walk horse round until he has stopped blowing.
Remove boots and bandages.
Check legs for injuries – if cut or scratched, wash with warm water and apply cleansing agent.
In hot weather, sponge horse down with cold water.
Wash neck (whatever the weather) if horse has sweated profusely.
In cold weather, wipe over the rest of the horse with damp sponge.
Scrape off excess water.
Dry ears with towel (the type used to dry hands rather than tea-cups).
Wipe eyes and nose with another sponge or cloth.
Pick out feet and remove studs.
Apply ointment or poultice if necessary.
Offer small amount of water.
Prepare horse for journey by putting on travelling boots, etc.
Feed small hay-net.

The horse is given his hard feed one to one and a half hours after he has completed the cross-country. If he is the last of our horses to go and the journey is less than two hours, he would probably wait to be fed at home in the peace and quiet of his own stable. On longer journeys we give all the horses a hay-net of 4-5 lb to eat while travelling and a hard feed to whichever horse is due for one. If we did not have mangers built into the lorry, we would be unlikely to attempt some makeshift arrangement, which usually results in food being tipped on to the floor and wasted; instead, the hard feed would wait until our return home. On journeys lasting three hours, we make one stop to offer the horses some water. We also check their temperature every quarter of an hour, by our usual method of putting a hand under the rug to feel their shoulders and loins to make sure they are neither too hot nor too cold. Once back at home, the horse's legs are checked again for any sign of swelling, bruising or any other type of injury, and appropriate action is taken if necessary.

SUMMARY

General: Arrive at least one and a half hours before dressage test.
Have correct clothes, tack and equipment for each phase.
Remove hunting tie pin before cross-country.

Feeding: Hay ration reduced until after cross-country.
No hard feed less than one and a half hours before being ridden.
Allow three and a half to four hours between hard feeds.

Dressage: Ride for one hour before test, using about half an hour for dressage schooling.
If extra time required to calm horse down, lunge for half an hour or lead in hand for up to one hour.
During half-hour of dressage schooling, work on achieving smooth transitions, correct shape, calmness, suppleness and obedience.
Make yourself known to the dressage steward.
Keep protective boots on until last minute.
Remember to get rid of whip before entering arena.
During test, keep thinking ahead to next movement.
Prepare for transitions three strides in advance.
If horse is difficult, stay calm.

Show jumping: During course walk, decide on pace required and where to turn into fences.
If possible, watch others jumping before getting mounted.
Start riding about half an hour before your turn (or one hour if dressage test ridden the previous day).
Make yourself known to collecting-ring steward.
Jump practice fence (about four times) when six horses still to go before your turn.
Keep horse moving (walk on loose rein when not jumping).
Final practice jump(s) when the second-last rider before you has almost completed the course.
During round, keep thinking ahead to the next fence.
Be sure to go through finish.

Cross-country: Have last mental run through course before mounting.
Allow time to ride horse to start (at walk), leaving twenty minutes for warm-up on arrival.
If dressage and show jumping ridden the previous day, allow one hour for warm-up.
Set off to ride all cross-country fences in a positive way.
Keep thinking ahead to next fence.
After completing course, avoid pulling up too quickly.
Dismount when horse has stopped.
Loosen girths, surcingle and noseband, and run stirrup irons up leathers.
Time the recovery rate.

Horse care: See details opposite.

12

FROM NOVICE TO INTERMEDIATE

The horse will gradually be able to start tackling novice courses at a faster pace, taking the quick routes at fences that offer alternatives. You might let him tackle a corner at his first event, assuming that it is an easy one, but I would be more likely to wait until his third outing – and I would not try a corner then unless I had complete confidence that he would stay straight and be obedient.

If the horse is competing on consecutive weekends, there is no necessity for a mid-week canter work-out. His normal programme for the week might then be as follows:

Monday	rest day
Tuesday	light hack
Wednesday	hack and dressage
Thursday	hillwork
Friday	hack and jumping lesson
Saturday	flatwork and short hack
Sunday	competition

When planning your own programme, you need to bear in mind that one-day events improve the horse's fitness quite dramatically. Once he has begun competing, you probably need do no more than keep him ticking over. Even when the horse is aiming for a three-day event, I would not canter between one-day competitions that are on consecutive weekends. The horse needs to be given four easy days after an event; you should also avoid any strenuous work after his rest day.

If the horse began competing as a five-year-old, I will not consider riding him in an intermediate class until the following year. He will have his winter rest, go through the process of getting fit again and start the spring season with maybe five novice events, including one open novice. The number of outings will depend on his physique and the going; he would certainly do no more than three events on consecutive weekends – and he would do those (at a steady pace) only if the going was very good. The decision as to whether or not to attempt an easy intermediate class at the end of the spring season

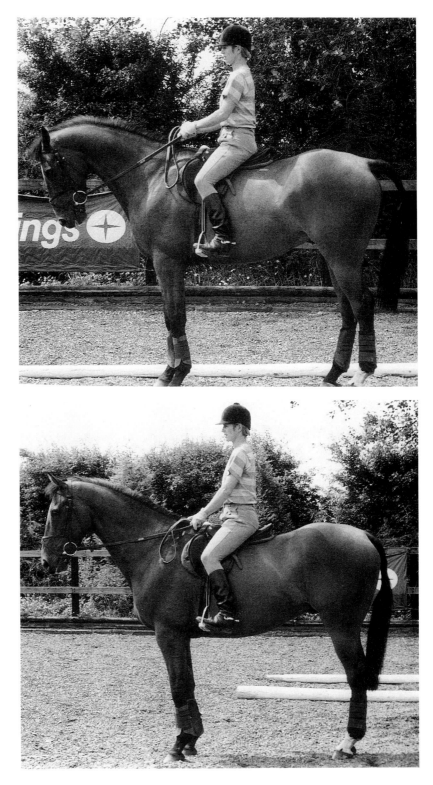

Good and bad halts. The incorrect halt (above) shows the horse overbent and not standing four square

will depend on how well he is going across country. Once again you have to listen to the horse.

NEW MOVEMENTS

We aim to teach the new movements required in intermediate tests about six months before the horse performs them in competition. This obviously requires a bit of guesswork, but nothing has been lost if we get it wrong and he is not ready to tackle a more difficult cross-country course in six months' time. In some cases, if the horse is straight and doing correct turns and circles, I might start shoulder-in at walk at least a year earlier. It is only because we are training a pentathlete, instead of a specialist in one discipline only, that we often need to bide our time before introducing new movements. In eventing we always have to be careful to avoid asking the horse for too much at once.

If you ask for a lateral bend to the left while in halt, the horse will invariably fall in by moving his shoulders in that direction. That is why you need your weight and your legs to achieve lateral flexion without shoulder movement. Gymnastic exercises, such as shoulder-in and travers, will help to improve the horse only if you are secure and balanced within the aid. If you are crooked, he will become so as well – in the process losing his flexion, tempo and impulsion.

Shoulder-in at walk is the first new lateral movement the horse learns after leg yielding. It requires him to move on three or four tracks, with his inside hindfoot following in (or close to) the track of his outside forefoot. It is useful in helping to establish control over the horse's forehand and quarters, as well as encouraging him to use his hocks and become more supple.

The best way to start shoulder-in is from a circle or corner, because you will already have the correct bend through the horse's body from head to tail. When the horse returns to the side of the arena from a circle, he can be asked to continue on the same curve until his inside shoulder is off the track as if starting another circle. He is then in the correct position to perform shoulder-in along the side of the school, with the whole length of his body flexed around the rider's inside leg and bent away from the direction in which he is moving.

The rider maintains the same flexion by use of the inside rein, while the outside rein stops the horse continuing on the circle and corrects excessive bending. The inside leg is applied on the girth, asking him to move his forehand forward and away from it. The outside leg, used behind the girth, maintains impulsion and prevents the quarters from swinging outwards. Do not ask for more than a few steps at a time when the horse is first learning this movement. It requires him to make quite an effort, since he has to bring his inside hindleg well forward under his body in order to carry his own and his rider's weight during this exercise.

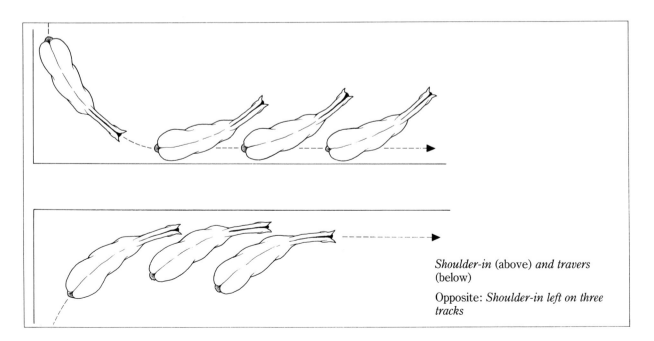

Shoulder-in (above) *and travers* (below)

Opposite: *Shoulder-in left on three tracks*

110

The horse should maintain his rhythm and impulsion, without leaning to the outside of the arena. Though his forelegs cross over during this exercise, his hindlegs should not do so; when he crosses his hindlegs, he is avoiding making the effort required from his inside hock. This is more likely to occur when the rider asks for too much bend or too wide an angle; the horse's hindlegs should virtually remain on the track they would normally take if he were moving straight ahead. Having completed the shoulder-in steps, the horse's forehand should be brought back to the track so that he moves straight ahead rather than continuing with the same bend on a circle. Otherwise he will learn to anticipate circling at the end of this movement. Once he understands what is required of him, the horse can be asked to perform the same exercise at trot.

Travers (or quarters-in) is a useful exercise although not included in eventing dressage. It helps to increase the horse's attentiveness to the rider's legs and gives improved suppleness in his rib cage. In this movement the horse's quarters are off the track and his hindlegs cross over, whereas his forelegs do not. He is bent slightly around the rider's inside leg, towards the direction in which he is going.

This exercise can also begin with a circle, which will put the horse into the correct position to start the movement. Instead of straightening his quarters as you complete the circle, they should be kept inside the

Left: *Shoulder-in right on four tracks*

Below: *Travers right*

track by the rider's outside leg, applied behind the girth, so that they follow on a different track from the forehand. The inside leg is used on or near the girth to keep the horse moving forward, while maintaining impulsion and bend. The inside rein keeps the horse moving in the correct direction, while the outside rein controls his speed and the amount of bend. The rider should put extra weight on the inside seat-bone.

You should always bring the horse's hindlegs back on to the track before reaching a corner, and you must avoid asking the horse to perform this exercise for too long, otherwise he will become a little too free with the unaccustomed mobility of his hindquarters and may be more difficult to keep straight in his basic work. Travers will probably be easier on the left rein, because of the tendency in most horses to prefer taking contact with the left hand. As with shoulder-in, we ask for this movement in walk first and then trot.

The *half-pass* would normally be attempted at walk only while the horse is still a novice. It requires him to move diagonally, so that he goes forwards and sideways at the same time, with each outside leg crossing over in front of its inside pair to make four separate tracks. You can get the correct position for half-pass in the same way as you would for shoulder-in – that is, by riding a circle and continuing on the same curve after returning to the side of the arena until the horse's inside shoulder is off the track. Thereafter the two movements take the horse in different directions. For half-pass he moves across the school on the diagonal, with his body bent slightly towards the direction in which he is going. Impulsion and forward rhythm must be maintained.

The rider's outside leg drives the horse sideways, while the inside leg asks for forward movement and impulsion. The inside rein asks for the correct bend, and the outside rein controls the forward movement and, if necessary, corrects the amount of bend. You should be looking the way the horse is going, with shoulders turned slightly in that direction and a little more weight on the inside seat-bone, with inside hip forward.

The movement is incorrect if the quarters are leading. In other words, for right half-pass, which is normally the easier direction, the horse's forehand should be slightly further to the right and in advance of his quarters. His head should not be tilted; this fault usually occurs because the horse has not been taught to stay straight and maintain an even contact on both reins in his basic flat work.

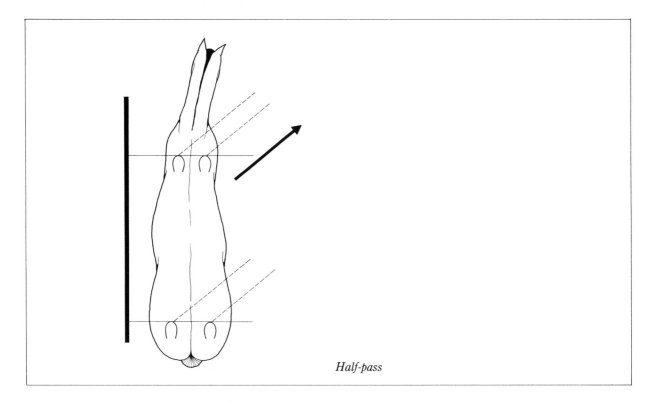

Half-pass

Medium paces will be required in trot and canter. By now the horse will have learnt to shorten and lengthen within both; in the process he will have taken some medium strides. They are longer than those used for working paces, but shorter than those required for the more advanced extended work. We will be looking for a rounder outline and improved impulsion from the hind-legs, which have to be properly engaged before the horse is capable of medium paces. If his hocks are not underneath his body but are trailing behind him, he will lose his balance and rhythm, move on to his forehand and produce quicker (rather than longer) strides. It is the elevation within these strides that gives him the necessary time to lengthen. The rider has to activate the horse's hindlegs to stoke up the engine before asking for medium paces. Once achieved you should allow a little with the hand without losing contact.

Transitions become more demanding at intermediate level. Halt to trot and walk to canter are now included in the upward transitions and trot to halt in the downward ones. They require more energy than the simple transitions used in novice tests, but the principle remains the same. It is important to alert the horse, by using one or two half-halts, so that he knows something different is about to be required of him. He should then be attentive to your aids given through your legs, weight and use of the retarding rein. He is therefore aware of the slight increase in emphasis that tells him, for instance, that you want him to come back from trot to halt rather than trot to walk.

The *simple change* is not so much a new movement as taking less time for something the horse has done already. He has to canter on part of a circle with the inside leg leading, come back through trot to walk for a few strides as he changes the diagonal and then strike off into canter with the opposite leg leading. He has already learnt the aids for striking off on one particular leg, but will obviously need extra impulsion to do this after the transition down to an active walk.

He will also have to learn *five-metre loops* at canter, this time without changing legs. This movement is an easier version of the counter-canter which is required at advanced level and is the first time the horse is asked to canter on a curve with the outside leg leading. We teach this in easy stages, moving only 2.5 metres off the outside track at first so that the curve is gentle. The horse should be bent in the opposite direction to the curve he is following. The position of both horse and rider remains on the leading leg as regards aids and flexion. The horse is encouraged to change direction with the outside rein and inside leg. You have to take care that he stays true to the bend and neither falls in with the shoulder nor swings out with his quarters.

Rein-back is also required for intermediate tests. We are inclined to leave this until the last of the new movements to be learnt, because we always want the horse to be thinking of going forward and it can therefore work against us; he can also use it as a form of resistance. We teach rein-back by having someone on the ground who can help to explain exactly what the rider is asking the horse to do. Without such assistance, he is likely to become confused. It is when he fails to understand what is required of him that he is likely to start rearing.

The rider gives the voice command 'back', and the usual aids. This means moving your weight slightly forward to give the horse's back full freedom, applying both legs on the girth and using your hands, with a give and take, to restrain any forward movement. On no account should the horse be pulled backwards.

The person on the ground can reinforce these aids by pushing with a hand in front of the horse's shoulder or, maybe, giving a light tap with a stick in the same area. He is likely to put his head up like a periscope when first asked to back and it helps to be aware of that. If he takes only one step back, make much of him before asking for another one. It will help him to know exactly what you want when these aids are applied and you will soon be able to dispense with the voice command. As the horse becomes more familiar with the movement the aids will gradually become less obvious.

DECIDING ON THE FIRST INTERMEDIATE CLASS

It is easy to persuade yourself that a horse is ready for his first intermediate after he has done, say, eleven novice events. In theory that is probably right, but it does not necessarily work out in practice. I prefer to take no notice of how many or how few events the horse has contested and concentrate instead on the feel he gives me over cross-country fences. Unless he collects the points that upgrade him too quickly, which can be a big problem, the decision to enter for an intermediate will depend on his confidence and character, not miles on the clock.

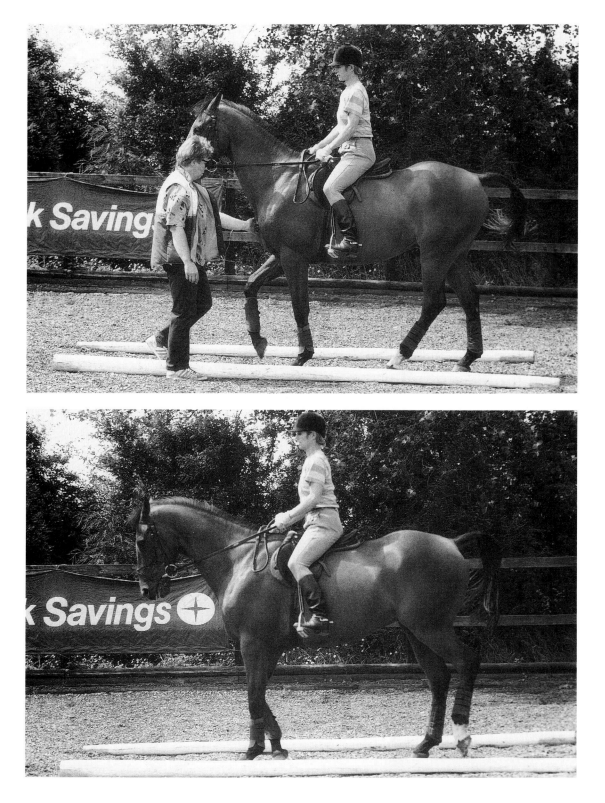

Teaching the horse to rein back using poles on the ground to keep him straight. The handler encourages him to move backwards by tapping him lightly on the shoulder

We like our horses to do their first intermediate before they upgrade; if they find the bigger fences slightly unnerving, you can then restore their confidence by going back to novice events. The decision to tackle an intermediate has to be based on each horse's confidence across country. You can ride the dressage test without doing him any harm and the extra two inches on the show jumps are hardly going to give him the heebie-jeebies, but if he makes a mistake across country you would have good reason to feel depressed. A stop would mean that he now knows how to refuse; a fall could seriously undermine his confidence.

I am careful to choose one of the smaller intermediate courses, with plenty of alternative routes, for the horse's first attempt at this level. I would be unlikely to consider an open intermediate, since it caters for all grades, including advanced, and is usually more difficult.

Canter work-outs

Because the intermediate course is longer, the horse needs to be slightly fitter than he was for novice one-day events. When training on flat ground, he might therefore move up from three five-minute canters to three of six minutes, still with a break after each one. If you are able to use an uphill incline for work-outs, it may be more effective to go from three six-minute canters to two of seven minutes. The actual programme needs to be adapted to the individual horse as well as the terrain; some get fitter on three canters and two breaks, while others are better suited by two canters and one break.

I rely as much on the horse's breathing as I do on my stopwatch when deciding on the length of these breaks, which would never be less than one minute or more than three. The actual time comes somewhere between these two parameters. If the weather is hot, the horse will be blowing harder and longer. He is therefore given a slightly longer rest than he would have on a cold day.

It continues to be important to time the recovery rate and be flexible with one's programme. You still do not want the horse to be three-day-event fit for a one-day test, nor do you want him to be struggling in any way at the end of the cross-country. If the recovery rate is the same for the longer canter work-outs, he is probably at the right level of fitness for an intermediate one-day event. Once into intermediates, he can be kept ticking over with just two seven-minute canters (with the usual break between) on weekends when he is not competing.

The horse responds to the rider's aids, remaining straight as he moves back between the poles

Jumping

The horse will be jumping considerably faster over novice cross-country courses than in the show-jumping arena. This extra speed results in a flatter jump; we therefore need to regain his natural bascule. This is done through gymnastic exercises, which also improve his suppleness and the elasticity of his muscles. The grids described in Chapter 9 – and your own variations on the same theme – will be of particular value to the long-striding horse. The shorter-striding and more athletic type would probably derive greater benefit from canter combinations on varying distances.

A combination suitable for a horse that is still at novice level would have three fences that gradually increased in height. The first might be at 3 feet 3 inches (0.97 metre), with the next two at 3 feet 6 inches (1.07 metre) and 3 feet 9 inches (1.15 metre). A distance of 26 feet (7.9 metres) would require a longish non-jumping canter stride between elements. As the horse gains experience, the heights and distances can be varied so that he learns to shorten and lengthen his non-jumping strides.

Four- to six-bar jumping, over between four and six vertical fences of about 3 feet 6 inches (1.07 metres), is another good exercise. It encourages the horse to be tidy in his jumping and again, by varying the distances, to adjust the length of his stride whenever necessary.

Perhaps you have noticed some imperfections in his style. Maybe he loses power by drifting to one side as he approaches a fence, thus reducing the forward thrust that enables him to clear the obstacle easily. Placing poles, as mentioned in Chapter 5, can be used to correct this tendency – and they can be brought a little closer together so that they give the horse less room for drifting.

It could be that the horse wastes time and effort by jumping too high. Normally this means that he is failing to fold up his legs sufficiently to clear the fence from a lower parabola. His body has to go higher to compensate for his trailing limbs. He can be trained to fold up his legs, but you have to be careful that he does not lose his natural bascule and begin jumping with a hollow back. Gridwork is the best way of curing the first problem without creating a different one.

The horse that consistently jumps too high will invariably land further away from his fences than a horse

with a lower parabola. If you gradually shorten your distances within the grid, he will realise that he has to find some way to land closer to the fence he has jumped. He therefore has to jump lower. When he first experiments with this solution, he may hit the fence. The only alternative left to him is to keep the lower parabola and fold his legs away. Similar results can be achieved by putting a place pole on the ground 9-10 feet (2.7 – 3.05 metres) after the fence, so that he has to land a little shorter to get inside the pole and avoid treading on it. In order to do this, his body has to be lower; if he is to clear the fence, his legs have to be folded out of the way.

The horse has to work hard in grids and all your efforts will be undone if you ask him to carry on for too long. If you do encounter a major jumping problem, it will not be solved by continually working on it. Quite often it is much better to go hacking for a few days and then come back to jumping when the horse is mentally and physically refreshed.

His technique and confidence should be improving, through schoolwork and competitions, while he is competing at novice level. Before riding him in an inter- mediate event, I would aim to take him schooling over some intermediate fences. I might also ride him in some slightly more ambitious show-jumping contests, but only if he happened to be fairly exuberant by nature. You can overdo show jumping to an extent where the more you do, the less tuned up the horse becomes. Often he will be much better when fresh to this discipline, so I normally aim to have two or three show-jumping shows over a period of six weeks before eventing starts and leave it at that for the rest of the season.

Cross-country course walk
The intermediate fences will certainly be bigger than anything the horse has tackled at novice level, but they will probably contain the same ingredients as those he has jumped before. If you think carefully enough, you can normally associate each fence with something similar which the horse has already tackled in a lower or easier form. Once the association is made, you can consider how you rode the easier version – and how the horse jumped it.

Make sure your horse has sufficient confidence to take the big step up from novice to intermediate

Horses are creatures of habit and I am sure they remember jumping the mini versions of the more difficult fences they meet as they go up through the grades. If you can also relate to some past experience, you will feel more confident about jumping the fence and have a better idea as to how you should ride it. There could be a more difficult approach or landing which needs to be taken into account, so you may have to tackle it slightly differently to the one in the past which had basic similarities.

If the horse has successfully negotiated the quick routes at novice level, there is no reason why he should not do the same in his first intermediate. You should not, however, attempt to play the hero. If the course designer has a bright idea which seems horrific to me, I will certainly opt for a slower alternative on my green intermediate horse, if one is available.

THE COMPETITION

The first intermediate contest is likely to tell you whether or not your basic training has been a success. Flaws in that department tend to become more transparent as you move up through the grades, because the horse cannot perform the more difficult movements unless the foundation is right. You will also be given further clues about his courage and confidence. It is not unusual for him to be slightly unnerved by his first experience over an intermediate cross-country course, which is why I always like to have the option of going back to novice afterwards. I normally aim for an easy intermediate at the end of the spring season before the horse has upgraded, and unless he appears to be in his element over the bigger obstacles, I would take him in one or two novice events at the start of the autumn. After that I would hope that he is able to tackle more intermediates with renewed confidence.

This horse is gaining all-important confidence over one of the bigger novice courses

SUMMARY

New movements required for intermediate tests are taught six months (or more) before horse competes at this level.

Decide whether the horse is ready by the way he goes across country.

Try to compete in intermediate before horse has upgraded.

Choose small intermediate course for first attempt.

Increase time for canter work-outs to three at six minutes, with breaks between.

Continue to time the recovery rate.

Use gymnastic jumping exercises to improve suppleness and elasticity.

Work to improve jumping style.

School over intermediate cross-country fences before competing in intermediate event.

Go back to one or two novice events (unless upgraded) if horse needs to regain confidence.

Aids for new movements
Shoulder-in:
Start from turn or circle when horse's forehand has moved off the track.

Weight on inside seat-bone.

Maintain bend with inside rein.

Ask for lateral movement with outside rein.

Inside leg on girth asks horse to move away from it and go forward.

Outside leg behind girth maintains impulsion and controls quarters.

Finish by straightening and then move straight ahead.

Travers (schooling exercise):
Start from turn or circle before horse's quarters are back on the track.

Weight on inside seat-bone.

Inside leg on or near girth maintains impulsion.

Outside leg behind the girth keeps quarters off the track.

Inside rein asks for direction and flexion.

Outside rein controls speed and bend.

Half-pass (at walk only until more experienced):
Start from shoulder-in position, then move across school on the diagonal.

Slightly more weight on inside seat-bone with inside hip forward.

Inside leg on the girth for forward movement and impulsion.

Outside leg behind girth drives the horse sideways.

Inside rein asks for correct bend.

Outside rein controls speed and bend.

Medium paces (trot and canter):
Create impulsion with legs.

Prevent this energy escaping into a faster speed with give and take of hands, without loss of contact.

Five-metre loops at canter:
Horse remains bent on the side of his leading leg.

He is asked to follow a curve in opposite direction with use of rider's inside leg and outside rein.

Rein-back:
Start with assistant on ground to reinforce the aids.

Weight slightly forward.

Legs applied behind the girth.

Give and take with hands to restrain forward movement.

13

CLOTHING AND EQUIPMENT – INTERMEDIATE AND ADVANCED

By now the rider's wardrobe will include a red or black jacket (for men) and a black or blue coat (for women) in order to compete in intermediate events. There is no obligation to add anything more to your own outfit than light-coloured gloves and a pair of spurs (both of which you may already have) in order to compete at the higher levels.

You do, however, have the option of wearing a top hat and tail coat in the dressage phase of advanced one-day events and intermediate or higher levels of three-day eventing. Men have an additional expense if they exercise this option, because they have to get white breeches and black boots with mahogany tops to complete the outfit.

The top hat and tails – whether borrowed, hired or bought second-hand – are obviously not essential, but they do help the overall picture and make you feel the part. The tails may flap a little, so you might like to practise at home in your tail coat. If, however, you go hacking in a long Australian mac during wet weather, the horse will already be accustomed to feel the movement of your clothing on his flanks.

Correctly dressed for the show jumping on Griffin (above) *and for the cross-country on Master Craftsman*

BITTING

I have already mentioned the bits I would try on a novice horse if an unjointed rubber snaffle did not prove satisfactory. These are a jointed snaffle in rubber, then metal, followed by a loose-ring snaffle and a French bridoon. I would hope that one of these was a success and that I could stay with it forever, but it will not always be the case.

If I wanted more control I would probably try a Magenis or Copper D Roller, followed by a Dr Bristol. These three stronger varieties of the snaffle can be effective on a horse that pulls with his head tucked in – usually as the result of being ridden in draw reins at some stage.

The horse that pulls with his head in the air is easier to correct. In this case I would use a rubber Pelham, with a loose curb chain or one with rubber backing. The curb chain encourages the horse to bend from the poll, which automatically lowers his head. If something stronger is needed to control the horse and bring his head down, a gag could be the answer – although it does occasionally have the reverse effect and encourage the head to go higher.

Though the stronger bits may make the rider feel more secure, they can have a detrimental effect on the horse's performance across country. You want him to be forward-thinking, so that he can go out and attack the fences with confidence. If he finds the mouthpiece uncomfortable or too strong, he will be concentrating too much of his attention back to the rider's hands and too little on the fences ahead. You do not want him to be too light on the rein; he needs to be happy on a reasonable contact so that he can take you into the fences.

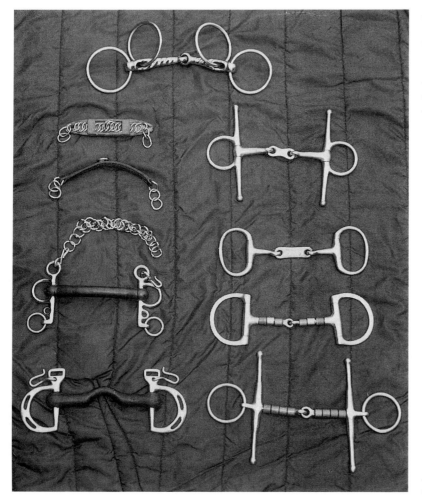

Bits and curb chains that can be effective on a horse that pulls. Top: *Scorrier.* Left (top to bottom): *rubber-backed curb chain, leather curb strap, vulcanite Pelham, vulcanite Kimblewick.* Right (top to bottom): *French bridoon, Dr Bristol, Copper D Roller, Fulmer copper roller snaffle*

Barnsby-Leng general purpose and cross-country saddles

STOPWATCH

You will need a stopwatch when you compete in three-day events, but do make sure that you can read it when you are on a horse and moving at speed. The figures may seem as clear as daylight while you are standing still, but they can turn into a useless blur when you attempt to read them during the speed, endurance and cross-country phase. A spare stopwatch will also be necessary; it will be too late to buy or borrow a replacement if the first one goes wrong on the day.

I always wear my stopwatch over my jersey and an inch or two above my wrist, where there is nothing that can accidentally stop it. Pressing the wrong button by mistake can be very costly, so practise at home to make sure that you can avoid this mishap, and that you can read the figures.

OTHER EQUIPMENT

It makes sense to double up on every essential item of equipment before competing in a three-day event. You will have spent months preparing for the contest and would find it galling, to say the least, if you had to retire because part of your tack had broken and you had no replacement.

You have the option of using a double bridle for the dressage phase of advanced events, but I have very rarely done so. It obviously gives you more control and collection, but I suspect that it might give too much. We are not looking for anything like the degree of collection required for Grand Prix dressage and, rightly or wrongly, I feel things can go wrong if I get more collection than I need by using a double bridle. The horse needs to accept the bit with confidence and be forward-

Ready to start the dressage on Night Cap. Note the rider's tail-coat and the straight front flap of the dressage saddle

thinking for his jumping.

I would prefer to carry on using a simple snaffle bridle with an ordinary cavesson noseband, but it has to be said that I have rarely achieved this beyond novice level. More often than not, I use a Flash noseband instead of the cavesson, which gives me a little more control and avoids the possibility of the horse crossing his jaw or opening his mouth.

I like to use white girths for the major three-day events. Since they are purely cosmetic and a pain to keep clean, you may prefer to spare yourself the effort and expense! A sheepskin noseband can be of practical benefit in the show jumping, as I found with Master Craftsman. He was bred to race over steeplechase fences, which could mean taking off 15 feet in front of the fences and landing another 15 feet away from them. Because of his breeding, Crafty has a tendency to bascule too late, so that the highest point of the parabola

comes after the fence instead of immediately above it. The sheepskin encourages him to lower his head in order to see where he is going. This in turn encourages an earlier bascule and shorter landing.

A minimum weight is required in certain contests (including the cross-country phase of advanced one-day events) so you will need a weight cloth and lead unless you are heavy enough to make the minimum of 11 stone 11 lb (75 kilos) without them. I normally practise with the extra weight for a couple of canter work-outs, but not necessarily for the jumping – unless I have a lightweight horse and want to see how he will carry the extra pounds over fences. Usually dead weight is easier for him; unlike the live weight of the rider, it is less inclined to move and throw him off balance.

We occasionally grease the horse's legs at one-day events, depending on his style of jumping and the ground. It could do no harm – and it might do a lot of good – if you were to use it every time your horse jumps a cross-country round. Should he hit a fence, the grease will help his legs to slide over it.

Our horses always have their legs greased for three-day events. Normally we use Vaseline – but you do get the odd one who is allergic to it, so we need to check beforehand. If there is an allergy, wool fat is used instead, and applied sparingly during the ten-minute halt. There is no reason why your horse should look as though he is ready for the frying-pan! The grease (applied mainly to the stifles, inside the back legs, the knees and forearms) is a bore to remove. You will need a blunt knife and washing-up liquid to help get rid of it.

My three-day event equipment also includes an Easyboot (or similar product) which can be used on the second section of roads and tracks if the horse happens to lose a shoe on the steeplechase. It has a metal clip, rather like a ski boot, and can be fitted far more quickly than a normal shoe. A measuring wheel is another useful item of equipment to take to three-day events, but you should be able to spare yourself the expense by finding a friend who has one.

We also need a bootlace on cross-country day, but it goes nowhere near the horse's feet. It is used to secure the bridle by tying it to the top plait on his neck. If you do have a fall, it is all too easy to pull the bridle off the horse; with the bootlace to secure it, you will at least have the option of remounting and carrying on!

Leaving the start box for an advanced cross country, with the necessary weight-cloth and weights

SUMMARY

Consider whether it is necessary to practise at home in tail coat (if worn).

Keep bit as mild as possible.

If more control needed for horse that pulls with his head tucked in, one of the following bits may prove effective: Magenis, Copper D Roller or Dr Bristol.

If horse pulls with his head up, a pelham and loose curb chain or one with rubber backing may be the answer.

A gag, which is more severe, normally lowers the horse's head – but it can sometimes have the reverse effect.

Make sure you can read your stop-watch when galloping.

Double up on all essential equipment.

Practise with lead weights, if required, to achieve minimum weight.

Decide on type of grease to be used on horse's legs and make sure he is not allergic to it.

A measuring wheel is necessary for walking the steeplechase and cross-country courses. If you don't possess one, try to find a friend who does. Dot and I found such a friend in Clarissa Bleekman, who is walking the course with us

14

PREPARING FOR THE FIRST THREE-DAY EVENT

If I had only one horse to ride and everything went according to plan (which rarely happens), my youngster would do a maximum of ten novice events as a five-year-old, with more novices and two or three intermediates the following year leading up to a novice three-day event. I would want him to enjoy his first three-day test and he has a better chance of having fun over a novice course, which is the shortest and least demanding of all. It is only because the advanced horses have to take priority at certain times of the year

that our novices usually gain their first three-day experience at intermediate events. We are careful to choose one with a lenient cross-country course.

This might well be a one-star CCI (the international equivalent of an intermediate three-day event), so we apply for the horse's passport almost as soon as I start thinking in that direction. It may take some time to come through from the International Equestrian Federation (FEI) and I don't want any worry about whether it will arrive on time.

A nice frame in trot, showing harmony between horse and rider

FLATWORK

I have ridden a variety of different tests at intermediate three-day events (or one-star CCIs); on one occasion, we had to do the FEI test that was used at Badminton. You will therefore need to find out – as early as possible – which test is to be used, so that you have plenty of time to practise all the movements.

The requirements of the test should not, however, be the only factor which determines when the horse is taught new movements. Generally speaking, he learns them when he is ready – which might be more than a year before he has to perform them in eventing. Meanwhile he can use them at dressage shows, which is an excellent way of giving him arena experience and monitoring his progress. Though I have left some of the more difficult movements and transitions to Chapter 16, you may decide to begin tackling them well before the horse does his first novice or intermediate three-day event. Indeed, some of them may be included in

the test, in which case the horse will need to learn them at this stage.

Whatever level he has reached in his training, the horse has to be given time to get his hocks engaged before he is asked to perform any lateral movements or other demanding exercises. This might take only five minutes with a short-based horse and anything up to forty minutes for one with a long base. Master Craftsman comes into the latter category and he always requires plenty of basic work to get his hocks engaged. When working him in before a dressage test, I would probably wait until the last ten minutes before practising any lateral movements.

FITNESS PROGRAMME

All our horses follow the same initial programme, whether or not they are being aimed for a three-day event. It is only when they reach one-day fitness that they go their separate ways, with a completely different routine for those who need to become three-day fit. You can reach this goal in a number of different ways, using the facilities that you have available.

Hills are a tremendous asset; they improve the horse's lungs, heart and muscle tone, enabling you to get him fit with fewer canter work-outs. The ideal place for faster work would be all-weather or grass gallops with a gradual uphill incline. You may not have this facility, in which case you will have to improvise. Two different charts, which were both used to produce horses that were fit enough for advanced or championship three-day events, are included in Chapter 17. You may be able to adapt one – or possibly use parts of both – to suit your own needs.

If the horse has never run in a three-day event before, it may be more difficult to get him fit. His programme could therefore be the same as that used for the advanced horse who is getting ready to cover a longer distance. Thoroughbreds, however, are rarely a problem in this direction, so their work would probably be slightly less. Suggested reductions for novice and intermediate three-day events are given with the two charts in Chapter 17.

STEEPLECHASE

If you have been getting close to (or within) the optimum time at one-day events, you will already have been doing some galloping. Another gear, however, will be necessary to get inside the time required for the steeplechase section of a three-day event. You need to practise at the faster speed and learn to gauge the miles per hour, metres per minute or seconds per furlong, according to which method of measurement suits you best. Using miles per hour means that you can check your speed alongside a car, as mentioned in Chapter 9. For metres per minute you will have to use markers and a stopwatch – but you can dispense with conversion tables, since this is the way in which speeds are given in the rule book. Seconds per furlong are of use if you are able to work the horse on gallops with furlong markers; alternatively, you can easily measure the distance and put up your own markers at home.

The faster speed should not be a problem if you are riding a Thoroughbred; he already knows how to gallop because it was bred into him, so he needs to concentrate on the endurance aspect. The half-bred, who is capable of cantering for long distances at a slower speed, needs to work on maintaining a faster pace.

You will probably have had the chance to jump some steeplechase fences while riding across country at one-day events; if so, the horse has no great need to go schooling over a steeplechase course. It would, however, be of benefit to you as a rider, especially if you are fairly inexperienced.

Above: *At this stage your canter/gallop work-outs change in order to build up to three-day event fitness*

Left: *The roads and tracks make the three-day event a test of endurance as well as speed. Make sure that your horse has done sufficient fitness training to be able to cope with the endurance aspect*

Right: *If you have never ridden over a steeplechase course, it will help to have some practice at the speed required*

FITNESS OF RIDER

The cross-country, speed and endurance phase of a three-day event is much more tiring than a one-day contest. You will therefore need to do exercises or other activities to build up your own strength, no matter how many horses you are riding each day at home. You can choose anything that takes your fancy – skipping, running, swimming, sessions on a standstill bike, or whatever – and you need to do it at least three times a week.

FEEDING

We have always been loath to give feeding charts, because quantities vary so much for each individual horse. As already mentioned, you have to judge the amount of hard feed he needs by his appearance and the feel he gives you when ridden. If a horse has already competed in a three-day event from Ivyleaze, we would have the advantage of being able to refer back to the quantity of hard feed he was receiving at that time – and the notes which tell us how well he fared on it.

Using the rough guidelines of 1 lb of hard feed per day for every mile the horse is covering, you would obviously expect the quantity to be increased for the longer distance in a three-day event and the preparatory canter work-outs. This is usually (although not automatically) true. Since we are always aiming to get the horse fit enough for the job in hand on the minimum quantity of hard feed, we would very rarely give more than 12 lb a day and it could be much less.

The quantity of bulk food depends on his waistline rather than his level of fitness. If he has a weight problem, he will obviously not be allowed to gorge himself on grass all day. His hay and 'slops' will also be given more sparingly, since we do not want him to be burdened with surplus weight during the competition.

PRACTICE FOR THE HORSE INSPECTION

It is all too easy to make a sound horse look lame. He only needs to turn his head – normally towards the person who is trotting him up – in order to start moving on an angle, which invariably makes him appear unlevel. I always practise the trot up at home, leading the horse from the wrong side so that it will not be a habit for him to turn his head to the left. Apart from wanting his head

and neck to be absolutely straight, I need to assess his best speed. The Ground Jury insists on working (rather than medium) trot, but the miles per hour can vary within that pace. Some horses shorten if they go too fast; others look very sluggish (and rather strange) if they trot up slowly. Quite a few do not trot well in hand, maybe because they are gawping at everything in sight or because they need the extra impulsion from the rider's legs and look like slobs without it. Practice at home may not make perfect, but it will certainly help.

TIMETABLE

A three-day test, especially one with two days of dressage, might seem quite leisurely in theory when compared with your one-day outings. In practice, it can become fairly hectic. The horse will need exercise, possibly twice a day if he is feeling scatty; you need to walk the cross-country at least three times, the steeplechase at least twice and take a second look at the roads and tracks, after having been driven round them once in a crowded vehicle. These all have to be fitted in with the briefing, horse inspection, one short final gallop and the competition itself. The horse will also require a certain amount of attention in his stable!

Once aware of the overall pattern, we do at least have time to plan the finer details of our programme one day at a time. This will be done each evening, when making detailed plans for the following day.

A tack box helps to keep the equipment tidy when travelling

CHECK-LIST

In addition to all the items required for a one-day event (see pages 91-92) I would take the following:

For the rider:
Top hat and tails (optional)
Stopwatch (and spare)

For the horse:
Spares of all essential equipment
Easyboot
Weight cloth and weights

Vaseline or wool fat
Rubber gloves
Blunt knife and washing-up liquid
Sheepskin and Flash nosebands
White girths for dressage (optional)
Bootlace (for tying bridle to top plait)
Animalintex (see page 148)

Other essentials:
Horse's passport (if required)
If hot, check that ice will be available

SUMMARY

Apply for horse's passport, if required.

Check on dressage test to be used and learn any new movements required.

When schooling on the flat, make sure the horse's hocks are engaged before he is asked to perform lateral movements or other demanding exercises.

Work out fitness programme (see charts in Chapter 17).

Practise at speed required for steeplechase.

Remember that Thoroughbreds need to work on endurance aspect.

Half-breds need to work at maintaining a faster speed.

Rider requires some fitness training.

Horse will probably need an increased ration of hard feed because of extra distance being covered.

Practise for horse inspection.

Check that all necessary equipment is available and in good condition.

Practise canter work-outs with your weight-cloth (if required) to make sure that it is comfortable for both horse and rider – and that the weight is evenly distributed

15

FIRST THREE-DAY EVENT

We normally arrive at novice or intermediate three-day events the day before the briefing, unless we are travelling abroad. For an overseas fixture I like to allow an extra two days so that the horse has time to recover from his journey. The arrival time is planned to allow for a quiet hack when we reach the venue, so that the horse has a chance to unwind before he settles into his temporary stabling. The following day's routine, which has to be planned round the times fixed for the briefing and first horse inspection, will include going out for one or two hacks on the horse and walking the cross-country course on foot.

Unless the horse has a thoroughly laid-back attitude, I will probably decide to take him out twice and give him time to soak up the atmosphere. It will be far more stimulating than anything he has seen or heard at one-day events, with many more marquees, vehicles, flowers, flags and people. The sight of all this extra activity may not worry him nearly as much as the additional noise. The horse has much sharper hearing than a human; he can catch the slightest click of your tongue or a quietly spoken word while training. Strange sounds seem to alarm him far more than unfamiliar sights, so he needs the chance to hear as well as see what is going on around him. I rarely attempt any flat-work with my horse on the first day. He needs time to settle into his surroundings, and if I tried to school him before he was relaxed, it would probably end up in a battle – which is the last thing I want at this stage.

THE DAY OF THE BRIEFING

Having a less than perfect memory, I believe in taking a notebook with me to the briefing so that I can jot down any relevant items of information. These may involve fences with interlocking penalty zones and will certainly include details as to where we can exercise and gallop. We may also be told about tack checks and dope tests.

Immediately after the briefing competitors pile into a convoy of vehicles to be driven round the roads and tracks. With so many people and vehicles, it is not always possible to see where you are going or the position of the kilometre markers. Often you can do no more than get a feel of the terrain. You have to go back before cross-country day to get a clear view of the route and the markers. I like to drive around, but some people prefer to ride. Whichever means of conveyance you use, you need to be sure of the route; it is easy to by-pass a turning flag, which would be a very disappointing way to get eliminated.

Between the two sections of roads and tracks, we all pour out of the vehicles and walk the steeplechase course. This usually turns into a time for gossiping rather than a careful study of the fences, so I will go back once or twice to give it more concentrated attention. By then I hope to have learnt the locations of the quarter, half and three-quarter points of the course, through the help of a reliable friend who has walked round with a measuring wheel. These places will be pinpointed in my mind when I walk round again. The information that I wear on my arm when setting out on the speed, endurance and cross-country phase will tell me the number of seconds I should take to reach each of these three points and the finish.

I give the horse his final practice trot up on the day of the briefing and first inspection. He is then plaited up; oil is put on his hooves and diamond shapes on his quarters so that he will look smart when he appears in front of the Ground Jury. We allow half an hour for him to be walked round beforehand to loosen and relax his muscles. He wears a rug or light sheet depending on the weather and, because he is so fit and may be feeling skittish, he wears exercise boots on all four legs. These are whisked off at the last moment; at the same time any mud or gravel is removed from his feet. Even tiny stones can cause mild discomfort and make the horse slightly unlevel, which could be enough for him to be failed by the Ground Jury.

CROSS-COUNTRY COURSE WALK

The time fixed for the horse inspection will dictate whether I walk the cross-country beforehand or afterwards. I try to avoid going in a group when I am looking at it for the first time. I prefer to sit down and eat a sandwich, while most of the other riders set out together on foot to inspect the fences. My concentration is ruined if I go with the others; I begin to absorb their ideas instead of focusing on my own first impressions. I therefore walk either on my own or with Dot and, maybe, a friend. I do not, if I can help it, discuss the course with them.

The first impression is enormously important because you are seeing the course as the horse will see it on cross-country day. By then it will be much more familiar to you, because you will have walked it two or three more times, whereas the horse will not have his first view of the course until the actual competition. I try to concentrate on my horse's likely reaction to each fence and the way I intend to ride him. Combination fences sometimes cause me a few moments of panic before I have worked out my line, but there is usually one route I prefer on the first walk round – and, oddly enough, I very rarely change my mind. When I walk round the second time, I am more than happy to listen to everyone else's views; at that stage I want to glean as much information about the course as possible. Having absorbed the opinions of other riders, I need to adapt them to my own horse and his individual needs – taking his length of stride into consideration as well as any doubts or fears he may have.

I normally walk the complete course three times. As well as knowing every detail of the route that I plan to take, I want to be familiar with the alternatives. Sometimes a particular route proves hazardous on the day; maybe it has become dangerously slippery because of overnight rain, or perhaps the distance is not working out quite as well as I had anticipated. It is no good being warned of an unexpected hazard unless you know the way to go in order to avoid it. Knowing the alternatives will also be important if you have a refusal, because it might then be prudent to take an easier route.

It helps to have some idea of the number of people likely to turn up on cross-country day. If there are likely to be big crowds, you need to use your imagination to see how they will affect your view of the fences. If the course is roped off, you should also consider whether the position of the ropes will have any effect on the way you approach each obstacle. At certain fences, there may be crowds leaning against the ropes and they could completely block your view of the obstacle as you approach it. Remember, too, when you are walking round that everything will happen much quicker when you are on a galloping horse.

FINAL PREPARATIONS FOR DRESSAGE DAY

On the evening before the dressage, I make a point of checking all the equipment and making sure that my own clothes are ready and that my boots are clean.

A few other details also need to be considered in advance, such as where to put one's number. It is no good attaching it to the bridle shortly before you are due into the arena, only to find that the horse shakes his head because he doesn't like it being there. Nowadays I sew mine on to the numnah, where it is completely out of the way. It will need to be taken off and sewn on to a clean one after the cross-country.

If your horse is wearing a Union Jack, that too has to be tried on beforehand with the saddle on top. There is otherwise the risk of a last-minute panic when you tack up for the dressage and discover that it doesn't fit. You may then be ten minutes late getting mounted, which means that you are upset and the horse senses it, so he is unsettled as well. Although some people function better when they are feeling slightly hassled, most of us need to be thoroughly organised to stay ahead of ourselves and avoid flapping.

The contents of our dressage bucket are likely to include:

Fly spray and applicator (having checked that this is a permitted spray)
Omnibus schedule with dressage test
Hoof pick
Sponge and cloth
Stencil and brush for putting diamond shapes on quarters
Spare bits
Spare bridle
Drink (for rider)
Spare spurs
Boot polish and duster
Saddlesoap and sponge
Leather punch

In cold or wet weather, there would also be a rug available for the horse and a jacket or mac for the rider.

DRESSAGE

The plans I make for the morning of the dressage test depend on the individual horse. He might be better for an early-morning hack or a gallop; he may need only to be walked out in hand at that stage. It is important to know what best suits your own partner and to be aware that his behaviour may be adversely affected by the atmosphere.

The serious work begins about one hour and ten minutes before the time for my test, when I start riding in. Though some horses take longer, I regard this as the ideal time. It allows for forty minutes of proper dressage schooling interspersed with periods of walking on a loose rein, which would occupy another twenty minutes. The remaining ten minutes are for smartening up. At that stage I change my coat while the horse is

given a quick wipe over to remove foam from his neck and bit; his hooves are oiled, feet picked out, diamond shapes put on his quarters and, finally, his tail bandage and exercise boots are removed.

There can be an uncomfortably thin dividing line between a nice active test and boiling over. The horse is fitter than he was for one-day events and there will be more people to create an exciting atmosphere; he might light up when he hears applause as the competitor before you leaves the arena. As always, you have to ride him as he is on the day, concentrating your attention on the next movement and making sure that you prepare him for it three strides in advance. Whatever the horse does, you must keep your cool. He is far more likely to become overwrought if he senses that you are uptight.

FINAL PREPARATIONS FOR CROSS-COUNTRY DAY

Every item of tack and equipment needs to be checked on the evening before the cross-country. We get out everything that will be needed and go through it, checking that all the items (including the spares) are in good order, deciding on studs to be used, making sure that we have the right bridle, bit, saddle, numnah, weight cloth and lead, girths, surcingle, etc. We also check the bandages, tendon protectors and over-reach boots, as well as the items that will be taken to the start of the steeplechase course and to the ten-minute-halt box before the start of the cross-country.

The steeplechase bucket will probably contain:

Spare shoes with studs already fitted
Easyboot
Spare bridle and reins
Spare surcingle and girths
Small first-aid box
Bandages
Scissors, needle and cotton
Leather punch
Spare stopwatch
Spare stick

All these items will be taken to the ten-minute-halt box once I have departed on phase C, the second section of roads and tracks. The following will be taken directly to 'the box':

Drink for the rider (non-alcoholic and non-fizzy!)
Glucose drink for the horse

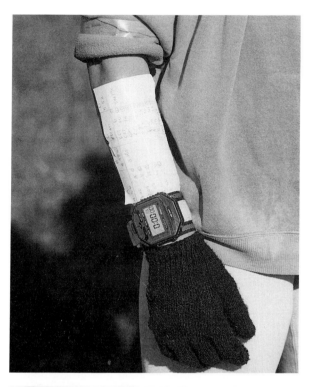

Charts and stopwatch will help this competitor to finish within the time on the roads and tracks, and the steeplechase

Leave yourself time after weighing out, so that the equipment can be checked before you set out on phase A

Spare saddle and stirrup leathers
Spare numnah
Stud spanner and studs
Towels
Sponges
Vaseline or wool fat
Rubber gloves
Headcollar and lead-rope
Spare over-reach boots
Towels
Sponges
Scraper
Buckets (2)
Programme with course plan
Coat for rider
Sweat sheet
Rugs
Ice packs (if hot and/or humid)

As well as checking the equipment, we have to work out our programme for the day. It includes the time the horse will be plaited and when his bandages will be put on, with sufficient time allowed for them to be sewn in place without anyone's thumbs being pricked because it has to be done in haste. We also need to know when the horse will be fed and how much he will be given, which will depend on his starting time for phase A. His hay ration is always cut right back before the cross-country, though he would have had an extra 2 lb or so to eat between six and nine o'clock the previous evening. He has just 2-3 lb during the night and, whatever time he is due to start, only a handful of hay before his hard feed the following morning.

My own times for the actual event, which will be sellotaped to my arm the following day, have to be written out after consultation with the programme. Three-day events can vary, with some roads and tracks more lenient than others, so you always need to check the times. My charts are worked out with the intention of reaching the steeplechase one or two minutes early and of having an extra two minutes in hand before the cross-country. I believe in keeping the details as simple as possible. For phases A and C, the two sections of roads and tracks, I need to know how long it should take to reach each kilometre marker. At most events I aim to take four minutes per kilometre, which is slightly faster than the time allowed.

Writing out the charts does not exactly tax my brain. I simply put: 0-1 (kilometres) = 4 (minutes), 1-2 = 8, 2-3 = 12 and so on. Since I will be trotting all the way on phase A, there will be no variations between the markers unless the time happens to be generous, allowing for a five-minute kilometre which would include some walking. On phase C, where I always do some cantering and walking, I include five-minute and three-minute kilometres, which I mark with an asterisk. For the steeplechase, I simply write down the time it should take to reach four points on the course – a quarter, half and three-quarters of the way round, plus the finish.

These details will be sellotaped to my arm just below my elbow, before I set out on phase A. Whether or not there is a cloud in the sky, I always keep winding the tape around my arm until the charts are completely covered. If it should happen to rain, they cannot be ruined.

I work out my cross-country times by deciding where I should be at the end of each two-minute period, again with the help of some reliable friend who has been round the course with a measuring wheel. I have this information before I walk the course the second and third times. I can therefore look for some particular feature – it might be a large tree or a barn – which will help me to fix these places in my mind. Some riders work out where they should be at the end of each minute on the cross-country. I find that too complicated because it means remembering so many places on the course, so I feel happier with my slightly simplified version. The cross-country times are not attached to my arm. They are written on a card so that I can have a last look at them during the ten-minute halt and make sure that they are indelibly printed on my mind.

SPEED AND ENDURANCE

I like to be on the horse ten minutes before we set out on phase A. If we are going early, he will have been led in hand for at least twenty minutes beforehand. If our starting time leaves us in the second half of the competition, he will have been hand-walked for half an hour in the early morning, before most of the spectators arrived. The horse will know that this is the big day and he may produce some fireworks in his excitement. With this in mind, we always have a lungeing cavesson and lunge line on the horse while he is hand-walked. If he does play up, the person leading has plenty of room to play with on the lunge line. With an ordinary halter, one sharp flick of the horse's head can be enough for the handler to lose the lead-rope – and the horse.

Unless he feels as though he needs a short period of canter to help him settle down, I normally trot the whole way for the first section of roads and tracks.

Some riders give their horses a pipe-opening gallop at the end of phase A before reaching the steeplechase, but I am not among them. I keep trotting, trying to think of nothing else except reaching each kilometre marker at the right time (but rarely succeeding). The steeplechase is looming ever nearer and I find myself wishing that it was over; it may be exhilarating to gallop over steeplechase fences, but I find it nerve-racking at a three-day event because too much depends on getting it right. By arriving one or two minutes early, I have time to check my girths and make sure everything is in order before setting out on phase B.

Mistakes most often occur on the steeplechase through the rider seeing a long stride and going for it. The horse may think he is too far away and put in another stride where there is no room for one, falling as a result. If I see a good stride I would ride for it, but the long ones are best ignored. It is better to sit quietly and try to let the horse decide; I would rather he fiddled and popped over the fence than ride for a long stand-off.

If you are required to make two circuits of the steeplechase course, you may find that your newcomer to three-day eventing applies the brakes when he reaches half-way. This is a normal tendency in novice horses; the steeplechase is new to them and, having been slightly surprised at being asked to jump at a faster speed than ever before, they expect to finish when they get back to the start box. They fail to understand that they are required to do a second circuit.

This is also potentially dangerous and you have to be cautious. You should ask yourself whether the horse is genuinely tired or simply confused at being asked to go round a second time. Usually the inexperienced three-day eventer slows down because he thinks he has reached the finish, in which case you need to shake him up a little so that he regains his momentum. If you suspect he is jaded, he can be eased for ten to fifteen strides – but he must be stoked up again before he reaches the next fence.

Unless the going has become deep on the inside track, I find the best place to be on the steeplechase course is close to the rails. It means you can go a little slower because you are taking the shortest route. If there are any sharp bends, I would still hug the rails but slow down a little into the turns and pick up again coming out of them. This gives the horse a little relief during his long gallop. During this phase I will again be thinking of my timing; I want the horse to finish just

Ready for the start of phase A, with weight-cloth in place and number attached to breastplate

within the time, without being over-stressed. I also remind myself to be very careful about the last fence and to ride it positively; it is easy to think that the steeplechase is over before you have jumped the last. Once it really is finished, you need to avoid pulling up too quickly or dropping the reins. The horse should come gently and quietly back to a balanced canter and then to walk. If it is hot, I will be handed a bag of ice which can be rubbed along the horse's neck to help him cool off.

There is a special area at the end of the steeplechase where someone can check that his bandages and shoes are still securely in place and that there are no cuts or grazes. We use white bandages, so that blood is instantly visible if the horse cuts a leg. If this is the case, we obviously need to check that the injury is not severe and that the horse is sound before I carry on. I am fully aware that time lost at this stage will have to be made up on the second section of roads and tracks, so I am anxious to avoid any delay.

If the horse loses a shoe, there should be a farrier in the vicinity who can quickly nail on one of the spares from the steeplechase bucket – but I normally prefer to use the Easyboot for phase C and make sure that somebody arranges for a farrier to be at the ten-minute halt when I arrive there. By arriving two minutes early, I know that I will have twelve minutes in the 'box', so will not have to make up for lost time if the horse is re-shod there before the cross-country.

On the second section of roads and tracks, I tend to canter and walk as well as trotting. These paces are less jarring and I think the horse appreciates a change. As on phase A, I try to think of nothing else but reaching the kilometre markers at the appointed time (again without great success – the cross-country course has a habit of intruding on my thoughts!).

TEN-MINUTE HALT

A vet will check that the horse is sound and not unduly distressed as we complete phase C and come into the ten-minute-halt box; unless there is some obvious problem, he will not need to be looked at again before we set out across country. Once I have been given permission from the vet to dismount, the rest of the Ivy-

leaze team goes into action to deal with the horse, while I get information as to how the course is riding – from the *chef d'équipe* (if I am in a team), otherwise from Dot or one of my fellow competitors who has already jumped the fences. I then have a short time to sit down and relax, have my drink, take a last look at the course plan and my times for reaching those pre-appointed places on the course.

It is much harder work for those looking after the horse. Unless I had fearful problems on the steeple-chase and have decided that the bit needs to be changed, the bridle is left on (with the noseband un-done) and a lead rope is attached to the bit. The girths and surcingle are loosened sufficiently to allow the sad-dle to be raised so that the horse's back (as well as his ears and head) can be towel dried. Some people re-move the saddle, but I prefer to leave everything on the horse.

If the weather is hot, he is offered a couple of sips of water – as a mouthwash rather than a thirst quencher. Perhaps because they know that the job is not yet com-pleted, they rarely want to take a deep draught of water at this stage. The horse is also given a small drink of glucose. In hot weather, ice is applied to the pressure points – on top of his head, down his neck and between his back legs.

Unless it is particularly hot and humid, the horse will be washed down only under his throat, along his neck and between his back legs. Care has to be taken to avoid getting anything else wet, especially the bandages which are likely to be soaked if the washing down is over-enthusiastic. The horse's legs are again checked for cuts or bruises and his feet are picked out; the bandages, studs, shoes and tack are also checked and grease is applied to his legs. The back studs will probably be changed if the going is soft. We avoid doing the roads and tracks on large studs, because it causes excess jarring and the horse's feet would be at an angle for the entire journey, both of which would affect his

Left: *Time to sit down and have a drink during the ten-minute halt*

Below: *A sip of glucose for the horse during the ten-minute break*

fetlocks and hindlegs. This is all done quickly because we do not want the horse to be standing still for long. Once finished, he is walked around quietly – with a rug on if the weather is cold.

I like to be alerted to the time five minutes before I am due to start the cross-country, so that I can get mounted four minutes beforehand, which gives me the chance to check my stirrups and have a trot. Some riders like to wait until one minute before they start, but I prefer to have longer, so that I can have my trot to remind the horse that the day's work is not yet over. It will also help to get his adrenalin flowing, his blood circulating and his muscles warm, so that he is ready to tackle the cross-country. You cannot expect him to go straight from a standstill into a gallop and start jumping fences.

CROSS-COUNTRY

Though I set out to get within the time on both steeplechase and cross-country, I will abandon the attempt if it means pushing a tired horse. It is always important to bear in mind that the first quarter of the course will ride slower because you have had to get started, and that the time can always be made up. You should know your horse well enough to realise when he is genuinely tired; you should also recognise the occasions when his

Horses have to be brave to jump into water. Welton Houdini shows that he can do it with his eyes closed!

146

apparent lethargy is simply a reluctance to go away from home. If you push a genuinely tired horse you are asking for trouble; it is far better to incur a few time faults than to risk taking him beyond his limit. At some stage on the course he will need a breather, which could mean taking it easy for 15 or 30 strides. It is up to you to assess just how long to give him.

As at a one-day event, both rider and horse should be forward-thinking. That means giving positive consideration to the fence ahead, not harping back to any hiccups you have left behind you. You need to know exactly how you are going to ride each obstacle before you come to it, so your mind needs to be focused in the right direction. If you are lucky enough to find yourself in harmony with a brave, careful and generous horse, it will be a thrilling ride.

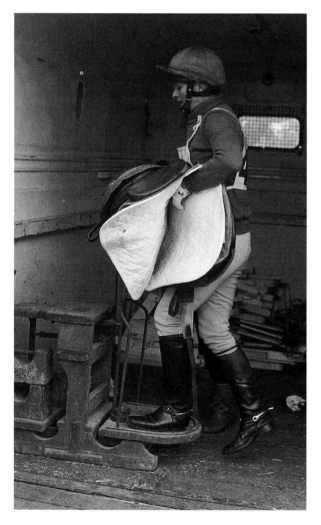

HORSE CARE

When the horse has finished the cross-country, we like to get his tack, boots and bandages removed swiftly so that he can be sponged down as quickly as possible. This is usually done from a bucket rather than a hose-pipe, because we can then adjust the temperature of the water if necessary. We would gladly use a hose if we were sure that the water would be really cold in hot and humid weather, and tepid to warm on a freezing day.

The first priority in hot weather is to get the horse's temperature back to normal, by applying ice packs on the pressure points and by sponging him down. If using a bucket, it will contain some ice to keep the water really cold. The sponging process continues until the water is cool as it comes off the horse; we then stop immediately.

At the 1973 European Championships at Frauenfeld in Switzerland, where it was exceptionally hot and humid, it took all of half an hour to get Night Cap's temperature back to normal. He was also blowing for longer than usual, which you have to expect under such conditions. On a cooler day, we anticipate that the horse will have stopped blowing about fifteen minutes after the cross-country and that his temperature will have come down before that.

Once he is cool enough, excess water is removed with a scraper and the horse is rubbed dry with towels. He is offered a small drink of water when he has stopped blowing heavily, but is not allowed to gulp it down; if he is very thirsty, he will be given a sip every five to ten minutes. Occasionally the horse does not want to drink at all, so we use a wet sponge to give him a mouthwash. We then put on a sweat sheet and walk him round quietly until his breathing is completely back to normal.

Once he has recovered from his exertions, he is allowed to pick some grass before being taken back to his stable. We will obviously have kept an eye open for any sign of injury, but his legs needs to be checked more thoroughly before the grease is removed using a blunt knife and then warm water and washing-up liquid. More grease will tend to come through to the surface later that day and again the following morning,

All competitors are required to weigh out and in before and after the speed, endurance and cross-country phase

requiring repeated washing.

We do not give the horse any pain-killing 'bute', but we normally apply cold poultices to his legs after the cross-country phase of a three-day event. Animalintex, which is the easiest type of poultice to use, will help to ease any bruising and make him feel more comfortable. You do occasionally come across a horse who is allergic to it, so you need to check beforehand. Otherwise, he can end up with a leg that is puffy from Animalintex rather than injury.

The horse can now be left in peace to have some hay and a full drink of water before his hard feed, which is given one and a half hours after completing the cross-country course. We will, however, bring him out for a ten-minute hand-walk every hour for the next three hours. He will also be trotted up in the evening to check that he is still sound.

Injuries, such as cuts or punctures, obviously need to be treated. Having checked that there are no remaining thorns (or anything else potentially dangerous), the wound has to be cleaned with warm water before an antiseptic ointment is applied. We will call the vet if the wound is deep, or if it contains any dirt or gravel. Should we find any sign of heat or swelling, we use gamgee that has been soaked in ice-cold water. This is wrapped around the affected area and kept in place by bandaging over it. The process is repeated every hour, with further applications of ice-cold gamgee.

On one occasion Priceless hit his stifle at Burghley and we spent hours on end applying hot towels and ice-packs alternatively before he was left in peace for the night. We do not believe in staying up all night to get the horse through the final vetting. He might have a hot poultice applied at midnight to relieve bruising for something like a big knee, but we would leave him until five o'clock at the earliest before giving any further treatment. The horse needs his rest, and if he cannot be left alone for five hours, it would be better not to present him to the Ground Jury.

We are always up early the following morning. It is all too easy to be lulled into a false sense of security because the horse seemed perfectly sound in the evening, only to find that he has stiffened up overnight. Most horses are fairly stiff after the cross-country, and some are much worse than others. We had one experience of the effect this can have during a three-day event at Breda in the Netherlands. The horse had been fine at his evening trot up after the cross-country, but was distinctly unlevel at 5.45 the following morning. Everybody shook their heads and said he would never pass the inspection. We nevertheless walked him in

hand for a while and he seemed a little better; he had some massage at breakfast time, and when I rode him later that morning he seemed to be back to normal. He was duly passed by the Ground Jury and was never known to be unlevel again.

You need to know how supple the horse is under normal conditions. Some youngsters can be as stiff as the seasoned compaigners, so age is not necessarily an accurate guide. If you know how the horse usually moves, you will obviously have a better chance of knowing when he has returned to normal. Nothing can be done if there is something radically wrong with him, but stiffness can generally be dealt with through massage and exercise if you have left yourself sufficient time.

The bigger horses tend to stiffen up more than the smaller ones. The size of the box may be a contributory factor: if your horse is big and the box is small, he will virtually be doing a pirouette the whole time. He therefore gets stiff because he is unable to walk forward and use his shoulders properly. Lungeing can sometimes help, but not always. Working on a smallish circle can actually make the horse worse, whereas he might have improved had he been ridden on a larger area. If he is still very stiff after light exercise, including some trot and canter, he will be withdrawn. The horse could easily damage himself if asked to show jump in this condition.

If there are no problems, our normal routine would be to give the horse a trot up first thing in the morning. Afterwards I might go for a forty-five-minute hack – with maybe half an hour of walking, followed by a little trotting and, perhaps, a short canter all on a nice long contact. Having loosened up, the horse will feel more comfortable when he is put away to have his breakfast before being prepared for the final horse inspection. Needless to say, we would not present him for the vetting unless he was fit and sound.

SHOW JUMPING

The programme rarely gives information as to when the course will be open for inspection, so you have to find that out for yourself and be ready at the appropriate time. You also need to be suitably attired, since you normally have to be in riding kit when you walk the course.

Inspecting the show-jumping fences is much the same at the first three-day event as it was when the horse took part in his first competition – except that

The horse will be tired on the third day of a three-day event and may feel quite different over his fences. It is a great bonus to have a reliable show jumper, such as Priceless who had only one rail down during his five years in major championships

you will now know his reactions rather better. If he has a tendency to drift towards the collecting ring, it should by now have become easier to work out, with the help of past experience, where you should turn into an obstacle to compensate for any drifting. You should also be more familiar with the way he jumps combination fences, and with the length of his stride. These factors determine the pace required for each obstacle, which is particularly crucial at combinations. By approaching the first element at the correct pace, you arrive at the right take-off point for those that follow.

The extra experience does not, however, make you foolproof against mistakes. I would expect to walk the course three times and, if possible, watch some other competitors jump before I get on the horse. Apart from seeing how the course is riding, I am still anxious to listen to the starting signal so that I know what it sounds like.

If the horse has already gone for a hack that day, I work him in for one hour before he jumps, mostly at walk. His muscles need to be kept loose, but you don't

want him on his knees with fatigue after the previous day's exertions. I normally start my practice jumping when there are eight horses to go before my turn; I then have my last couple of jumps when there are two left in front of me. The number of fences I jump depends on the horse. He may need to unloosen by having a couple more jumps than was necessary at a one-day event, but I have to be careful to avoid wearing him out. In that respect, the fewer I do the better. When he is not jumping, he must be kept walking; there should be no standing still in the collecting ring.

Do not forget to salute the judges when you ride into the arena. Once you have your signal to start, you will (as always) be concentrating your attention on where to turn and how you will approach the fence ahead.

SUMMARY

On arrival, take horse for a quiet hack to give him a chance to unwind.

On day of the briefing, horse would probably benefit from two hacks rather than one – to get used to strange sights and sounds.

First horse inspection: allow half an hour for horse to be led in hand beforehand.

Keep exercise boots on his legs until the last moment. Remove any mud or gravel from his feet just before trot-up.

Walking the course: Remember your first impression of the fences, this will be how the horse will see them on cross-country day. All observations and information on the fences must be adapted to the individual horse.

Be familiar with the alternatives, whether or not you plan to take them.

Consider whether your view is likely to be restricted by the crowds.

Make sure you know the route on the roads and tracks. Decide places on steeplechase and cross-country courses which you should reach at specific times.

Dressage: Check all your equipment the evening before. Decide whether the horse would benefit from an early morning hack or short gallop before his test. Allow about one hour and ten minutes for riding-in (40 minutes for proper schooling, 20 minutes for walking on a loose rein and 10 minutes for smartening up).

Speed, endurance and cross-country: Check all equipment the evening before.

Write out charts for time to be taken on roads and tracks, plus steeplechase.

On morning of the cross-country, horse is led out in hand for 20-30 minutes.

Rider mounts about ten minutes before the start of phase A.

Steeplechase: Do not attempt to ask the horse to stand back at the fences.

If allowing horse to reduce speed for a short distance, make sure he regains his momentum before the next fence.

Ride the last steeplechase fence positively.

Avoid pulling up too quickly or dropping the reins.

Ten-minute halt: Ask the vet for permission to dismount.

The horse's noseband is undone and a lead-rope attached to the bit.

Girths and surcingle are loosened.

The horse is towel dried.

He is given a few sips of water and a small drink of glucose.

In hot weather, ice is applied to the top of his head, down his neck and between his back legs.

He is washed down under the throat, along his neck and between his back legs.

His legs are checked for cuts and bruises and his feet picked out.

Bandages, studs, shoes and tack are checked – and studs changed if necessary.

Grease is applied to his legs.

Horse is walked round quietly.

Rider mounts four minutes before start of cross-country, which allows time for a quick trot.

Cross-country: Remember the horse will need a short 'breather' at some stage.

If he is genuinely tired, make sure you do not push him beyond his limit.

Concentrate on correct speed, balance and accuracy on approach to each fence.

Horse care: Remove tack, boots and bandages.

Sponge horse down.

In hot weather, first priority is to get horse's temperature back to normal.

When he is cool enough, excess water is removed with a scraper and the horse is towel dried.

He is offered a small drink of water.

Horse is walked round (in a sweat sheet) until breathing has returned to normal.

His legs are checked thoroughly and, if any injury is found, appropriate treatment is given.

Grease is removed from his legs.

Cold poultices are applied to his legs.

Horse is given water and hay in his stable, followed by hard feed.

He is brought out for a ten-minute hand walk every hour for the next three hours.

He is trotted-up in the evening.

A poultice may be applied at night to relieve bruising.

The horse is trotted-up early the following morning.

He is given light exercise to loosen up – and massage, if necessary to relieve stiffness.

Show jumping: Horse is worked in for one hour, mostly at walk.

Jump practice fence when eight horses are still to go before your turn.

Have last two jumps when two horses are still to go.

Keep horse moving at walk when not jumping.

Remember to salute the judges.

During round, concentrate on the fence ahead.

16

INTERMEDIATE TO ADVANCED

The move from intermediate to advanced one-day events is a major step for the horse. We do, however, have the advantage in Britain of being able to use open intermediate classes as a stepping-stone between the two – and even when upgraded, we can always come back to them if the horse needs to regain his confidence.

He will have to be established at intermediate level, which will probably mean contesting about four competitions without any problems, before I consider the next step. I will then find some open intermediates, which are usually slightly larger than intermediate tracks but not as big as advanced. The horse will probably have contested about ten competitions at either intermediate or OI level before I consider an advanced class. As his rider, you have to go by your own gut reaction to decide whether he is ready for the bigger challenge.

Master Craftsman did his first advanced in the spring of 1987 when he was still only a seven-year-old, which is considerably younger than most. Obviously we can all make mistakes, but I could see no reason why he should not go ahead. He had the right character and confidence to attempt it – and he proved that he was able to cope. Another horse of the same age might not

have been ready to move out of novice classes until that autumn. You have to give each individual as much time as he needs. He must not be hurried out of his rhythm across country and he must be secure at each level before he moves up the next rung of the ladder.

I always choose a suitably encouraging advanced track, with plenty of alternatives, for the horse's introduction to the highest level of one-day eventing. In that way he can learn to tackle higher fences without necessarily having to answer bigger questions.

WORK ON THE FLAT

By now I would hope that the quality of the horse's paces is more secure, that he has more weight on his hindlegs and a greater degree of lateral bend from head to tail. We are looking for a horse with a shorter base, plus more impulsion and elevation within his work. At this stage I can probably start to be a little greedier in the accuracy at markers, so that transitions are made at a precise spot rather than close to it. In theory, the more the horse is on his hocks, thereby lightening his forehand, the lighter the contact will become on the reins – though there always must be a contact, whether he is doing Grand Prix dressage or a novice one-day event. In practice, the weight on the reins will depend as much on the preference of the individual horse as on his stage of training.

As always, we start teaching new movements at least six months before the horse is likely to perform them in a dressage arena. He will normally start half-pass at trot when he is just into intermediates; having learnt the movement at walk as a novice, he is already familiar with the aids. He also has to learn counter-canter on a serpentine, which is an extension of the five-metre loops included at intermediate level.

Counter-canter requires the horse to follow the curve of a circle, while bent in the opposite direction and leading on the outside leg. The first loop of the serpentine will be in true canter, with the inside leg leading, and the rider should stay in the same position to maintain the correct bend for the counter-canter loop. If, for instance, the horse was required to lead on his near (left) leg, the rider's weight would be on the left seat-bone, while the left hand and right leg ask for a bend to the left throughout the whole serpentine. On the counter-canter loop the rider asks for a change of direction (but not of bend) by use of the right rein supported by the left leg.

Both *extended walk and canter* have to be learnt for advanced tests. They follow on from the medium paces, which the horse has already learnt, and require greater length of stride and energetic impulsion from the hindquarters. The horse's head and neck have to be stretched further forward because, as already mentioned, his feet cannot strike the ground further ahead than his nose. In extended walk, his hindfeet touch down well ahead of the hoof prints left by the forefeet.

The rider's legs have to create the extra energy for extended paces, with the hands then allowing for the necessary stretching of head and neck but still maintaining contact. You will be asking for greater extension than you have requested for medium paces, which is possible only because of the extra impulsion and elevation the horse acquires through training. You should not ask for too much at once, or ask for it in the same place each time. You want the horse to be constantly listening for the messages you give through the aids rather than anticipating them.

The horse's repertoire will also have to include the more difficult transitions of *canter-halt* and *halt-canter*. Moving into halt without any trot or walk strides will require the usual half-halts to prepare the horse for the transition. His training will have taught him to be alert and listening; he will learn to distinguish your aids for downward transitions by the amount of emphasis you put on them; they will obviously be lighter for canter to trot and stronger for canter to halt. He will also recognise the aids for striking off into canter and, as long as you have created enough energy through the use of your legs, he should respond to this message whether it is given in halt, walk or trot.

At this stage we would probably teach *half-pirouette*, in which the horse's forehand moves round his hindlegs in a half-circle. This is a useful gymnastic exercise, which helps to give control over the horse's quarters and forehand. You can work towards this movement by schooling in small circles which gradually decrease in size, without the horse losing either impulsion or rhythm. The movement will require him to flex in the direction he is moving, with about the same amount of bend as for shoulder-in.

To begin a half-pirouette from walk, the rider would restrain the forward movement with the outside rein. The inside rein then leads the forehand round, while the outside one controls the speed and, if necessary, corrects the flexion. The inside leg is applied on the girth to create impulsion and stop the horse falling in. The outside leg, used behind the girth, prevents him from swinging his quarters out – thereby avoiding the effort required to perform the movement correctly. His inside hindleg, which acts as the pivot, should move in such a small half-circle that it appears to remain on the same spot.

CANTER WORK-OUTS

The additional distance for the cross-country section of an advanced one-day event means that another increase is needed in the time for canter work-outs. These will build up to three seven-minute canters (on flat ground) or two of eight minutes (on an uphill incline) with breaks in between. The horse can then be kept ticking over at one-day-event fitness with two seven-minute canters on weekends when there are no competitions. As always, his recovery rate will be timed when he has finished cantering. I would not run him more than twice on consecutive weekends at intermediate or advanced level, except on the rare occasions when I feel my horse needs more experience and I know the going is good. If I do run him three weeks in a row in order to further his education, I will not go fast across country.

More often than not, the horse will be aiming for a second three-day event – which will probably be

Left half-pass in walk

Right half-pass in walk

another (or first) intermediate or the international equivalent, a one-star CCI. Once he has contested his first one-day event of the season, he will therefore move on to one of the programmes (or a combination of them) described in Chapter 17.

JUMPING

Grids continue to be a means of developing the horse's technique and overcoming any problems in his jumping. Since he has reached a higher level, the difficulties incorporated in each line of fences should seem no more demanding than those he encountered when he was an inexperienced youngster going through grids that were suitable for a novice.

Different distances, used judiciously, will teach him to shorten or lengthen his non-jumping strides. Place poles can also be used (see diagram on page 156), to encourage him to stay straight and jump with a rounded bascule. He may need correction because he has discovered a method of clearing fences without making the effort to use himself by rounding his back.

Priceless was a past master at this; he had learnt that he could take off two feet before the correct place and so clear the fence with a flat back. This meant that he also landed two feet further away, which might not

have mattered too much over single fences but could have been a problem in combinations. Priceless, however, had that sorted out as well. Having landed too close to the next fence, he used to take a minute non-jumping stride so that he could put in another flattish jump. When we put a place pole 9 feet (2.74 metres) in front of the second element in a double, he was obliged to take a proper non-jumping stride and so use himself correctly.

Four- to six-bar jumping is a useful exercise for teaching the horse to be tidy and mentally active. At advanced level I would have each fence at about 3 feet 11 inches (1.2 metres). The distances between them can be varied in order to teach the horse to adapt the length of his non-jumping stride. Combinations can also be employed for this purpose, using different heights and distances.

At the early novice stage, the fences in a combination will have to get progressively higher. Once the horse has a few events behind him, this rule no longer applies; you can begin to play around with different heights and distances. At advanced level I might, for example, have a combination with the first fence at 3 feet 6 inches (1.07 metres), the second at 3 feet 10 inches (1.17 metres) and the third at 3 feet 9 inches (1.15 metres). A distance of 23 feet (7 metres) between the first two elements would require one short non-jumping stride; 38 feet (11.6 metres) between the

Opposite and above: *Advanced grid work using poles to keep the horse straight, as well as place poles on the ground, which encourage athleticism and a better style of jump. Some horses require full freedom of head and neck in grid work, without interference or support from the rider*

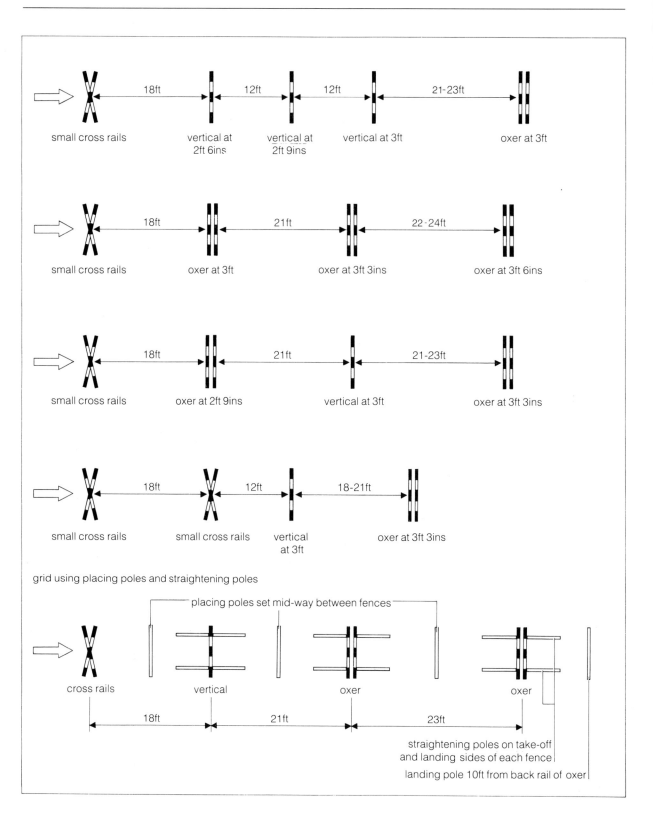

small cross rails   18ft   vertical at 2ft 6ins   12ft   vertical at 2ft 9ins   12ft   vertical at 3ft   21-23ft   oxer at 3ft

small cross rails   18ft   oxer at 3ft   21ft   oxer at 3ft 3ins   22-24ft   oxer at 3ft 6ins

small cross rails   18ft   oxer at 2ft 9ins   21ft   vertical at 3ft   21-23ft   oxer at 3ft 3ins

small cross rails   18ft   small cross rails   12ft   vertical at 3ft   18-21ft   oxer at 3ft 3ins

grid using placing poles and straightening poles

placing poles set mid-way between fences

cross rails   vertical   oxer   oxer

18ft   21ft   23ft

straightening poles on take-off
and landing sides of each fence
landing pole 10ft from back rail of oxer

second and third elements would allow for two long strides. The following week I might change these distances, making the first one 26 feet (7.9 metres) for one long stride and the second 34 feet (10.4 metres) for two short ones. I would also change the heights, always remembering that the higher the fences the greater the distance required between them – and vice versa.

The combination can be used as part of a small course which also includes single fences. The horse has to learn how to cope with the different shapes of these single obstacles by getting in close to spread fences and backing off at verticals. If he goes beyond the correct take-off point at a vertical, the highest part of his bascule is likely to occur beyond the fence instead of above it. If he is jumping a true parallel, the highest point should be reached above and between the two top rails, hence the need to take off a little closer.

Some horses habitually get too close to verticals, mainly because they are not solid in appearance. A spread fence commands far greater respect and encourages him to back off simply because it looks so much more imposing. At verticals, the horse often goes a foot (0.3 metre) beyond the point where you have asked him to take off, making it harder for him to clear the fence because it requires a greater degree of athleticism. He can be taught to back off by putting a small fence about 6 inches (0.15 metre) in front of the vertical. Alternatively, you can put a pole on the ground about 2 feet (0.6 metre) in front of the fence so that he takes off in front of it and discovers, in the process, that it is easier to clear this type of obstacle by standing back the extra foot or so. Do not be tempted to put the pole any further forward, because he might mistake it for a place pole and therefore think that he has to go across it before taking off. If he continues to leave his bascule too late, you can try putting another pole 10 feet (3.05 metres) away from the landing side of the fence. This will encourage an earlier parabola because the horse will need to land in front of the pole.

Now that he has reached a higher level, I take a different sequence of practice fences during my show-jumping warm-up. I start the advanced horse with a vertical followed by a smallish square oxer – or, in other words, a spread fence with both front and back rails at the same height. This requires him to make the highest part of his parabola above and between the two

Grids for intermediate and advanced horses. Straightening poles can be used on the ground or propped with one end on the fence. All distances can be shortened or lengthened by one foot depending on the horse and height of the jumps

rails. I then jump an ascending oxer, which has the back rail 1-1½ feet (0.3-0.45 metre) higher than the front. He now has to leave his parabola until later, otherwise he may trail his hindlegs and hit the back rail. If he does touch it, he will learn by his mistake and remember that he needs to arc correctly, keeping his hindlegs well in the air. The oxer will be squared up again for my next jump to remind him that he also has to jump the first rail cleanly. Finally, as the rider before me enters the arena, I will have my last jump over a vertical.

Because the time allowed is tighter, you have to be prepared to take shorter turns in the show-jumping phase of advanced competitions. Assuming that the basic schooling is correct, this should not be a problem. The horse will have become more athletic through training, so he no longer needs the same amount of space for his approach.

CROSS-COUNTRY

It is easy to be intimidated by an advanced course unless you start by considering each problem separately. I always like to look at the fence on its own before I consider the outer problems, although these will obviously have to be taken into the reckoning when I decide how to ride it.

I will certainly not want the horse to throw a huge leap at any fence with a drop. If he is landing on to a slope, the further out he jumps the bigger the drop before he touches down and the greater the strain on his forelegs. As already mentioned, I am also anxious to let him see where he is going before he takes off. At advanced level, any fence that incorporates a drop is therefore approached in a short active canter, with plenty of impulsion. In this way you can adjust the horse's stride easily to get close to the fence, so he can see over the top and is comfortable about jumping it. You are looking for a nice rounded jump that does not take you too far away on the landing side.

Typical drop fences include coffins, sunken roads and jumps into water. Problems at these obstacles invariably arise because the rider has approached at the wrong speed, usually by going too fast. That encourages the horse either to take off too early or to put on his brakes, because he wants to see where he is going before launching himself into the unknown. The correct pace depends on the distances in combination fences (such as a coffin) and whether you are approaching a spread or an upright. If the course builder has been kind to the horses, you should not have to jump a spread fence with a drop. It requires a faster pace than an upright and puts greater strain on the horse, because the extra speed produces a greater impact on landing.

The same guidelines apply when you are jumping a drop fence into water, whether it be a vertical or a spread. If the horse stands off a long way back at the fence, he will enter the water at a faster speed and therefore experience more of a dragging sensation, which could cause a fall. I always aim to get fairly close to the obstacle, but I do not want the horse to land too steeply; he should learn to put his forelegs out in front of him as he makes his descent, which will help to reduce the dragging effect. Once he has landed, experience will have taught him to expect a flat surface under his feet.

When jumping a drop, you need to straighten your arms to allow for the extra length of rein the horse requires as he stretches his head and neck. Usually that is enough, but there are rare occasions when you have to slip your reins a little to avoid interfering. You also have

to open the angle of your body so that it is more or less perpendicular as the horse makes his descent, ideally with your shoulders no further back than your hips. The lower legs should be forward, with heels well down to take the impact on landing.

It can be a costly mistake to lean forward again too early. If the horse is going to stumble, he normally does so within the first stride; by regaining your normal position as soon as he lands, you therefore run the risk of shooting straight over his head. It is safer to wait for a couple of strides, then move forward and gather up the reins. Sometimes you have to jump a fence at the bottom of the drop, but the same thing applies. There is no time to gather up the knitting; it is better to stay with the contact and position you have, so that the horse can keep flowing forward and remain in balance.

If you decide to tackle a corner, you will have to make careful preparations when you inspect the fence on foot. This means working out an imaginary line (as shown on the diagram) which will take you over both

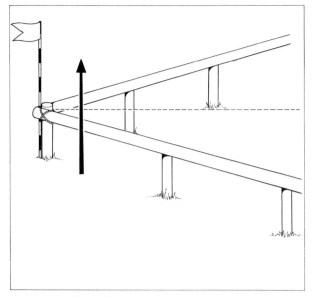

The imaginary line over a corner

your chosen route from the saddle. It is too late to try looking for the angle when you are on the horse; you need to be on the correct line from at least 12 strides away and your eye should stay on the fence, so that you can make any necessary adjustments of stride in plenty of time. If you leave it until the last minute, the horse will be thrown off balance and may well run out.

It is the rider's responsibility to come into every fence at the correct pace. The horse will then take his cue from the person on his back and learn to know the type of fence to expect. More pace is needed for wide spreads or combinations requiring a long stride, but you should not encourage him to stand off. If you are jumping a wide ditch or water with no fence above it, you want to take off close to the edge and so keep the amount of effort required to the minimum.

At uphill steps, you should aim to get fairly close. If the horse stands back, he will land rather flatly and want to apply his brakes. By taking off close to the first step you will get a more rounded jump and land in balance, giving yourself room either to push or to check for the next jump up.

At steps going downhill, the horse should be allowed to come in quietly and drop down without any hassle. The rider's position should be the same over this type of obstacle as all other drop fences, with arms straightened to allow the horse sufficient freedom of his head and neck without losing contact. Having come down the steps at a steady pace, you may have another fence to jump at the bottom – and it could be on a long distance. You will therefore have to use your legs as soon as you land from the final step in order to create the necessary impulsion for the fence ahead.

arms of the fence at the same distance from the corner flag. Having assessed the angle, you have to find some means of recognising the correct line when you come to ride it. This means finding something to look for on the fence itself, then lining it up with an object (usually a tree or a telegraph pole) in the distance.

The same applies to jumping angles. Having assessed where the distance between angled fences is best suited to your horse, you will need to find some way of lining it up so that you will be able to recognise

Left: *Master Craftsman wears a weight-cloth for an advanced one-day event. Make sure you don't make the big step up from intermediate to advanced too early*

We all feel elated after a good round across country!

SUMMARY

Use open intermediate classes as a stepping-stone to advanced.

Decide whether the horse is ready for advanced by the way he goes across country.

Choose an encouraging track, with plenty of alternatives, for his first advanced.

Work to increase impulsion and elevation in flatwork.

Increase time for canter work-outs to 3 at 7 minutes or 2 at 8 minutes, with breaks between.

Continue to time recovery rate.

If aiming for a three-day event, revise fitness programme after his first one-day contest.

Use grids to develop horse's jumping technique.

Use different distances to teach horse to shorten and lengthen his non-jumping strides.

Place poles encourage straightness and a rounded bascule.

Four- to six-bar jumping helps the horse to be tidy and alert.

Horse is taught to get close to spread fences and back-off at verticals.

During warm-up for show jumping, take practice fences as follows: vertical, square oxer, ascending oxer, square oxer, vertical.

On the cross-country course, aim to get close to drop fences and approach them in a short active canter.

Choose the correct pace for the approach, depending on the width of the fence and distances in combinations.

Work out your exact line if planning to jump a corner or angle.

Aids for new movements

Counter-canter with near (left) leg leading:
Weight on left seat bone.
Left hand and right leg ask for bend to the left.
Right hand supported by left leg asks horse to move in required direction.

Extended walk and canter:
Rider's legs create energy.
Hands then allow for horse's head and neck to stretch, while maintaining contact, so that he can achieve extension.

Canter-halt:
Prepare horse with half-halts.
Give aids for downwards transition, with slightly more emphasis than for canter walk.

Halt-canter:
Use legs to create energy.
Give usual aids for strike-off into canter.

Half-pirouette (gymnastic exercise) from walk:
Restrain forward movement by use of inside rein.
Inside rein leads forehand round.
Outside rein controls speed and corrects bend.
Inside leg, applied on the girth, creates impulsion and prevents falling in.
Outside leg, behind the girth, prevents quarters swinging out.

Master Craftsman clears a footbridge, which required the same accuracy and straightness as a corner

Beneficial makes a big splash. You should never think that you have successfully negotiated this type of obstacle until you are out of the water

Griffin displays perfect technique. It would be wonderful if all my horses jumped the same way over every fence!

Master Craftsman shows that he is forward-thinking, which is always a great asset

17

PREPARING FOR A CHAMPIONSHIP THREE-DAY EVENT

By now I would hope that my equine pentathlete has developed all his skills and that he shares something of my own joy in setting out across country. He has been moving up the rungs of the ladder slowly and, in the process, he should have acquired increasing confidence in his own ability and learnt to appreciate that I am anxious to look after him (and myself!). There will have to be mutual trust between us before we attempt the ultimate goal and contest a championship three-day event.

The number-one priority is that he should be confident and happy across country; my own gut reaction will tell me whether or not this is the case. If I believe he is ready, I still have to keep an open mind during the time of preparation. This will include some advanced one-day events, which are the best means of telling whether he has the necessary self-assurance to tackle a championship cross-country course. If he lacks confidence, he is likely to have a refusal or a fall which will undermine him even more.

It is rare for a horse to benefit from a cross-country mistake, but it does occasionally happen when you have a brave and confident jumper who never so much as considers refusing. Master Craftsman answers that description and he certainly learnt to be more careful

after he clobbered the fourth cross-country fence at the Seoul Olympics and we nearly parted company. He had never hit anything that hard before and he has obviously remembered the experience, without being too upset by it.

NEW MOVEMENTS

The horse may already have learnt the full repertoire of movements required in eventing dressage. These include *extended trot*, which is a continuation of medium trot and requires even more impulsion and elevation. As always, this is produced by the use of the rider's legs, which have to stoke up the engine before the movement begins. Impulsion is needed to drive the horse forward; elevation is necessary in order to give him sufficient time in the air for his extended strides. It is therefore important to have these two essentials before allowing with the hand (while maintaining contact) and so releasing the power as you ask him to move into extended trot.

The horse may begin to run when you are first teaching this movement, in which case you have to slow down and repeat the process. He will normally get the message quite quickly; having reached the stage in his training where his hocks are well engaged, he realises that this is something he can do naturally. The strides – and the outline of the horse – should become longer, without loss of rhythm or change of tempo.

Counter canter has already been learnt on a serpentine, when the horse was required to lead on the outside leg during the second loop. He now has to be able to strike off into canter, with the leg nearer the outside of the arena leading, while moving on a straight line. This means applying the normal aids to canter on a particular leg (see Chapter 4 summary) and maintaining the same position when you reach the corner of the school. If turning right there, the horse's left (near) leg will be

leading and he should be bent a little to the left – in the opposite direction from the way he is going. As on the counter canter loop of his serpentine, the rider's right rein and left leg ask for a change of direction but not of bend.

Right: *You need to slip the reins and adopt an upright position to jump safely into water. It has to be said that in this example I have rather overdone it!*

Below: *Every rider needs instruction for all three phases*

REFUSALS

Though I do everything in my power to avoid refusals, they do sometimes happen – and they are not necessarily the end of the world! If you examine the reasons that led to the horse stopping and try to be constructive, it is even possible that good might come out of it and you learn by the mistake. You may realise that the horse was not ready for that type of fence, or that it was beyond his scope. It may therefore give you a new attitude as to how you need to ride him in the three-day event, which could mean taking some slower routes in order to jump a clear round.

There is no point in making excuses. If you come to the conclusion the mistake was due to rider's error, you have to own up to it no matter how demoralised you might feel. If you can find no fault in your own riding – or your judgement – you have to try to discover what other reason may have caused the horse to stop.

I had to go through this mental process after Griffin refused at a one-day event coffin during the build-up to his first Badminton. This meant remembering my own gut reaction to the fast route through the coffin when I walked the course; I had felt that the distances between the elements were wrong and that it would be silly to attempt it. I nevertheless went against my instincts. The horse was due to run at Badminton, so I felt he should go the quick way just to prove he was ready for the big challenge. In retrospect, I had no right to attempt it, so I had to own up to bad judgement and put the blame fairly and squarely on my own shoulders. The experience was to help at Badminton, however, because it gave me an insight into how I should ride the horse. I was less foolhardy this time and, having taken some of the slower routes, Griffin jumped a clear round to finish tenth.

BITTING

As a general rule, horses pull less at a three-day event than they do at one-day horse trials; they are more settled simply because they have done the steeplechase and the roads and tracks. I therefore prefer to use a slightly milder bit when it comes to the full-scale test. Unfortunately, however, the theory is not foolproof. Griffin had been strong at one-day events before I took him to his first Badminton, where I expected him to pull less. In fact the reverse was true and I felt distinctly under-bitted on the Badminton cross-country. If the horse is pulling you are bound to be slower because

it takes longer to set him up for each fence, and I probably had an extra ten time penalties as a result.

The one place where I prefer to be almost over-bitted is on the gallops where I do my work-outs. Once the horse learns to pull to an extent where he is going faster than you wish, the extra speed can become a habit. If I found he was too strong on the gallops, I would certainly use a bit that gave me more control when I did my next work-out; I might then go back to the previous bit as long as I felt that I would be back in control.

In common with most other riders at three-day events, I believe in having a stronger bit on hand in the ten-minute halt box. I do not often use it, but it is there as a precaution in case the horse had been out of control on the steeplechase. Apart from anything else, it helps my peace of mind to know that I can change the bit if I wish to do so.

IN CASE OF INJURY

If your training programme is interrupted through injury, you may be forced to withdraw from the competition – though much will depend on the timing. It would matter less if the horse had already contested two one-day events, because they will have brought him on in fitness and he will not lose too much by walking for a week on a reduced ration of hard feed. But if he were to miss two runs as the result of lameness – or be off work for more than a week – it would be better to accept the disappointment and withdraw from the three-day event. Both his fitness programme and his preparation will have been badly disrupted, and in my opinion it would be asking for trouble to attempt a three-day event (particularly a championship) under such circumstances.

If a minor injury occurs at a less crucial time, I would want the horse to be sound for at least a week before running in a one-day event. He would also need to do a canter work-out beforehand, and be perfectly level when trotted up the following day.

THE TRAINING PROGRAMME

The horse will be tested in five departments – dressage, steeplechase, endurance, cross-country and show jumping – so his preparation has to take them all into account. The actual time allowed for each one depends, to a large extent, on the individual horse. He may, for instance, need a good half-hour of loosening-up work before his hocks are sufficiently engaged to attempt any lateral work or other movements which also require a considerable amount of impulsion.

You need to be flexible. If he is not going well in the arena, it is sometimes better to put him away and bring him out again later, so that you avoid a battle. It is remarkable how the horse can improve after a couple of hours in his stable. I would not, however, make a habit of putting him away every time he misbehaves, because he might begin to see this as a way of avoiding work. For the same reason, I would also try to get him to co-operate in some easy movement before returning him to his box.

If he is to be fit enough for a three-day event, the horse will need at least two canter work-outs per week, unless he has competed in one-day trials. We allow four fairly easy days after events to give him time to recover and the best part of a week before doing any more fast work. We also avoid any strenuous work after his day off.

Ideally, I would aim to ride the horse in three advanced one-day events. He might have contested one open intermediate beforehand, but that will depend on the horse. If he tends to be over-cautious, the OI will give his confidence a boost. If he is ultra-brave, it would probably be wiser to do only the advanced contests which have substantial fences that he will have to respect.

As already mentioned, Thoroughbreds are easier to train for speed. They need to work on the endurance aspect at cross-country pace, whereas the half-bred has to learn to maintain a faster pace. These factors have to be borne in mind when you work out your fitness programme for the horse. You will also need some extra form of exercise to get fit yourself, since riding on its own is insufficient preparation for the rigours of a three-day event.

The horse's schedule has to take account of the facilities available, which is why I am giving two separate charts. You can adapt either one to your own needs or use a combination of both. The key points to remember are that you must have sufficient canter/gallop work-outs and competitions – and that you need to allow time to practise all disciplines. The horse still requires at least twenty-five minutes' walking and five to ten minutes' trotting before he begins a canter work-out. You will continue to time his recovery rate, as explained in Chapter 9, in order to monitor his fitness.

Chart One was used for training a horse in the United States on flat and firm ground. Because of the distances involved in travelling to events, the horse spent some time away from home, but the facilities were similar

It is all too easy to overtrain the horse at this stage. A spell in the field works wonders for his mental attitude, helping to keep him relaxed and happy

throughout his build-up to a two-star three-day event.

This system follows the Interval Training method, beginning with two five-minute canters and gradually building up to three of nine minutes. A break of three minutes is allowed between each canter or gallop. Because it involves slower and longer canters than Chart Two, it is helpful for building up stamina in Thoroughbreds and avoids the problem of them becoming over-excited from too much galloping. There were no hills to help get the horse fit and, in order to give him sufficient work, travel days had to count as his rest days towards the end of the programme.

Chart Two made use of an uphill incline for canter work-outs while I was preparing a horse for Badminton. By using faster speeds as well as the uphill slope, it was possible to use shorter distances than those in Chart One because the horse was working harder during his work-outs. This puts less strain on his limbs, but the system would not be recommended for hard ground. The faster speeds would make it too punishing on the horse's feet. If the going is satisfactory (or if you can use all-weather gallops), Chart Two will help the non-Thoroughbred to gallop at the speeds required in a three-day event.

Breaks of two to three minutes are given between each canter or gallop. This is mainly because it takes about two minutes to walk down the hill on the all-weather gallops that I am lucky enough to use. I would never canter downhill because it puts too much strain on the horse, so the breaks are there whether I want

Master Craftsman at an advanced one-day event, which forms an essential part of the build-up to a three-day championship

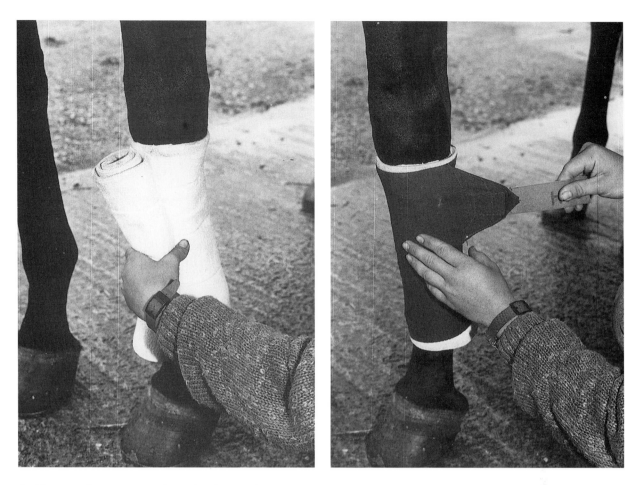

Accidents can happen, so we always bandage our horses during the run-up to a three-day event

them or not. I would probably make some changes if I were to use a full circular gallop, but, never having done so, I have no idea what they would be.

Chart Two is a combination of Interval Training and the method used for getting racehorses fit. It allows time to practise all the disciplines, which would not be possible if I followed more closely the racehorse programme and cantered three times a week. I tried that once and, though it was certainly effective in getting the horse fit, I found it left insufficient time for dressage and jumping. So I now have two canter sessions a week, plus one session of hillwork which has the same desired effect on the horse's lungs and heart. He can do some jumping or dressage on the same day as the hillwork, which would not be possible if he were doing a more strenuous canter work-out.

Sometimes, if the horse does not have much Thoroughbred blood – or if he needs to be more keyed up mentally – you may feel that a third canter day is essential. If using Chart One, however, you need to be careful about increasing the work. The horse is already cantering for a longer time and over a greater distance than those following Chart Two, so his condition could deteriorate. If I were adding a third work-out to Chart Two, I would give the horse two one-mile canters at 545 metres per minute, which would be approximately three minutes each.

The last five work-outs in Chart Two have four different speeds over a distance of one mile, with the third as the fastest. The reason for not leaving this until last is that I want to avoid galloping the horse at speed on tired legs.

You can normally reduce the work when preparing for a *novice* or *intermediate* event. You should, however, bear in mind that it can be difficult to get a horse three-day-event fit for the first time and he may therefore need as much work as those preparing for a championship. If this were not a problem, I would make the following changes.

Chart One: reduce each canter/gallop by one minute. Chart Two: use exactly the same system until four sets of fast work are introduced in week 15. Change all work-outs from this stage to: one mile at 545 metres per minute, one mile at 690 m.p.m. and one mile at 545 m.p.m. (approx 3, 2¼ and 3 minutes).

Chart One

Weeks 1-3:	Walking (¾–1½ hrs)
Week 4:	Hacking and dressage
Week 5:	Jumping (small grids) with dressage and hacking

Week 6
Monday	30 mins dressage, 45 mins walking
Tuesday*	2 × 5 mins at 400 m.p.m.
Wednesday	30 mins dressage, 45 mins walking
Thursday	Jumping (grids and single fences at canter)
Friday	30 mins dressage, 45 mins walking
Saturday*	2 × 6 mins at 400 m.p.m.
Sunday	Rest day (turned out)

Week 7:
Monday	35 mins dressage, 50 mins walking
Tuesday*	6 and 7 mins at 400 m.p.m.
Wednesday	40 mins dressage, 45 mins walking
Thursday	Jumping (single fences and grids at canter)
Friday	45 mins dressage, 45 mins walking
Saturday*	2 × 7 mins at 400 m.p.m.
Sunday	Rest day (turned out)

Week 8:
Monday	45 mins dressage, 45 mins walking
Tuesday	Travel: 24-hr journey to clinic and event
Wednesday	Rest day (with hand walking)
Thursday	1½-hr hack
Friday	45 mins dressage, 45 mins hacking
Saturday*	2 × 5 mins at 400 m.p.m. and 1 × 5 mins at 500 m.p.m.
Sunday	1¼-hr hack

Week 9:
Monday	30 mins dressage, 1 hr walking
Tuesday	Dressage clinic (lessons)
Wednesday	Dressage clinic (lessons)
Thursday	Jumping (single fences at trot and canter)
Friday	45 mins dressage, 30 mins hacking
Saturday	1½-hr hack
Sunday	Rest day

Week 10:
Monday	45 mins dressage, 45 mins walking
Tuesday*	3 × 6 mins at 400 m.p.m. (last 5 mins at 500 m.p.m.)
Wednesday	45 mins dressage, 45 mins walking
Thursday	Jumping (over courses)
Friday	1 hr dressage, 30 mins walking
Saturday	**First event:** dressage and show jumping
Sunday*	**First event:** cross-country

Week 11:
Monday	Rest day: 1 hr hand walking
Tuesday	1½-hr hack
Wednesday	1 hr dressage, 30 mins walking
Thursday	1 hr dressage, 30 mins walking
Friday	1 hr dressage, 30 mins walking
Saturday*	3 × 6 mins at 400 m.p.m. (last 5 mins at 500 m.p.m.)
Sunday	1½-hr hack

Week 12:
Monday	1 hr dressage, 30 mins walking
Tuesday*	2 × 6 and 1 × 7 mins at 400 m.p.m. (last 5 mins at 500 m.p.m.)
Wednesday	1 hr dressage, 30 mins hacking
Thursday	Jumping (grids)
Friday	45 mins dressage, 45 mins hacking
Saturday*	3 × 7 mins at 400 m.p.m. (last 5 mins at 500 m.p.m.)
Sunday	45 mins dressage, 45 mins hacking

Week 13:
Monday	1 hr dressage, 30 mins hacking
Tuesday*	3 × 7 mins at 400 m.p.m. (last 5 mins at 500 m.p.m.)
Wednesday	Travel: 8-hr journey to next event
Thursday	Jumping (grids and single fences)
Friday	1 hr dressage, 30 mins walking
Saturday	**Event: dressage and show jumping**
Sunday*	**Event: cross-country**

Week 14:
Monday	Rest day: 1 hr hand walking
Tuesday	1½-hr hack
Wednesday	45 mins dressage, 45 mins hacking
Thursday	1 hr dressage, 30 mins hacking
Friday	45 mins dressage, 45 mins hacking
Saturday*	3 × 8 mins at 400 m.p.m. (last 5 mins at 500 m.p.m.)
Sunday	1 hr dressage, 30 mins hacking

Week 15:
Monday	45 mins dressage, 45 mins hacking
Tuesday*	3 × 8 mins at 400 m.p.m. (last 5 mins at 500 m.p.m.)
Wednesday	Light jumping (single fences)
Thursday	Travel: 6-hr journey to next event
Friday	1 hr dressage, 30 mins walking
Saturday	**Event: dressage and show jumping**
Sunday*	**Event: cross-country**

Week 16:
Monday	Travel: 11-hr journey home
Tuesday	1½-hr hack
Wednesday	1 hr dressage, 30 mins hacking
Thursday	1 hr dressage, 30 mins hacking
Friday	Light jumping (single fences)
Saturday	45 mins dressage, 45 mins hacking
Sunday*	9 mins at 400 m.p.m., 9 mins at 450–570 m.p.m., 9 mins at 500–690 m.p.m.

Week 17:
Monday	45 mins dressage, 45 mins hacking
Tuesday	1 hr dressage, 30 mins hacking
Wednesday*	9 mins at 400 m.p.m., 9 mins at 450–570 m.p.m., 9 mins at 500–690 m.p.m.
Thursday	1 hr dressage, 1 hr hacking
Friday	Jumping (single fences and course)
Saturday	1 hr dressage, 1 hr walking
Sunday*	9 mins at 400 m.p.m., 9 mins at 450–570 m.p.m., 9 mins at 500–690 m.p.m.

Week 18:
Monday	Travel: 4-hr journey to three-day event
Tuesday	45 mins dressage, 1¼ hrs walking
Wednesday	1 hr dressage, 1 hr walking
Thursday	1 hr hacking (morning), 30 mins hacking plus dressage (afternoon)
Friday	**Dressage test**
Saturday	**Speed, endurance and cross-country**
Sunday	**Show jumping**

* fitness programme (allow 3-minute break between each canter/gallop)

m.p.m. metres per minute

Chart Two

Weeks 1-3:	Walking (¾–1½ hrs)
Week 4:	Dressage and hacking
Week 5:	Light hillwork, jumping (small grids) with dressage and hacking

Week 6:

Monday	Rest day
Tuesday	1½-hr hack, dressage or lungeing
Wednesday*	2 × 1 mile at 500 m.p.m. (= 2 × 3 mins)
Thursday	1½-hr hack, lungeing
Friday*	Hills and dressage
Saturday	1½-hr hack, flatwork, jumping (grids)
Sunday*	2 × 1 mile at 500 m.p.m. (= 2 × 3 mins)

Week 7:

Monday	Rest day
Tuesday	1½-hr hack, dressage or lungeing
Wednesday*	1 and 1½ miles at 500 m.p.m. (= 3 and 4½ mins)
Thursday	1½-hr hack, lunge over poles
Friday*	Hills and dressage
Saturday	1½-hr hack, flatwork and jumping
Sunday*	1½ and 1¼ miles at 500 m.p.m. (= 4½ and 4 mins)

Week 8:

Monday	Rest day
Tuesday	1½-hr hack, dressage or lungeing
Wednesday*	2 × 1½ miles at 525 m.p.m. (= 2 × 4½ mins)
Thursday	1½-hr hack, lunge over poles
Friday*	Hills and dressage
Saturday	1-hr hack, dressage, jumping (grids)
Sunday*	2 × 1½ miles at 525 m.p.m. (= 2 × 4½ mins)

Week 9:

Monday	Rest day
Tuesday	1½-hr hack, dressage
Wednesday*	1½ miles at 525 m.p.m. and 1½ miles at 545 m.p.m. (= 4½ and 4 mins)
Thursday	1½-hr hack, lunge over poles
Friday*	Hills and dressage
Saturday	Show-jumping show
Sunday*	2 miles and 1½ miles at 525 m.p.m. (= 6 and 4½ mins)

Week 10:

Monday	Rest day
Tuesday	1½-hr hack, lungeing
Wednesday*	2 × 2 miles at 545 m.p.m. (= 2 × 6 mins)
Thursday	1½-hr hack, lunge over poles
Friday*	Hills and dressage
Saturday	Show-jumping show
Sunday*	2 × 2 miles at 545 m.p.m. (= 2 × 6 mins)

Week 11:

Monday	Rest day
Tuesday	1½-hr hack, dressage or lungeing
Wednesday*	2½ miles and 2 miles at 545 m.p.m. (= 7 and 6 mins)
Thursday	1½-hr hack, light lungeing
Friday*	Hills, plus dressage or jumping
Saturday	1½-hr hack, dressage
Sunday*	**First one-day event** (Open Intermediate)

Week 12:

Monday	Rest day
Tuesday	1½-hr hack
Wednesday	1½-hr hack, lunge over poles
Thursday	1½-hr hack, dressage, light hillwork
Friday	1½-hr hack, jumping
Saturday	1½-hr hack, dressage
Sunday*	1 mile at 545 m.p.m., 1 mile at 570 m.p.m., 1 mile at 650 m.p.m. (= 3, 2¾ and 2½ mins)

Week 13:
Monday   Rest day
Tuesday   1½-hr hack, lunge over poles
Wednesday*   1 mile at 545 m.p.m., 1 mile at 570 m.p.m., 1 mile at 680 m.p.m. (= 3, 2¾ and 2½ mins)
Thursday   1½-hr hack
Friday*   Hills, plus dressage or jumping (grids)
Saturday   Light hack, dressage
Sunday   **One-day event** (Advanced)

Week 14:
Monday   Rest day
Tuesday   1½-hr hack
Wednesday   1½-hr hack, lunge over poles
Thursday   1 hr hack, light hills, dressage
Friday   1½-hr hack, jumping
Saturday   Hack, dressage (lesson)
Sunday*   **One-day event** (Advanced)

Week 15
Monday   Rest day
Tuesday   1½-hr hack
Wednesday   1½-hr hack, dressage (lesson)
Thursday*   Hillwork and hack
Friday   Hack, short dressage, gridwork
Saturday*   ½ mile at 400 m.p.m., 1 mile at 545 m.p.m., 1 mile at 690 m.p.m., 1 mile at 545 m.p.m. (= 2,3,2¼ and 3 mins)
Sunday   1½-hr hack

Week 16
Monday   Rest day
Tuesday   1½-hr hack, lunge over poles
Wednesday*   ½ mile at 400 m.p.m., 1 mile at 545 m.p.m., 1 mile at 690 m.p.m., 1 mile at 545 m.p.m. (= 2,3,2¼ and 3 mins)
Thursday   1½-hr hack
Friday   1½-hr hack, light gridwork
Saturday   1-hr hack, dressage
Sunday*   **One-day event** (Advanced)

Week 17
Monday   Rest day
Tuesday   1½-hr hack
Wednesday   1½-hr hack, lunge over poles
Thursday*   Hillwork, hack
Friday   Hack and dressage (lesson)
Saturday   1½-hr hack, jumping
Sunday*   1 mile at 500 m.p.m., 1 mile at 545 m.p.m., 1 mile at 690 m.p.m., 1 mile at 545 m.p.m. (= 3¼, 3, 2¼ and 3 mins)

Week 18
Monday   Rest day
Tuesday   Travel to three-day event, 2 × 1-hr hacks
Wednesday   Hack in morning, dressage in afternoon
Thursday   Hack in morning, dressage in afternoon
Friday   **Dressage test**. Pipe-opener – ½ mile at 680 m.p.m.
Saturday   **Speed, endurance and cross-country**
Sunday   **Show jumping**

* fitness programme (allow 2–3-minute break between each canter/gallop, depending on weather conditions and how hard the horse is blowing)
m.p.m. metres per minute (times given are approximate)

SUMMARY

Decide if the horse is ready by the way he jumps across country. If he has a refusal, try to assess the reason constructively.

If the horse is too strong during canter and gallop work-outs, use a stronger bit but aim to change back to a milder one.

Remember that horses usually pull less on the cross-country at a three-day event, though there are exceptions.

Plan fitness programme according to facilities when working out your chart.

Aim to ride in three advanced one-day events during your build-up to a championship, possibly preceded by an open intermediate.

Continue to time recovery rate after canter/gallop work-outs.

Chart One:
This method is used on flat and hard ground.

It is helpful for building up stamina in Thoroughbred horses.

For a novice or intermediate three-day event, reduce each canter/gallop by one minute (unless the horse needs the extra work).

Allow 3-minute break between each canter/gallop.

Chart Two:
This method makes use of an uphill incline for canter work-outs and steeper slopes for a weekly session of hillwork.

It is helpful for encouraging non-Thoroughbred horses to gallop at the speeds required.

It is not recommended for hard ground, because the faster speeds would make it too punishing on the horse's feet.

For a novice or intermediate three-day event, reduce final work-outs as shown on page 168 (unless the horse needs the extra work).

Allow 2-3 minute break between each canter/gallop.

Aids for new movements
Extended trot:
Rider's legs create energy for increased impulsion and elevation.

Hands then allow (while maintaining contact) so that the power created is released into the extended movement.

You may be part of a team at a championship. If so, remember that you are now riding as a team member and not as an individual

18

THE ULTIMATE TEST

I prefer to arrive at championship three-day events two days before the briefing, if time permits and the organisers are prepared for horses and people turning up early. Since most championships run from Thursday to Sunday, with the briefing on Wednesday, this normally means getting there on a Monday afternoon. I like to have time to unpack on arrival and to take the horse out for a quiet hack so that he can survey his surroundings.

Horses are not easily fooled; they know that a big competition is coming up as soon as they arrive at the venue. As a result, they are often quite loopy the following day. I rarely do any schooling the day before the briefing; instead, I go out for one or two really nice hacks. If the horse is behaving like a complete nutcase, I might even take him out three times – for no more than forty-five minutes each time, most of which would be walking.

I know that I feel the benefit, just as much as the horse, from having that complete day to unwind and get my bearings. The day of the briefing is always fairly hectic. I therefore try to plan my programme with a view to avoiding any situation in which I might find myself panicking against time, thereby causing hassle for everyone else. I would prefer to ride half an hour earlier than necessary, rather than have any worry about getting to the briefing on time. If I find myself with half an hour to spare, so much the better; I can sit down, relax and read a newspaper. I also make sure that I have enough time to eat; if you find yourself in too much of a hurry to stop for food, you invariably end up feeling hungry and bad-tempered.

Equally important, we make sure that whoever is looking after the horse knows exactly what is required. It is unfair to expect anyone to read your mind, so I write down the exact times I will be riding, what tack the horse should wear and when he has to be plaited up and ready for the horse inspection. The Ivyleaze team believes in communication as well as careful planning!

The details given in Chapter 15 are common to all three-day events, so there is no point in repeating them. This chapter is therefore concerned with the extra problems that may be encountered in championships, mainly because of the enormous crowds who turn up to watch them.

173

DRESSAGE

There is a tendency for all of us to feel we must try to improve our horses' dressage while we are at a championship and waiting to ride the test. This is mistaken; we cannot improve at such a late stage and would be better employed trying to keep the horse relaxed and happy, so that we can hold on to what we already have.

Much of his preparation for the arena can be done without any dressage. This includes mooching about, hacking and anything else that helps him to unwind mentally while he soaks up the atmosphere. You know that he is capable of performing all the movements in the test, but he will not do them satisfactorily if he is tense.

The biggest battles I have had at championships were the result of spending too long in the practice arena. Nowadays I try to do no more than half an hour all told while I am at the event. The horse tends to become claustrophobic if you spend too long there, as I know to my cost. His movements then become restricted as tension seeps in. I may not have had a disagreement with him all year but his tension, combined with my own anxiety to do a good test on such an important occasion, can result in a serious battle of wills.

Most horses are more settled if they go out for an early-morning hack on the day of the dressage test. I was up with the sparrows to ride Master Craftsman before he did his test at the Seoul Olympics and I know he was much better for the outing. It is always a good idea to plait up the horse before going out for the first time. He will be well aware that plaiting means something important is about to happen, and if it is done well in advance there is time for the message to sink in.

All horses are affected, to a greater or lesser extent, by the electrifying atmosphere of a championship three-day event. Some positively enjoy it; others become introverted and nervous. Night Cap came into the latter category and we racked our brains trying to find a way of getting him to relax before the dressage. It was noise which upset him most, particularly the sound of clapping from the stands.

Having tried various ploys with little success (four days at the Bath and West Show, visits to local football matches, a clapping rent-a-crowd at home and brass-

Master Craftsman at Badminton. You need to be aware that big crowds create an electric atmosphere

*Always make sure that your horse's
head is straight when you trot him up
for the horse inspection*

band music in his stable), we discovered a more effective solution. The horse was given a couple of hours to get used to the atmosphere, during which time he was led around the collecting-ring and allowed to pick some grass. In the past we had used similar tactics, but for a shorter length of time, and Night Cap had then been taken back to the stables. This tended to undo all the good work because he became overwrought again when he returned to the collecting-ring area. By keeping him there, he was able to continue listening to the clapping until he became bored by it. He was much less tense as a result and therefore able to show the judges that he was capable of performing a really good test.

SPEED, ENDURANCE AND CROSS-COUNTRY

There are normally two fences that alarm me when I walk the cross-country at a championship three-day event for the first time. This is especially true of Badminton, where the declared aim of Colonel Frank Weldon (who was course designer and director there for many years) was 'to frighten the living daylights out of the riders without hurting any of the horses'.

As at every stage of eventing, I have to look at each fence in a positive way – first on its own and then considering the problems surrounding it. Normally you can relate each obstacle to something similar the horse has jumped in the past (even if it is only a diminutive version), which will give you encouragement and help you to know how to ride it. Invariably the problem fences begin to look less alarming once you have done some positive thinking. The only time I can recall being completely flummoxed was at the Seoul Olympics where, for the life of me, I could not figure out a route across the Wondang Walls. It was an immense relief when the first element of this combination was removed, because it then seemed jumpable.

I walk championship courses four times – on the day of the briefing, on both days of dressage and on the morning of the cross-country. By the time I ride round it, I should be familiar with each fence and know exactly how and where I plan to jump it. I should also know all the alternatives available, in case there is some good reason for abandoning my chosen route.

On most cross-country courses there is an area in front of each fence which allows you to straighten up and get your line right. Badminton is an exception; the ropes there are positioned cunningly and there is far less room to sort yourself out. Quite often the fences are out of sight until you are almost on top of them. You can find yourself galloping towards an obstacle and all that is visible is a bulge in the ropes, with people leaning over it to obliterate your view. I am convinced that there would be at least 25 per cent more clear rounds at Badminton if there were no ropes and no spectators.

You have to use your imagination when you walk the course and consider how your view will be altered when the crowds pour into the Duke of Beaufort's park. A fence might be visible from a long way back when you are looking at it without many people around, but they could be standing ten deep on either side of the ropes on cross-country day. If you have failed to consider this aspect – and the much faster pace you will be going when you are on your horse – you could find it alarmingly disconcerting on the day.

The other imperative is (as ever) to be aware of your own and your horse's capabilities and limitations, so that they can be taken into account when you plan how to ride the course. In an ideal world I would always want to tackle big cross-country fences on a horse that answered the same description as Priceless: fairly small, with enormous scope, and incredibly athletic. Unfortunately, such horses are not often to be found, so we all have to accept certain limitations and learn to adapt to them.

From the time he starts to event, the long-striding horse will more than likely find galloping and jumping spread fences easy, but he might lack the athleticism that would help him through a short coffin. The short-strider will probably find spreads more of a problem, but he should be able to make snappy turns – so it might be advisable for him to follow a twisty alternative route where one is available.

Unless you are going early, it should be possible to watch the early runners on closed-circuit television. This can be useful, but it can also be dangerously misleading if you are watching a horse that is totally different from your own. You could, for instance, watch a short-striding horse through a water complex and make the mistake of relating it to your own long-striding partner who happens to be much bolder, which is something I have done myself.

Information about how the course is riding can be potentially dangerous for the same reason. If you do get advice, it must come from somebody who knows your horse well and can be relied upon to give you all the relevant details. It is no good being told how a horse jumped through a combination if your informant fails to mention that the animal was short-striding and that he was looking both chicken-hearted and knackered!

Sometimes you do find a double or combination rides

differently from the way you had expected. The two sets of white rails into the lake at Badminton in 1989 came into this category. In theory the distance between them should have been exactly right for one normal stride, but both the white rails and the water encouraged horses to back off and it rode as a long stride. It was therefore important to approach it with rather more pace than had at first seemed necessary, otherwise the horse was liable to try putting in a second stride. A number of them did this, usually with painful results.

Once you are on your way, riding along the first section of roads and tracks, the steeplechase fences will be the first obstacles to worry about. By now the horse will have done enough three-day events to realise that he quite often has to do two circuits on a steeplechase track. If he slows down at the end of the first circuit, it is therefore more likely to be through tiredness or unsoundness than misunderstanding. You need to make a rapid assessment as to whether he is lame or, perhaps, feeling the effects of the weather or the ground. At the same time, you must not underestimate the fence ahead. If you let him ease up for a short distance, he must get back into gear so that he will have enough power and momentum to clear the obstacle.

There will not be a vast number of spectators watching the steeplechase, but the cross-country, when you reach it, is likely to be awash with people. Riders inevitably become infected by the atmosphere, which increases one's nerves before the cross-country. Once started, however, you are concentrating too much on the fences to be conscious of the crowds. You know they are watching only to the extent that you want to be seen to give a good performance – which, if anything, helps you to ride better. If I happen to hear clapping after I have jumped a difficult fence, it gives me a tremendous lift.

With Ian Stark, Lorna Clarke and Anne-Marie Taylor (now Evans). We all have to check and re-check our line of approach to each fence, as well as making sure that we know all the alternative routes

The horse, on the other hand, can be seriously distracted by the people. He can start looking at the crowds instead of concentrating on the obstacles and then start spooking. There is a danger that he will back off both the crowds and the fences, which can be a real problem and there is nothing you can do about it. These horses tend to become introverted and anxious when there are large crowds. I had expected Griffin to react this way when I first rode him at Badminton and was delighted when he turned extrovert instead, which meant that the crowds helped rather than hindered him.

As always, it is the rider's responsibility to prepare the horse for each fence. He needs your help to establish the correct speed, balance and accuracy on the approach; it is too late to put him right once you reach the obstacle. The correct pace going into a bounce will depend on the distance between the elements, but you should always aim to take off close to the first part so

Above: *Master Craftsman as a comparatively young and inexperienced horse competing in the Olympic Games at Seoul*

Right: *The show-jumping phase is extremely nerve-racking and can mean the difference between success and failure*

that you do not land too near the one that follows. Ideally, the horse should touch down exactly half way between the elements; he will then be well placed to bounce over the next part of the fence.

Sometimes the horse begins to lean on the bit towards the end of the course when he is tiring, which makes him feel very heavy in front. The rider must be able to use legs and hands to get him back on his hocks and off his forehand, otherwise he will be in serious danger of hitting one of the remaining fences. This is one of the reasons why the rider needs to have done some fitness training!

SHOW JUMPING

I normally walk the show-jumping course four times at a championship, which helps me to overcome the terror of losing my way! We are all well aware at this final stage of the competition that the advantages of a superlative dressage and heroic cross-country performance can easily be laid to waste in the show-jumping arena. Every fence has to be studied carefully, often in the knowledge that each rail on the floor is likely to move you down in the placings. There is normally far more nervous tension before the show jumping than the cross-country, which is bound to communicate itself to the horse.

The parade of competitors before the show jumping can also prove rather too stimulating for your partner, despite his efforts of the previous day. Having become over-excited while in the arena with all the other horses, it can be a real problem to get him to concentrate when you go back in there to jump the fences. It is worth remembering that the calmer you can keep him during the parade, the better he is likely to be in the final phase of the competition. Some horses thrive on the charged atmosphere of the big occasion and jump better for it; others can lose their concentration and become very spooky. Riders are obviously aware of the crowded stands before they jump but, once in the arena, there is fortunately so much to think about that most of us manage to forget the people.

Only one person can win, but plenty of others are likely to feel equally ecstatic when the competition is over. If your horse has responded gamely to the ultimate challenge, you have to be thrilled with him. And when all the clapping is over and you come down to earth, you will still be left with a deep-rooted sense of satisfaction.

SUMMARY

(To be used in conjunction with summary for chapter 15 on page 150)

Dressage:

Do not spend too long in practice arena.

If horse is tense, give him plenty of time in the collecting-ring before his test so that he can get used to the atmosphere.

An early morning hack before the test can also help him to settle.

Speed, endurance and cross-country:

When walking cross-country course, look at each fence on its own before considering the problems surrounding it.

Consider the position of the ropes. They may allow limited space for straightening up before the fence; if people are leaning over them, your view may be obliterated.

Take your horse's limitations into account when planning how to ride each fence.

If watching on closed-circuit television, be sure to relate what you see to your own horse's length of stride. The same applies to any information received.

If the horse begins to lean on the bit through tiredness, use legs and hands to get him back on his hocks.

Show jumping:

If there is a parade of competitors beforehand, try to keep the horse as calm as possible during it.

The trot-up on the last day of a three-day event is almost another phase in itself. Griffin has just passed this hurdle at the World Championships in Stockholm, where his gleaming coat and bright eye prove that he was at peak fitness

19

OVERSEAS TRAVEL

Horses have a far easier journey when they travel by air rather than road and sea. Because they are physically incapable of vomiting, a rough sea crossing can be particularly distressing and you could have a very sick horse with a high temperature at the end of it. Enforced inactivity at a time when the horse is three-day-event fit can also cause serious problems unless his hard feed is reduced and you make sure he gets some exercise.

FOOD FOR THE TRAVELLER

The horse has his normal amount of hay and other bulk food when making a long overseas journey, but we always reduce the hard feed two to five days beforehand, and we allow the same length of time to bring him back to his normal ration. The actual quantity – and the time span during which the hard feed is reduced – will depend on the length of the journey, how well the horse travels and the facilities for exercise en route.

Our plans have to be adjusted if there is an unexpected hold-up due to bad weather. We would not want to sail with the horses if a gale is blowing – and it is unlikely that we would be allowed to do so. Waiting for the next sailing (and calmer seas) can add half a day or more to the time between departure and arrival.

We had one such hold-up when we took *Griffin* to the Boekelo three-day event in the Netherlands. He was due to be on the night ferry from Harwich, which would have meant arriving at Boekelo at about four o'clock the following afternoon. We planned to give him half his normal ration of hard feed; he had been ridden that morning and it should have been possible to give him an hour's ridden exercise when he arrived. The plan had to be amended when the lorry was not allowed on to the night ferry; *Griffin* would have to spend the night in it parked at the docks, before sailing the following morning. His hard feed was therefore cut right back to two pounds, because we would arrive after dark and therefore too late for the horse to be lunged or ridden; his only exercise would be walking in hand.

If the horse is leaving home before daylight and arriving late the same evening, he will probably have his normal rest-day ration of hard feed on the day he is travelling. It is on longer journeys that we need to cut back further, especially if walking in hand is likely to be his only exercise. However, we have to bear in mind that he will probably lose condition if he has scarcely any hard feed for three days in a row.

This will not be a problem if there are at least five days to bring him back to his peak before the competition. The flight to Australia for the 1986 World Championships lasted thirty-three hours and Priceless's hard feed could be cut right back during the journey, since he would have four weeks before the competition began. Master Craftsman had twelve days in Seoul before competing in the Olympics, so he also had time for his hard feed to be reduced gradually before the flight and slowly increased to normal rations after he arrived.

Time is not usually on our side when we are competing on the Continent of Europe. If our journey by road and sea to one of these events is to take two days or more, we will try to find somewhere to lunge the horse each day he is travelling. He can then have a small amount of hard feed without running too much risk of encountering the problems associated with a build-up of protein. The most obvious of these is azoturia (also known as 'tying up'), which causes severe cramps in the horse's back and quarters when he returns to work.

When they are at home, all our horses have a minimum of ten minutes' grazing a day. It is rarely possible to lead them out to pick grass when they are travelling to an overseas event, so we make up this deficiency by feeding carrots when we are abroad. The carrots are a special treat for away trips; we do not feed them at Ivy-leaze, but they help to compensate for taking the horse away from the comfort and security of his own stable. They also add some interest to meals that may otherwise consist mainly (or totally) of 'slops'. It is still important for him to have his four feeds each day because he will be looking forward to meal-times.

If the weather is likely to be hot and humid, we automatically give electrolytes, which replace essential elements lost through sweating. We would start giving them before leaving home and continue until a few days after our return, following the instructions on the packet.

We like to take all the horse's food with us on overseas trips, though this is not always allowed. It is therefore important to check the regulations of any countries you will be entering, as well as making sure that you have all the necessary documentation. If we cannot take the food with us, we do our level best to obtain

Travelling by air. Horses have to be carefully monitored throughout the long journey to avoid such potential dangers as dehydration and sickness

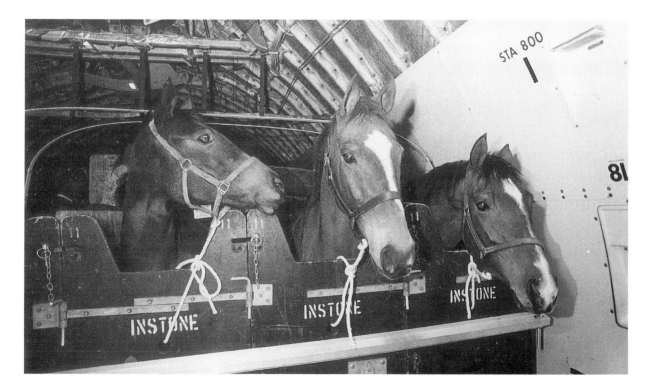

some in advance from the country of destination, so that it can be introduced gradually into his diet before he leaves home, thus avoiding any sudden change. We are not allowed to bring hay back into this country, but HorseHage is permitted because it is packed into sealed bags. We therefore make sure that we have some HorseHage with us, otherwise the poor horse will have nothing to eat when he arrives at the port.

Normally we give the same amount of hard feed on the outward and return journeys. The horse will be tired by the time he makes the trip home, so it is not the time to start deviating from a system. Tiredness makes him less resistant to germs, so there may be more potential danger at this stage than on the outward journey.

READY TO TRAVEL

For extra protection and to prevent the legs swelling, we always put gamgee and bandages under the horse's travelling boots when going abroad. As with most shorter journeys, he wears a light rug (when necessary) that is suitable for the weather and his own individual needs. Temperatures can change more

frequently when you are travelling a long distance, so regular checks are made to see whether the horse needs warmer or cooler clothing.

He will cope with the stresses of travel much better if there is good ventilation. A stuffy atmosphere is the main cause of stress, especially in aircraft which are invariably too hot. Low temperatures are not a problem; you can always put on extra rugs to keep the horse warm. It is when he is hot that you are likely to run into trouble, because heat has a debilitating effect which causes stress.

We do not use a tail bandage on these trips, for fear of it tightening or slipping to an area where it can cause pressure and prevent the proper circulation of blood. Horses have been known to lose their tails through having bandages put on too tightly, so we prefer not to take the risk. The tail is a delicate area, with no tough skin to protect it – and very little hair, because we remove most of it for the sake of appearance. Instead of a bandage, we use a tail guard which is attached to a light roller to keep it in place.

Unloading at the end of a successful trip

EXERCISE

We always exercise the horse before loading him into the lorry for a long journey, even if it means getting up at three o'clock in the morning and leading him round for half an hour by torchlight. If off-loading is allowed at the sea port, he has another half-hour of hand-walking before embarkation, and he may be taken out again at the end of the crossing.

There could still be two or three days of road travel ahead, depending on the destination. If this is the case, the horse is exercised each morning before setting out and again in the evening, when arriving at the overnight stop or the venue itself. We also stop at lunch-time and off-load to give the horse another short session, which means that he has a total of 1–1½ hours' exercise each day. We would hope to find somewhere suitable for lungeing in the morning or at lunch-time; he can then be exercised more vigorously than hand-walks allow. If he is left standing in the lorry all day, he can hardly be expected to arrive at the destination in peak condition.

REST-TIME

The horse will need a holiday when he returns home. This does not mean putting him straight out in the field; after competing in a three-day event, whether at home or abroad, he needs about a week to be let down slowly before he is turned out. At the start of the week he is hacked out for about an hour and a half. This gradually decreases to half an hour, and at the same time, his hard feed is slowly reduced. This avoids an abrupt change, which would be likely to upset his system.

The break will help to refresh him both physically and mentally. It may be beneficial for the rider as well! Though the horse still needs loving care and attention while he is turned away, it is obviously far less time-consuming than when he is in training. The spring season is always particularly welcome, because horses and humans have had a good rest.

Holiday time. The rider may fancy Barbados, but all the horse asks for is a nice big field

SUMMARY

Feeding:
Reduce hard feed 2-5 days before a long overseas journey and allow the same time to come back to normal ration.

On shorter journeys (24 hours or less) give normal rest-day ration while travelling.

If permitted, take food and hay for the whole trip.

Clothing for the journey:
Use gamgee and bandages under the travelling boots.

Choose a light rug (if needed) suitable for temperature and individual horse.

Check horse regularly to make sure he is neither too hot nor too cold.

Use a tail guard in preference to a bandage.

Exercise:
The horse should be exercised for at least 20-30 minutes three times a day – before setting out, again at lunch-time and on arrival at over-night stop or destination. Try to find somewhere to ride or lunge the horse for one of the three sessions (the other two can be hand-walking).

Rest-time:
Before turning the horse out for his holiday, gradually reduce hard feed and exercise over a period of about one week.

CONCLUSION

The training methods described in this book have been used successfully on a number of different horses, but they are not written in concrete. We are always learning and therefore must be ready to adapt. As Egon von Neindorff wrote, 'The horse already knows how to be a horse, the problems of horsemanship are entirely those of the rider.'

GLOSSARY
(including terms used in America)

Backing-off: refers to the horse shortening his stride to reach the correct point of take-off, instead of going beyond it. He does this with his hocks underneath him, maintaining impulsion.

Bandage: known as a leg wrap in America.

Bascule: derived from the French word for see-saw, this describes the movement of the horse as he clears a fence.

Bounce: jumping two fences without taking a non-jumping stride between them.

Box (loose): equivalent of the American stall.

Brushing: when the horse knocks a fore or hindleg with the one opposite.

Dressage arena: see diagrams.

Drop fence: any fence where the ground on the landing side is lower than the take-off.

Easy boot: a boot made of plastic that can be used, as a temporary measure, to protect the sole of the foot if the horse loses a shoe.

Falling in: describes a horse when he shifts his balance to the inside shoulder on a turn or circle, while moving his head to the outside. His feet normally follow his shoulder by drifting inwards.

Falling out: describes a horse when he moves his shoulder outwards on a turn or circle. When falling in or out, the horse will not be straight (q.v.).

Gamgee: cotton wool with a covering of gauze, which is used under bandages.

Hack: the equivalent of an American trail ride.

Half-halt: an almost imperceptible moment in which the rider's legs create energy in the horse, while the hands restrain him. It produces momentary collection and is a useful preparation for transitions.

Hard feed: energy-giving food that has a fairly high protein content (e.g. oats, event nuts and some mixes).

Large Dressage Arena 20m x 60m

Headcollar: known as a halter in America.

Horsebox: a van used for transporting horses.

186

Inside (or outside): refers to the inside (or outside) of the horse's bend when making a turn or circle – or when performing lateral movements.

Let down: the gradual decrease of hard feed and exercise which is followed by a holiday for the horse when he is turned out (or 'turned away') in a field.

New Zealand rug: a waterproof rug used on a horse when he is turned out in cold weather.

Numnah: a thick pad, which is fitted underneath the saddle to prevent rubbing. Unlike the smaller pads which can be used to improve the fitting of the saddle, the numnah covers the whole saddle area.

Over-reach: when the toe of a hindfoot strikes into the heel of a forefoot.

Over-reach boots: a bell-shaped rubber boot, used to protect the front heels from an over-reach injury. It is called a bell-boot in America.

Plaiting: known as braiding in America.

Spooking: refers to a horse that views unfamiliar fences with great suspicion, normally shortening his stride on the approach. He may then make a quick dart to get over the obstacle, losing his rhythm and often going crooked in mid-air.

Straight: the horse is said to be straight when his hindfeet follow in the same track as his forefeet, whether on a straight line or a circle.

Surcingle: also known as an over-girth, this passes over the saddle and round the horse's body to be secured by a buckle. Usually made of webbing or elasticated web, it gives extra security to the saddle.

Ten-minute halt box: also known as 'the box', this is an enclosed area where riders weigh out at the start of the speed, endurance and cross-country phase and weigh in at the finish. It is also used for the compulsory ten-minute halt before the cross-country.

Yard: the equivalent of an American barn, it refers to the entire stable area.

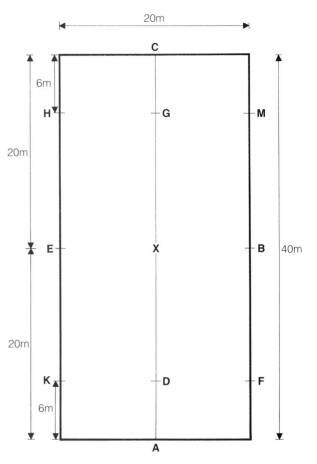

Small Dressage Arena 20m x 40m

INDEX